Ecology, Sustainable Development and Accounting

Accounting literature has viewed sustainability in terms of social, economic and environmental performances. There have been concerns that the relationship between sustainability, accounting and organizational performance cannot be explained unless we can deduce patterns of administrative behavior that chronicle management practices.

Ecology, Sustainable Development and Accounting argues that, despite the broader social and economic development dimensions of sustainability and the limitations of its extension to corporate and organizational behavior, an ecological framework is capable of providing the overall societal and community chronologies that describe corporate sustainable operations. Drawing examples from international development and federal government organizations, this book documents the link between ecology, corporate sustainable development, and sustainability accounting and reporting. It draws together the literature from several disciplines to elaborate the contribution of the ecological approach to sustainable development in the accounting literature.

This book will be of particular interest to students, academics and practitioners in the areas of environmental studies, ecological economics, sustainable development studies, and social and environmental accounting. The sociological and anthropological perspectives make this book the first of its kind to apply the population ecology of sociology to both the sustainability and accounting literature.

Seleshi Sisaye, PhD, is Professor of Accounting at Duquesne University, USA.

Routledge Explorations in Environmental Studies

Nuclear Waste Management and Legitimacy
Nihilism and responsibility
Mats Andrén

Nuclear Power, Economic Development Discourse and the Environment
The case of India
Manu V. Mathai

Federalism of Wetlands
Ryan W. Taylor

Governing Sustainable Urban Renewal
Partnerships in action
Rory Shand

Employee Engagement with Sustainable Business
How to change the world whilst keeping your day job
Nadine Exter

The Political Economy of Global Warming
The terminal crisis
Del Weston

Communicating Environmental Patriotism
A rhetorical history of the American environmental movement
Anne Marie Todd

Environmental Justice in Developing Countries
Perspectives from Africa and Asia-Pacific
Rhuks Temitope Ako

Climate Change and Cultural Heritage
A race against time
Peter F. Smith

A Global Environmental Right
Stephen Turner

The Coming of Age of the Green Community
My neighbourhood, my planet
Erik Bichard

Fairness and Justice in Environmental Decision Making
Water under the bridge
Catherine Gross

Carbon Politics and the Failure of the Kyoto Protocol
Gerald Kutney

Trade, Health and the Environment
The European Union put to the test
Marjolein B.A. van Asselt, Michelle Everson and Ellen Vos

Conflict, Negotiations and Natural Resource Management
A legal pluralism perspective from India
Edited by Maarten Bavinck and Amalendu Jyotishi

Philosophy of Nature
Rethinking naturalness
Svein Anders Noer Lie

Urban Environmental Stewardship and Civic Engagement
How planting trees strengthens the roots of democracy
Dana R. Fisher, Erika S. Svendsen and James J.T. Connolly

Disaster Risk Reduction for Economic Growth and Livelihood
Investing in resilience and development
Edited by Ian Davis, Kae Yanagisawa and Kristalina Georgieva

Energy Security Cooperation in Northeast Asia
Edited by Bo Kong and Jae Ku

Water Politics and Spiritual Ecology
Custom, environmental governance and development
Lisa Palmer

The Politics of Ecosocialism
Transforming welfare
Edited by Kajsa Borgnäs, Teppo Eskelinen, Johanna Perkiö and Rikard Warlenius

Peak Energy Demand and Demand Side Response
Jacopo Torriti

The Green Economy in the Gulf
Edited by Mohamed Abdelraouf and Mari Luomi

Ecology, Sustainable Development and Accounting
Seleshi Sisaye

Environmental Change and the World's Futures
Ecologies, ontologies and mythologies
Edited by Jonathan Paul Marshall and Linda H. Connor

Ecology, Sustainable Development and Accounting

Seleshi Sisaye

LONDON AND NEW YORK

First published 2016
by Routledge
2 Park Square, Milton Park, Abingdon, Oxfordshire OX14 4RN

and by Routledge
711 Third Avenue, New York 10017

First issued in paperback 2017

Routledge is an imprint of the Taylor & Francis Group, an informa business

British Library Cataloguing-in-Publication Data
A catalogue record for this book is available from the British Library

Library of Congress Cataloging-in-Publication Data
A catalog record has been applied for

ISBN 13: 978-1-138-06496-6 (pbk)
ISBN 13: 978-0-415-81635-9 (hbk)

Typeset in Goudy
by GreenGate Publishing Services, Tonbridge, Kent

In memory of
Eileen Sisaye Stommes, PhD
June 20, 1947 to July 10, 2006

Contents

Acknowledgments

I have been working on this book, *Ecology, Sustainable Development and Accounting*, since fall 2010. I signed a contract with Routledge in June 2012. I would like to acknowledge the support that I received while working on this book from Louisa Earls, commissioning and associate editor, Routledge Environment and Sustainability – Earthscan Series. Louisa was very instrumental in both the early and later stages in the preparation of this book. Over the years, I have worked with two previous assistant editors: Charlotte Russell and Bethany Wright. I have enjoyed close working relationships with the current associate editor, Annabelle Harris, and assistant editor, Margaret Farrelly. I would like to express my appreciation to the editorial staff of Routledge for their continued support and assistance over the years in the preparation and completion of the book. Without their support, this book could have not been published on a timely basis.

I am very grateful to the Emerald Publishing Group, particularly Chris Tutill, who generously granted me copyright permission to use my articles and book chapters. These articles and book chapters are listed in the Introduction to this book.

Duquesne University's sabbatical leave award during the fall 2014 semester enabled me to devote my time exclusively to work on the book. Deborah Kennedy has provided expert secretarial assistance over the years by typing the book chapters, and preparing the references and indices. I appreciate Debbie's kind assistance and support in all phases of the preparation of the manuscript, and would like to thank her for it. I have been fortunate to work with Petros Christofi on quality management and productivity, which has affected my research on sustainability reporting. Henry M. Musembi, my graduate assistant, has assisted in the final preparation of author and subject indexes.

I have benefited from my research collaboration with Jacob G. Birnberg, University of Pittsburgh. I have known Jake for over 30 years as a mentor, friend and colleague. He took the time to read and critique the manuscript, and provided extensive editorial changes and revisions. I am very grateful for his continued interests and support of my research. I owe Jake special thanks and appreciation for his intellectual contribution and moral support, which have been instrumental in completing the book and other research projects that I have undertaken over the years.

This book is dedicated to my late wife, Dr. Eileen Sisaye Stommes (June 20, 1947 to July 10, 2006). Eileen was not only my wife, she was a friend, colleague and research partner. She shaped my interest in and research on ecology and sustainable development, starting on our doctoral program in development sociology at Cornell University. I have benefited from her work and publications in international agricultural development programs in El Salvador and Ethiopia, and the United States federal government regulatory policies on agricultural redistricting and organic food legislation. She wholeheartedly supported my research and was instrumental in directing my sociological and anthropological disciplinary background into accounting research and scholarship. She spent her career in public service working in high-level policy-making positions at both the New York State Department of Agriculture and Markets and the United States Department of Agriculture. I am dedicating this book to the memory of her service, scholarship and lifelong contributions intended to make the world a better place.

Seleshi Sisaye
Duquesne University

Acronyms and abbreviations

2DS	2-degree scenario
AACSB	Association to Advance Collegiate Schools of Business
ABC	activity-based costing
AFD	French Development Agency
AICPA	American Institute of Certified Public Accountants
AOS	*Accounting, Organizations and Society*
BC	black carbon
BSC	balanced score card
CBC	community-based conservation
CCS	carbon capture and storage
CEO	chief executive officer
CERES	Coalition for Environmentally Responsible Economies
CIAR	*Community Impact Assessment Report*
COP	Communication on Progress
CPA	certified public accountant
CR	corporate report
CSR	corporate social reporting/responsibility
DJSI	Dow Jones Sustainability Index
DSS	Decision Support System
ECM	environmentally conscious manufacturing
EF	Ecological Footprint
EIA	environmental impact assessment
EMA	environmental management accounting
EMB	environmental mitigation banking
EMS	environmental management system(s)
EPA	Environmental Protection Agency
ESD	ecologically sustainable development
ESDI	environment and sustainable development indicator
ESI	Environmental Sustainability Index
EU	European Union
EVA	economic value added
FAO	Food and Agriculture Organization
FASB	Financial Accounting Standards Board

FMV	fair market value
FWF	Food Wastage Footprint
GAAP	Generally Accepted Accounting Principles
GCCI	Global Climate Change Initiative
GDP	gross domestic product
GHG	greenhouse gas
GRI	Global Reporting Initiative
IAASB	International Auditing and Assurance Standards Board
IBRD	International Bank for Reconstruction and Development (known as the World Bank)
IFRS	International Financial Reporting Standards
ILO	International Labour Organization
IRI	Initiative for Responsible Investment
ISO	International Organization for Standardization
IT	information technology
IWRM	integrated water resource management
JIT	just-in-time technology
LCA	life-cycle assessment
LDCs	least developed countries
LPI	Living Planet Index
MIT	Massachusetts Institute of Technology
MNC	multinational corporation
MSCI	Morgan Stanley Capital International Index
NFP	not-for-profit organization
NGO	non-governmental organization
NIPA	national income and product accounts
NIST	National Institute of Standards and Technology
NOAA	National Oceanic and Atmospheric Administration
NRC	National Research Council
NRTEE	National Round Table on the Environment and the Economy
OECD	Organisation for Economic Co-operation and Development
OLC	organizational life cycle(s)
PCAOB	Public Company Accounting Oversight Board
R&D	research and development
RCRA	Resource Conservation and Recovery Act
S&P	Standard & Poor's
SAA	Social Assessment Analysis
SAM	Sustainable Asset Management
SASB	Sustainability Accounting Standards Board
SDI	sustainable development indicator
SEA	social and environmental accounting
SEC	Securities and Exchange Commission
SEE	social, ethical and environmental
SER	social and environmental reporting
SF	structural functional

SIA	Social Impact Analysis/Assessment
SIAR	*Social Impact Assessment Report*
SIM	Social Impact Measurement
SOX	Sarbanes-Oxley Act
SRG	*G3 Sustainability Reporting Guidelines*
SSA	Social Soundness Analysis
TBL	triple bottom line
TIP	Technology Innovation Program
TQM	total quality management
UN	United Nations
UNDP	United Nations Development Programme
UNEP	United Nations Environment Programme
UNGC	United Nations Global Compact
USAID	United States Agency for International Development
USNMFS	United States National Marine Fisheries Service
WB	World Bank
WBCSD	World Business Council for Sustainable Development
WCED	World Commission on Environment and Development
WHO	World Health Organization
WI	Well-Being Index
WRI	World Resources Institute

Introduction

Ecology, Sustainable Development and Accounting is one of the few scholarly books available on the market in accounting. The book extends the ecological frameworks from sociology and anthropology to describe the theory and practice of sustainable development and accounting reporting systems. I have benefited from my multidisciplinary background in development sociology, ecological anthropology and organization management to contribute to behavioral accounting research on sustainability and accounting.

In my scholarly articles and papers, I have utilized industrial ecology, systems theory and ecological approaches along with the stakeholders and resource-based view of the firm to study sustainable development and accounting. The genesis of the ideas discussed in this book can be found in the four articles that are published in Sisaye (2011a, 2011b, 2012b and 2013) and the two book chapters in Sisaye (2012a and 2014, with J. G. Birnberg) by the Emerald Publishing Group. I am very grateful for Emerald copyright policies that enabled me to use the materials from these four articles and two book chapters throughout the book.

Ecology and sustainability

The ecological framework received prominence in the 1970s when economists suggested that existing natural resources create potential limits to growth (Davidson, 2000). They stressed that the current rate of population growth could adversely affect food and industrial production, the environment (pollution), climatic conditions and geographical locations. Organizational ecology research focused "on the broader environment – community, nation, ecosystem and planet" (Hansen, 2004: 66). It addressed the imbalance resulting from pollution, environmental degradation and damages to the ecosystem. The publication of the Brundtland Report (WCED, 1987) highlighted the importance of conservation and carefully managing non-renewable resources, and focused on strategies that call for developing alternative renewable resources (Gray, 2010: 802).

Sustainability emerged as the underlying framework for governmental, international development and business organizations to guide their programs in meeting the needs (satisfaction) of the current generation without sacrificing the needs of future generations (WCED, 1987). It provided a multidisciplinary perspective by linking the individual into communities/organizations and to the society at large – market, economy and industry – as well as national and international/global concerns.

An overview of sustainable development

Sustainable development is an interdisciplinary area of study. It is not a discipline *per se* because it has no established theory and research method. It is a subject that has attracted many different social, biological and environmental sciences disciplines. Historically, the subject of sustainability has its roots in the engineering sciences, particularly in civil and agricultural engineering. When engineers were designing roads, bridges, dams and irrigation projects, they were required by the host government officials and community elders that the projects focus on the long-term impact of sustaining development without altering the livelihood of the local population. In biology, the subfield of evolutionary biology examined the issue of sustainability among species: plants and animals.

Sustainability has its original basis in evolutionary biology which has been shaped by the Darwinian theory of evolution and natural selection. The approach became popular in economics (agricultural and resource economics), sociology (rural sociology and human ecology), anthropology (ecological anthropology) and organization management studies (population ecology) to explain the evolutionary growth and development process of communities and societies and its applications to international donor organizations. There have been parallel approaches of sustainability of environmental resources that are shared by governmental and business organizations.

Ecological approaches to environmental resources management

Environmental resource management utilizes an evolutionary focus for addressing sustainability, societal improvement and conservation, and recognizes the potential threats of industrial and population growth for environmental destruction. At the same time, people who are also concerned about environmental conservation attempt to limit industrial growth by focusing on natural resources conservation (Penn, 2003). Over time, environmental activism by various coalitions/groups emerged to ensure that industrial accountability and responsibility are enforced through governmental regulations.

When environmental resources management is viewed as an ecological issue, it becomes inherently a subject related to sustainability involving the interdependency among living systems. Sustainability then becomes a social and ethical issue that is concerned with defining acceptable ethical values and mores that will sustain the social relations of interdependence within living communities.

Resource management among humans entails a collective and interdependent process that has cultural and social implications. As Thiele (1999: 30) noted, it becomes an ethical or moral issue that "requires viewing others along with the self as integrated parts of a larger whole." Ethics then prescribes those values and "obligations" that "sustain the community." Ecological ethical issues and concerns have influenced sustainability accounting education and their integration in accounting and business curriculum.

Ethical concerns stress that sustaining natural and social community development becomes a duty that is required for continuous improved growth and future balanced development. There is an inherent conflict of interest among government agencies, business organizations and societies to sustain environmental resources for long-term continued growth and survival. To address these conflicting interests, there is a need for compromises and negotiations among contending interest groups. Regulatory government agencies issue laws and regulations to reinforce society's interests. They require business organizations to behave according to ethical and moral principles of sustainability and social soundness analysis (Sisaye et al., 2004). It is apparent that "today successful human adaptation entails engaging in sustainable practices and propagating mores that promote such practices" (Thiele, 1999: 33). Accordingly, ethics of sustainability advances the need for business organizations to adapt and learn about environment resources and manage them ethically and responsibly. It is this core issue of the accountability of business organizations regarding sustainable performance that is the core issue of this book.

An evolutionary analysis of sustainability suggests that there are benefits for business organizations to pursue sustainable environmental resource management policies. Sustainability provides a quality improvement plan that enables business organizations to develop competitive advantage. To remain competitive, business plans examine their resources, including geographical boundaries, employees, the communities in which they are located, and how the organization conducts its business. They focus on developing alternative sources of energy conservation, and managing non-renewable as well as renewable energy resources. It becomes imperative that business organizations are viewed as living systems that are able to adapt to their communities, both in terms of economic and social well-being as well as their cultural development.

In accounting, these constraints provide feedback on issues of quality productivity improvement assessment. The treatment of sustainability as an ordinary accounting expenditure where the costs are treated as expenses raises issues as to the feasibility of developing and implementing environmental resource management plans for the long term given uncertainty of economic/financial performance benefits and existing resource constraints and limitations. Nevertheless, organizations that focus on environmental resources management have emphasized innovations in which the management of activities as well as costs has become the basis for competitive advantage (Johnson, 1992; Porter, 1985).

Industrial ecology, which utilizes an organizational systems view towards environmental resource management, has linked economic and accounting data as quantitative indicators of improved performance for technical and material production output. Industrial ecology has thus broadened the focus of accounting and financial performances by including social, economic, market, political or strategic systems in industrial organizations. The analysis has focused on the systematic components of the organization's environment, including accounting systems. Consequently, environmental issues are broadly examined from the viewpoint of economics, ethics, law and the sociology of organizations (Hoffman, 2003).

Sustainable development and environmental resources management

Sustainable development addresses natural conservation and responsible use of environmental resources. It emerged as a national concern in the conservationist movement of the 1970s. Over time, it has evolved to encompass broader societal issues including "social justice, poverty, social exclusion, marginality, community participation, gender, health, human rights, and other socioeconomic needs and problems" (Bozzoli, 2000: 275). According to Zairi (2002: 1162), "sustainable development is based on a perceived need to address environmental deterioration and to maintain the vital functions of natural systems for the well-being of present and future generations." Sustainability integrates environmental resources and conservation issues into socio-economic and cultural development goals. Sustainability incorporates adaptation, continuity of change, innovation and growth, improved productivity and competitive performance, a focus on customer satisfaction, and meeting the needs of employees and stakeholders, as well as the community and the society at large.

In sustainable development, the basis of planning starts with identifying national objectives followed by the delineation of specific policies. While sustainability incorporates environmental factors and economics, its focus is on societal well-being, where individuals and groups share responsibilities in their utilization of natural resources. When culture has been incorporated as part of national strategic plans, it required "integrating policies, plans and activities of conservation, use and sustainable management of natural resources. It also meant identifying the organizations and institutions that would implement the recommended policies and operational principles" (Bozzoli, 2000: 276).

Historically, sustainable development is a subject that is of interest to anthropologists as it addresses development issues that encompass economic goals, social justice/equity, survival, responsibility of environmental management, and cultural development (Bozzoli, 2000; Stone, 2003). Sustainability is a holistic approach that promotes economic growth and prosperity to meet current demands but without sacrificing future generations' needs and priorities. Sustainability is a goal that has regional, national and global ramifications. Sustainability focused on the transfer of knowledge and resources from the developed to the developing economies. It encouraged flows of people, ideas, resources and materials from the well-endowed countries to those societies and countries that need aid and assistance (WCED, 1987). Accordingly, the sustainable development programs of international donor organizations' aid assistance has contributed to agricultural development, industrial growth and social equity among the recipient countries.

An ecological approach of sustainability in the accounting literature

It must be noted that sustainable development also is within the subject domain of sociology and anthropology. In the social sciences disciplines, sociology (population ecology) and anthropology (ecological anthropology) have been concerned with the subject of sustainability for many years. Accordingly, there is a substantial theoretical and practical set of approaches from organizational sociology and ecological anthropological disciplines which can be extended to the subject of sustainability accounting and reporting.

The basis of sustainability accounting can be derived from the Social Soundness Analysis (SSA) and Social Impact Assessment (SIA) analysis that are based on anthropological and sociological disciplines. SSA and SIA incorporated accounting income and performance indicators within the design and implementation of economic and social programs in developing countries. Both the United States Agency for International Development (USAID) and the International Bank for Reconstruction and Development (IBRD; referred to as the World Bank) use SSA and SIA, respectively, to study the feasibility and sustainability of economic development programs which they funded or supported in these countries. If the projects proposed are not supported by SSA and/or SIA sustainability analyses, the strategy is to revise and/or modify the project to make it sustainable; otherwise, to abandon it in favor of other proposed project sites. These approaches have influenced the strategic planning approaches of corporations by stressing the importance of sustainability and continued community economic growth in business ventures.

During the late 1960s and early 1970s, many accountants (and non-accountants) were aware of sustainability issues and became involved with social responsibility reporting and social audits. The approach did not receive business support when industrial development in the manufacturing sectors transferred from the developed to the developing economies. Corporate social issues and sustainable development issues were almost absent due to the availability of cheap labor and raw materials in the developing economies that supported industrial growth.

The 1980s and 1990s brought the realization that sustainability has broader local, national and international development implications. There have been concerns that the application of sustainability to business organizations has conceptual constraints. To this effect, some accountants have argued that sustainability is primarily an ecological and societal concept and its extension to corporate and organizational responsibilities has certain limitations. They have argued that sustainability has several social and ecological dimensions that transcend corporate organizational behavior and sustainable performance.

For example, Gray (2010) has questioned the concept of sustainability relationship to corporate performance unless it is possible to derive some form of organizational narratives that describe organizational behavior. Gray has raised three issues that questioned sustainability's applications to business organizations.

First, social and ecological justice is applicable to global as well as regional levels and their translation to the corporate level is questionable. Second, sustainability is a state of being that is complex where there is no single "sustainable position" or policy that a corporation can achieve. Sustainability outcomes are derived from collective value judgments involving "politics, preference, knowledge, religion and spirituality, understanding of the planetary ecology, morality" (Gray, 2010: 57). Third, and finally, sustainability efforts result from "interactions between organizations, individuals, societies and states" (p57). In other words, some organizations may behave in an "unsustainable" manner – for example, mining, natural resources extraction – while they compensate for their extraction through sustainable actions (p57).

Sustainability has thus several social and ecological dimensions that transcend corporate sustainable economic, social and environmental performances. Although these constraints exist, in this book, I have documented that the ecological framework would provide the societal and community narratives that describe corporate sustainability behavior. I show that the ecological framework is capable of providing the overall societal and community narratives that describe corporate sustainability performances. Accordingly, the book links corporate sustainable development to sustainability accounting and reporting.

Organization of the book

The book integrates multidisciplinary ecological approaches from sociology and anthropology to study business organizations as holistic living systems to analyze environmental problems in a manner where management policies influence their political acceptability, social impact and economic feasibility.

In this book, I discuss the common trends of sustainable development, environmental conservation and natural resources management among governmental and bilateral organizations. I extend the ecological approach to sustainability policies of business organizations; and accounting theory, scholarship, education and practice.

Chapter 1 introduces the general framework of ecology and relates to the literature in sociology and economics. Chapter 2 utilizes the sociology of population of organizations to describe organization growth and development and its link to sustainability and accounting. Both chapters describe the theory and practice of environmental resource management, which draws its fundamental principles from sociology (organizational and human ecology). As a philosophy for environmental resource management, both Chapters 1 and 2 recognize ecological sustainability system constraints and boundaries that affect the planning and implementation of improved productivity programs. While sustainable systems are considered dynamic and continually changing to adapt to existing societal changes, it is likely that the forces of nature and humans could become devastating to some systems, contributing to their eventual failure and/or death. Organizations' birth, maturity and death as they relate to sustainable development and accounting are discussed in these two chapters.

Chapter 3 documents the ecological anthropology and industrial ecology approaches to sustainability, where conservation and preservation of natural ecosystems have shaped the redesign of industrial production systems, business strategies, and quality and productivity management. It traces the impact that the ecological approach has in international development assistance programs in both the United States and Europe, and its application in international donor agencies among bilateral and multilateral organizations in developing economies. Ecological anthropology has shaped many of the international bilateral and multilateral organizations' agricultural and rural development assistance programs in the least developed countries (LDCs).

In Chapter 4, I present the bilateral and multilateral international development organizations and the United States federal government. The bilateral organizations include USAID and the Organisation for Economic Co-operation and Development (OECD), and the multilateral organizations are the World Bank, United Nations Development Programme (UNDP), the Food and Agriculture Organization (FAO) and the International Labour Organization (ILO), who have integrated sustainability as part of their development assistance programs to promote agricultural and industrial development and public health in the least developed countries of Africa, Asia and Latin America. The U.S. federal government agencies have also advanced sustainability to protect and sustain environmentally based development programs. The U.S. federal government organizations reviewed include the Environmental Protection Agency (EPA) and the Department of Commerce, which have established national guidelines to promote sustainability. The U.S. Department of Commerce has included the Malcolm Baldrige Award sustainability guidelines as one of several criteria used to recognize corporations' manufacturing and service excellence. The adoption of sustainable development by national and federal government agencies and bilateral and multilateral organizations has been extended to business organizations in the management of environmental and conservation programs.

In Chapter 5, I discuss the approaches of business organizations and how they have shaped and influenced sustainability policies and programs. Because business organizations as ecosystems are considered living organizational systems, they are expected to adapt, evolve and grow over time. Sustainability provides a framework for these organizations to respond to environmental constraints. Chapter 5 details how most corporations followed the USAID and World Bank models in their approaches towards sustainable business interventions in promoting social and economic development that yield long-term profitability to their shareholders.

Chapter 6 links the development of sustainability accounting to the sustainable development practices as described in the SSA and SIA frameworks of multilateral and bilateral international development organizations. It shows how sustainability accounting and reporting has recently emerged as one of the main competitive forces that business organizations employ to differentiate their products and services from others in order to attract and keep customers. Moreover, the press and media have popularized sustainability by publishing positive reports of organizations with sustainability programs. The accounting profession, particularly the American Institute of Certified Public Accountants (AICPA), in collaboration with the big four public accounting firms, have established guidelines for voluntary disclosure of sustainability information and data by corporations in annual reports and other published documents that are available online. The market for consulting firms has increased for improving accounting systems to better collect data and report sustainability performance.

In Chapter 7, there is a discussion of how colleges and universities have integrated sustainability coverage within existing business, management and accounting courses. Some of them have introduced standalone courses to cover the subject matter of sustainability accounting.

These trends in academia, business, government and international donor organizations have positioned sustainable development as one of the most important humanitarian, environmental, social and economic development programs. Sustainability has been advanced as national and international development objectives to promote and sustain equality, redistribution and creation of wealth, alleviation of poverty, better standards of living, preservation of natural resources and advancing democratic political reforms to ensure the full participation of citizens in the conduct of their governmental activities and affairs. Sustainability has become an important strategic goal for business organizations. In accounting, sustainability has broadened the issue of corporate social responsibility (CSR) to include environmental and ecological factors in triple bottom line (TBL) reporting for transparency and accountability of business performances to the various stakeholders. Sustainability accounting and reporting have now emerged as an important area of accounting education and scholarship.

References

Bozzoli, M. E. (2000). "A role for anthropology in sustainable development in Costa Rica," *Human Organization*, Vol. 59, No. 3, pp275–279.

Davidson, C. (2000). "Economic growth and the environment: Alternative to the limits paradigm," *Bioscience*, Vol. 50, No. 5, pp433–440.

Gray, R. (2010). "Is accounting for sustainability actually accounting for sustainability … and how would we know? An exploration of narratives of organisations and the planet," *Accounting, Organizations and Society*, Vol. 35, No. 1, pp47–62.

Hansen, S. (2004). "Resilience and sustainability," *Chartered Accountants Journal of New Zealand*, Vol. 83, No. 9, pp66–67.

Hoffman, A. J. (2003). "Linking social systems analysis to the industrial ecology framework," *Organization & Environment*, Vol. 16, No. 1, pp66–86.

Johnson, T. J. (1992). *Relevance Regained: From Top-down Control to Bottom-up Empowerment*. The Free Press, New York.

Penn, D. J. (2003). "The evolutionary roots of our environmental problems: Toward a Darwinian ecology," *The Quarterly Review of Biology*, Vol. 78, No. 3, pp275–301.

Porter, M. E. (1985). *Competitive Advantage*. Macmillan Publishing Co., New York.

Sisaye, S. (2011a). "Ecological systems approaches to sustainability and organizational development: Emerging trends in environmental and social accounting reporting systems," *The Leadership & Organization Development Journal*, Vol. 32, No. 4, pp379–396.

Sisaye, S. (2011b). "The functional–institutional and consequential–conflictual sociological approaches to accounting ethics education: Integration from sustainability and ecological resources management literature," *Managerial Auditing Journal*, Vol. 26, No. 3, pp263–294.

Sisaye, S. (2012a). "An ecological approach for the integration of sustainability into the accounting education and professional practice," *Advances in Management Accounting*, Vol. 20, pp47–73.

Sisaye, S. (2012b). "An ecological analysis of four competing approaches to sustainability development: Integration of industrial ecology and ecological anthropology literature," *World Journal of Entrepreneurship, Management and Sustainable Development*, Vol. 8, No. 1, pp18–35.

Sisaye, S. (2013). "The development of sustainable practices in complex organizations: Implications and potentials for integration into the accounting curriculum," *World Journal of Entrepreneurship, Management and Sustainable Development*, Vol. 9, No. 4, pp223–245.

Sisaye, S. and Birnberg, J. G. (2014). "Sociological approaches of organizational learning: Applications to process innovations of management accounting systems," *Advances in Management Accounting*, Vol. 23, pp1–43.

Sisaye, S., Bodnar, G. H. and Christofi, P. (2004). "Total quality management and sustainability reporting: Lessons from Social Soundness Analysis," *Internal Auditing*, Vol. 19, No. 5, pp32–39.

Stone, M. (2003). "Is sustainability for development anthropologists?," *Human Organization*, Vol. 62, No. 2, pp93–99.

Thiele, L. P. (1999). "Evolutionary narratives and ecological ethics," *Political Theory*, Vol. 27, No. 1, pp6–38.

WCED (World Commission on Environment and Development) (1987). *Our Common Future*, The Brundtland Report. World Commission on Environment and Development (WCED) and Oxford University Press, New York.

Zairi, M. (2002). "Beyond TQM implementation: The new paradigm of TQM sustainability," *Total Quality Management*, Vol. 13, No. 8, pp1161–1172.

1 Ecology, sociology and organization development

In general, the ecological approach has been broadly applied to address people, human and animal species, history, geographical locations, geology, climate, agricultural practices, technology, the environment, level of development, vegetation, societal change, culture and ethnic/local population characteristics, as well as organizational development and management.

While the ecological approach has its theoretical and methodological foundations in the biological sciences, it attracted social science research in the late seventeenth and early eighteenth centuries.

During the 1790s, Thomas Malthus applied an ecological evolutionary analysis of population growth to describe famine, poverty, food shortages and resources scarcity (Hawley, 1986). Darwin extended Malthus's essay on population to develop the evolution of population growth by natural selection (Hawley, 1950, 1986). Darwin's theory of evolution and natural selection has been further applied by social and behavioral scientists such as sociologists, anthropologists, economists, geographers and political scientists, amongst others, to explain societal growth and development, organizational change, political systems, cultural change, structures and management control systems.

For example, Hilborn et al. (1995: 47) noted that the theoretical foundations of ecology are in the biological sciences. They used the biological analogy to suggest that reproductive surplus and population growth occur under favorable conditions of sustainable harvesting. This assumes that there has to be a compensatory balance between surplus and mortality for new generations to maintain "balance of births and deaths" to sustain "reproductive output" (p47). There is competition for resources to support animal population growth, which determines the relationship between reproductive surplus and the size of the population in sustainable harvesting. However, when the ecosystem changes because of climate change, the environmental variation will change the reproduction surplus by changing the species. They gave examples from Northeastern Pacifics, where the increased abundance sustainability of pink salmon and Alaska pollock contributed to the decline of "populations of king and tanner crab, fur seals, and many bird species." This shifted the ecosystem "with a major readjustment in the reproductive surplus of many species" (p51). Humans, because of over-exploitation and harvesting, alter the environment and habitat, causing a decline in reproductive surplus and in extreme cases habitat loss due to extinction. Hilborn et al.'s study extends the Darwin theory of evolution and natural selection to explain reproduction surplus and death among the Northeastern Pacifics' pink salmon and Alaska pollock fish populations.

Evolutionary biology has developed the theoretical foundations of the ecological approach to study animal reproduction, growth and death. In addition to evolutionary biology, ecology has also surfaced in many social sciences disciplines: anthropology, sociology, economics and geography. These disciplines have emphasized the importance of ecological approaches in sustainable growth and development strategies. While the subject of the study and research problems may vary among the social science disciplines, most ecological studies have addressed populations or groups instead of units or individuals as their basis of analysis to study social, economic, cultural and political systems, as well as human organizations. In sociology, organizational ecology focuses on the broader environment – community, nation, ecosystem and planet. It addresses the imbalance resulting from pollution, environmental degradation and damages to the ecosystem.

An overview of the ecological approaches to organizations

Ecology focuses on populations of organizations and examines the effect that the environment, market forces, technology, natural resources and geographical locations have on organizational change and development processes. The human ecosystem becomes the dominating factor that shapes non-human ecosystems when humans and non-humans interact with their environment. According to Stepp et al. (2003), the human ecosystem's components include matter, energy and information. Ecology, whether applied in human, non-human or organizational contexts, uses a deterministic approach to explain evolutionary changes. Organizational ecology is a deterministic approach that places relative weights on internal and external environmental conditions as the underlying factors to explain organizational forms and structures, growth and maturity, as well as mortality rates.

Broadly speaking, the ecological approach considers the environment or physical habitat, level of technology (including culture), social organization and population characteristics (for the theoretical background see Duncan, 1961) in a given society. It examines the effect that environment and market forces have on the organizational adaptation process. It has shifted the nature of sociological organizational studies from that of a purely cultural explanation to one incorporating the environment as an interactive factor in the cultural practices of organizational systems. The ecological approach has thus enabled researchers to examine the impact of social and spatial groups, location, geology, level of technology and patterns of land use in the development of organization density and population. It recognizes that there are internal and external environmental constraints on organizational adaptation and change strategies.

Competition is one of those external constraints that enhances organizational learning and innovation to improve current performance. If the number of competitive organizations within a population increases, it creates resource constraints and intensifies the potential for acquisition. Through mergers and acquisitions, the weakest and underperforming organizations are selected out for death, and only the better performing organizations survive (Freeman, 1982; Pfeffer, 1985). Competition and access to resources shape organizational development and growth strategies.

Organizational ecology uses the Darwinian evolutionary perspective to explain the demographic process that contributes to its life cycles, including founding or birth, growth and death (mortality) over the internal adaptation process of change. In an evolutionary process, the number of trials for organizational forms to find better fit is assumed to continue until a point is reached where organizational learning contributes to an increase in population density to the environment without selection (Aldrich, 1979; Amburgey and Rao, 1996; Barnett and Hansen, 1996; Carroll, 1984). At the same time, the evolutionary process may create the conditions for inertia, allowing organizations to compete to secure the scarce resources needed for their sustained survival and growth. This evolutionary process implies that, in competition, there is selection and learning (Barnett and Carroll, 1995; Carroll and Barnett, 2004; Hannan and Freeman, 1977; Singh and Lundsen, 1990), as well as entry, exit, mobility and retention, depending upon organizational size and populations (Fujiwara-Greve and Greve, 2000; Hannan, 1998). Organizational ecology combines organizational inertia with environmental selection to provide a comparative analysis of the evolution of organizational forms and environmental selection mechanisms that govern competition and legitimation in industry life cycles: founding, growth and mortality rates.

Ecology and organization development

The ecological approach explains changes and developments within a population of organizations as dynamic and continuous processes. More importantly, the ecological framework suggests that environmental shifts lead to the development of new policies and procedures to address these issues at the institutional level. Any substantial shifts in the environment call for changes in strategies and policies to maintain organizational stability and functional adaptation. Ecology thus argues that the environment is an important factor in the organizational adaptation and selection process.

According to Frisbie et al. (1984), the ecological approach comprises four dimensions: population, organization, environment and technology. Of these four factors, technology has the most impact in shaping human population adaptation to change.

Technology

Technology plays an important role in the study of class relations, forces of production, division of labor and societal change evolutions/transformation. In human ecological theory, technology forms the basis for organizational competition, survival, resistance and change. According to Frisbie et al. (1984: 751), technology is based on a formulation "which recognizes three ecosystem flows – energy, materials, and information – as basic to the survival and adaptation of populations."

Technology is the main factor that accounts for most theories of societal evolution, including the radical and incremental approaches to social change. Technology not only increases the ability of organizations and society to adapt to change; it also improves their competitive advantage. The possession of advanced technology increases the competitive advantage in populations of organizations. If technology is consolidated, it not only expands the technology gap, but also contributes to the decline and mortality of organizations, which are inferior. Spatial distribution and geographical location affect the distribution and dispersion of technological development among societies, regions and populations of organizations.

Population

Ecology views organizations as communities having interdependency relationships among multiple and diverse populations. These interactions are complex and affect the rise and fall of organizational populations and shape the underlying conditions that promote their mutual homogeneity, diversity, stability, change and growth (Astley, 1985: 114).

According to Marple,

> as populations interact to provide organization for sustenance necessary for the group's survival, particular patterns of population distribution over space emerge and remain temporarily persistent, although change in the structure of these patterns must be seen. Organizations of human population often usually use technology to deal with changing environmental conditions (both physical and social) which enable them to survive. Human ecologists propose that organizations (defined as a collectivity) constantly attempt to bring themselves into an equilibrium with their environments.
>
> (1982: 107–108)

Organizational ecology

Organizational ecology "focuses on the demography of organizational populations (births and deaths of organizations)" (Baker et al., 1998: 173). The approach describes the "relationship between population density and rates of founding, failure and growth" (Barron, 1999: 424). The founding rate refers to "the rate at which new organizations are founded," the failure rate deals with "the rate at which existing organizations leave the population," and the growth rate addresses "the rate at which they grow or decline" (Barron, 1999: 424). The growth rate explains changes in organizational population – growth and decline over time. Organizational growth is faster at earlier periods and then slows down gradually.

Similarly, the likelihood for organization dissolution increases at the earlier stage of the organization life cycle rather than the later years. Organizational birth, growth and failure (decline) are caused by factors that are endogenous and exogenous to the organization (Carroll, 1984). Ecological researchers assume that organizational mortality or "failures are due to causes external to organizations" (Carroll, 1984: 84). Ecological research has shown that organizational death can be attributed to age (newness versus maturity), merger absorption or ownership transfer. Hannan (1998: 128) attributed the death of young organizations as liability of newness, because they are "vulnerable to environmental selection." He noted that aging provides an advantage against environmental vulnerability when there is turbulence and increases their chances to survive. Moreover organizations tend to grow over time as they age and "mortality rate declines with age" (p128). These organizations have a tendency to be inert and to resist change due to familiarity and stability in their social systems (Sisaye, 2006).

Hannan (1998) elaborated structural inertia as occurring when organization capacity for change is limited due to their inabilities to adjust to environmental changes. He referred to his prior work (Hannan and Freeman, 1977, 1984, 1989) to suggest that structural inertia occurs when organizations have very limited capacities to reshape their core structures (their forms) as the environment changes. If they are unable to change their core features, this will affect their chances to live in the short run (pp126–128). He advanced the view that variability and uncertainty in environmental conditions will change organizational forms and the selection process will affect the distribution of organizational populations.

According to Amburgey et al. (1993), the organizational inertia and change processes can be characterized as involving both adaptive and disruptive processes. While organizations can show inertia and reluctance to change, they are more likely to serve as forces for initiating change over time. Organizational changes may contribute to failures for some organizational populations, by increasing mortality failures. For other populations, the change may be accompanied by other additional changes. The impact of these changes depends on the life cycle of the organization – the immediate effects tend to be significant at early stages and decline at later stages.

The evolutionary theory describes a series of sequential stages (life cycles) of evolution in organizational development and societal changes over time. Carroll (1984: 73) suggested the developmental approach assumptions in evolutionary theory included an idea that "organizations change structurally over time and that the form of change is shaped by structural pressures and constraints." Organizations are considered to be "highly adaptive" and "structural changes occur in response to internal and external stimulations." In other words, there is a selection process in organizational adaptation. According to Carroll, ecological theories emphasized that "environmental conditions constrain the organization and shape organizational structure; however, external constraints such as size and technology also affect its structure" (p73). The approach assumes that survival depends upon the organization's ability for adaptability and resource sustenance as it interacts with the external environment. The extent to which organizations can adapt and change their strategies primarily depends on external environmental factors.

Environment

Environmental changes affect organizational systems, structure, strategy, functions, procedures and day-to-day activities. The impact of environmental changes upon the current performance of the organization depends on whether these changes are minor or significant. Whether the environmental impact is minimal or significant, organizations are primarily concerned with maintaining stability and continuity. The impact of external environmental factors – stable or unstable environment – varies according to the age of the organization and complexity of its structures. During periods of stability, when the impact of environmental changes is minimal, organizations are less likely to undertake a major change. They are able to implement incremental procedural changes that will sustain the current operations of the organization with or without changing (i.e., sustaining existing performance). In stable environments, older organizations have advantages over newer organizations since they have developed repetitive and fixed routines of handling their activities that are consonant with their environment.

On the other hand, when there are significant changes (i.e., in dynamic–unstable environments that contribute to low performance), current structures are unable to meet these changes. This requires a fundamental change in the organization's structure, strategy and human resources. Newer organizations are able to adapt easier than mature organizations "as old established procedures [of mature organizations] may no longer accomplish what they were initially intended to do" (Marple, 1982: 109). Altering well-established procedures can be very difficult and costly.

As organizations grow over time, they expand and tend to resist changing their procedures. For these organizations, gaining legitimacy is important. They attempt to gain visibility and exert environmental impact through mergers, acquisitions or corporate interlocking with other organizations (Aldrich, 1979). The size and age of organizations may accelerate or impede change process and technological innovations, and may contribute to their death.

Organizational continuity and dissolution can occur if there is a change in one or more domains of the organization communities. According to Thompson (1967), organizational domain refers to the organization's stakeholders, including the technology used by the organization, the product and/or services rendered, and the clients – stockholders, employees and others – whom it serves. When the organization changes one or more of its domains, it involves changes in the organization's core activities.

As Haveman (1992) noted, environmental changes can have either a considerable or a peripheral impact upon organizational core activities. When the changes are considered significant, it can have a negative effect on organizations' core activities of accountability, reproducibility and performance, which could increase mortality rates. On the other hand, if the changes are minimal and peripheral, it is likely to have a positive effect on improved performance by enabling organizations to enter into new markets or develop related products (Haveman, 1992: 48–75). It is this surviving tendency of organizations that causes inertia to persist over time as organizations develop and adapt their mission and strategy when they interface with their surrounding environment.

Wholey and Brittain (1986) argued that environmental conditions and slack resources shape organizational strategy as becoming either specialist or generalist. Organizations become generalist or specialist depending on environmental conditions: stable or volatile. When environmental conditions are stable, organizations become specialists. Volatile environmental conditions increase uncertainty, and organizations become generalists to diversify the risks associated with uncertainty.

When an organization diversifies, diversification – whether related or unrelated – changes some components or aspects of the organizational domain, which results in changes in organizational forms. Changes that have fewer impacts on the organizational domain are easier to undertake, and less threatening to organizational survival and performance (Haveman, 1992). Many organizations undertake related diversification of existing products and markets compared to unrelated diversification of new products, markets and customers. The effect from related diversification on the organizational domain is lower. When compared to unrelated diversification, related, diversification results in better organizational performance and adaptation (Haveman, 1992; Rumelt, 1974, 1982). Increases in organizational death and failure are more likely to be associated with unrelated, rather than related, diversification (Barnett and Carroll, 1995). Haveman (1992: 72) noted that "if organizations build on their original domain, financial performance is enhanced; if changes bear no relation to the competencies developed through experience in the original domain, financial performance is hurt."

The resource-based approach to the organizational domain puts an emphasis on organizations to capitalize on their existing competencies, particularly if it involves the innovation of new products and/or services. If innovation change focuses on the original domain of what the firm does best, it utilizes past knowledge, experience and technology for the future endeavors of new products and services. The resource outlay and the costs incurred for such innovations can be managed and controlled to improve future performance.

The resource-based view of the firm

The resource-based view of the firm has its theoretical and practical foundations in the ecology of organizations literature. In general, organizational ecology has addressed the relationship among organizational resource availability, environmental conditions and strategic management policies to address these issues. The resource-based approach suggests that organizations seek to develop/maintain a competitive advantage of the available resources to meet their demands and opportunities by aligning their strategic plans with the environment to develop a strategic fit and align organizational functional areas of management to achieve sustainable development objectives (Munck and Borim-de-Souza, 2012: 404–405). The resource-based view of the firm is based upon the organization's relationship to the natural resources environment.

Resource availability and adaptation strategies are shaped by internal and external environmental factors. The resource-based view assumes that firms have resources – material, financial and human – and capabilities (skills) to have competitive advantage over others. These unique, non-substitutable and difficult-to-imitate resources and capabilities (skills) shape corporate sustainable development. Firms' ability to control valuable resources that are non-substitutable and difficult to imitate provides competitive advantage and the capability to manage environmental threats and to sustain business performance (Barney, 1991; Porter, 1985; Rumelt, 1982).

Firms' competencies arise when they have an advantage over others in terms of "resources that are rare, non-substitutable, difficult to imitate, and valuable to customers" that are acquired due to "physical assets, employee skills, and organizational processes" (Buysse and Verbeke, 2003: 454). The management and sustenance of these unique resources and capabilities are affected by conservation and economic growth policies. Bansal (2005) identified "three resource based variables" – "international experience," "capital management capabilities" and "organizational slack" (ample resources) – as providing competitive sustainable development strategies (pp200–201). If firms possess resource distinctiveness, capability and slack, Bansal suggested that they can become instrumental in shaping the early stages as well as sustaining long-term corporate sustainable environmental programs.

The resource-based view of an organization emphasizes the importance of heterogeneity in a firm's ecological resources: physical, natural, economic and financial. It suggests that those firms who possess heterogeneous resources that are non-substitutable, difficult to imitate and are rare and valuable have a relative advantage to withstand external changes and adapt to them relatively easily compared to their competitors. When firms have both the resources and the complementary assets that provide access to both manufacturing and distribution facilities to reduce cost and improve the quality of products and services, they have acquired competitive advantage strategies from their competitors. These organizations have the resources to withstand externality costs associated with liability costs, legal fees or clean-up costs that are necessary to support improved organizational performance (Barney, 1988, 1991, 2001; Christmann, 2000; Rumelt, 1974).

The political economy of the environment shapes the availability and control of resources. Rudel et al. (2011: 222) noted that, "For sociologists, the political economy of the environment refers to how people control and, periodically, struggle for control over the institutions and organizations that produce and regulate the flows of materials that sustain people (corporations and the state)." Access and control of valuable resources are the key for managing the environment.

In the business management literature, the resource-based view of the firm has been derived from the ecological approaches of sociology and anthropology.

Given the co-evolution history of sustainability, it becomes apparent that the integration of sustainability into the accounting literature will be largely influenced by the resource-based framework of the organizational ecology of sociology and ecological anthropological literature (Sisaye, 2011).

The resource-based view of an organization has been commonly used in strategic management research to study how differences in resources among organizations affect their capabilities to undertake planning and control initiatives in response to environmental changes. It is assumed that organizational resources do provide the necessary support for "learning" and "exploration" when organizations engage in "exploitation" of knowledge that they have already acquired or when they try to use their resources to improve what they already have in existing products and/or services. According to Kraatz and Zajac (2001), organizations undertake plans to innovate only when the environmental change(s) create constant threats to the organization's survival and/or growth. However, the ability of these organizations to respond to environmental and competitive changes depends on the availability: slack or scarce ecological resources.

Economic development and population growth have created challenges to natural and environmental resources to sustain growth. Ecosystems cannot support business, market and industrial growth unless there is an environmental resource-based economic development policy. Hart (1995) suggested that the natural resource-based view of the firm is based on the notion that prevention pollution, managing product stewardship and sustainable development are inter-related and are strategically important to sustain competitive advantage. These resources may enable firms to have pollution control, product stewardship/differentiation and life-cycle analysis and/or sustainable development strategies. Sustainable development requires long-term strategies in developing technologies that are green and clean and preserve the environment as well as supporting strategic and moral leadership for the organization (Buysse and Verbeke, 2003: 455). The sustainable development strategy prioritizes moral leadership, legitimacy and shared vision, and has "a strong sense of social-environmental purposes" (Hart, 1995: 1002).

The resource-based approach to the organizational domain puts an emphasis on organizations to capitalize on their existing competencies, particularly if it involves the innovation of new products and/or services. If innovation change focuses on the original domain of what the firm does best, it utilizes past knowledge, experience and technology for the future endeavors of new products and services. The resource outlay and the costs incurred for such innovations can be managed and controlled to improve future performance. The ecological approach to organizational adaptation utilizes the selection process, whereby organizational resources are allocated in change programs where the original domain existed and competencies are well developed. The change process can contribute to the organizational evolution of survival or decline depending on the number of organizations within a given population.

Organizations can thus take advantage of learning and innovation as a competitive advantage to secure control of valuable and scarce resources (Sisaye and Birnberg, 2014). Although there are variations among organizations in their responses to environmental changes, those organizations that do survive and grow continue to develop new technologies and inventions in their industrial sectors. The resource-based view uses evolutionary economics to examine an organization's response to environmental changes.

As a resource-based view of the firm, evolutionary economics examines organizations' "resources, competencies and trajectories" (Durand, 2001: 398). It focuses on the internal pressures of environmental selection when examining forms of organizational behaviors and routines and their responses to environmental changes. Evolutionary economics thus provides a coherent and integrated framework to explain the social and economic development processes and sequences of organizational adaptation and change in the environment (Peukert, 2001). It has a micro focus on individual organizations and attempts to explain the behavior of organizations and their decisions in relation to environmental changes and requirements. The behavior of organizations is governed by the economic selection mechanism whereby individual decisions are made according to profitability rules of exogenous factors involving shifts in consumer demand and supplier input prices which can influence investment decisions (Nelson and Winter, 1974: 891, 893). In accounting, the evolutionary economics approach to a resource-based view of the firm is the predominant view that has influenced the financial accounting theory of profitability and economic return in tangible assets and capital investment decisions.

The underlying premise in ecological economics is that, when the environment changes, organizations rely on research and development or through a trial and error process of organizational learning to solve their problems. Nelson et al. (1976: 91–92) indicated that the process of change is governed by "an economic selection mechanism" that organizations employ selectively, including expansion when there is profitability and contraction when there is loss. The evolutionary dynamics of organizational populations, including birth, growth, maturity and death, are affected by economic resources where geographical location and spatial characteristics limit resource domain and availability.

Barnett and Carroll (1995) discussed two approaches to organizational change – the adaptation and the selection mechanisms of organizational change. Both evolutionary economics and the resource-based view of sociology described in this chapter examine organizational adaptation as a selection process, where organizational resources are allocated in change programs where the original domain existed and competencies are well developed. Chapter 2 extends the population ecology approach of organizations to describe the evolutionary process of organizations as entailing a selection of survival or decline depending upon the number and size of organizations within a given population.

References

Aldrich, H. E. (1979). *Organizations and Environments*. Englewood Cliff, NJ: Prentice-Hall.

Amburgey, T.L., Kelly, D. and Barnett, W.P. (1993). "Resetting the clock: The dynamics of organizational change and failure," *Administrative Science Quarterly*, Vol. 38, No. 1, pp 51–73.

Amburgey, T. L. and Rao, H. (1996). "Organizational ecology: Past, present, and future directions," *Academy of Management Journal*, Vol. 39, No. 5, pp1265–1286.

Astley, W. G. (1985). "The two ecologies: Population and community perspectives on organizational evolution," *Administrative Science Quarterly*, Vol. 30, No. 2, pp224–241.

Baker, W. E., Faulkner, R. R. and Fisher, G. A. (1998). "Hazards of the market: The continuity and dissolution of inter-organizational market relationships," *American Sociological Review*, Vol. 63, No. 2, pp147–177.

Bansal, P. (2005). "Evolving sustainability: A longitudinal study of corporate sustainable development," *Strategic Management Journal*, Vol. 26, No. 3, pp197–218.

Barnett, W. P. and Carroll, G. R. (1995). "Modeling internal organizational change," *Annual Review of Sociology*, Vol. 21, pp217–236.

Barnett, W. P. and Hansen, M. T. (1996). "The red queen in organizational evolution," *Strategic Management Journal*, Vol. 17 (Special Issue, Summer), No. 1, pp139–157.

Barney, J. B. (1988). "Returns to bidding firms in mergers and acquisitions: Reconsidering the relatedness hypothesis," *Strategic Management Journal*, Vol. 9, Special Issue, pp71–78.

Barney, J. B. (1991). "Firm resources and sustained competitive advantage," *Journal of Management*, Vol. 17, pp99–120.

Barney, J. B. (2001). "Is the resources based 'view' a useful perspective for strategic management research? Yes," *Academy of Management Review*, Vol. 26, No. 1, pp41–56.

Barron, D. (1999). "The structuring of organizational populations," *American Sociological Review*, Vol. 64, No. 3, pp421–445.

Buysse, K. and Verbeke, A. (2003). "Proactive environmental strategies: A stakeholder management perspective," *Strategic Management Journal*, Vol. 24, No. 5, pp453–470.

Carroll, G. R. (1984). "Organizational ecology," *Annual Review of Sociology*, Vol. 10, pp71–93.

Carroll, G. R. and Barnett, W. P. (2004). "Organizational ecology: An introduction," *Industrial and Corporate Change*, Vol. 13, pp1–2.

Christmann, P. (2000). "Effects of 'best practices' of environmental management on cost advantage: The role of complementary assets," *Academy of Management Journal*, Vol. 43, pp663–680.

Duncan, O. D. (1961). "From social system to ecosystem," *Sociological Quarterly*, Vol. 21, No. 2, pp140–149.

Durand, R. (2001). "Firm selection: An integrative perspective," *Organization Studies*, Vol. 22, No. 3, pp393–417.

Freeman, J. (1982). "Organizational life cycles and natural selection processes," *Research in Organizational Behavior*, Vol. 4, pp1–32.

Frisbie, W. B., Krivo, L. J., Kaufman, R. L., Clarke, C. J. and Myers, D. E. (1984). "A measurement of technological change: An ecological perspective," *Social Forces*, Vol. 62, No. 3, pp750–765.

Fujiwara-Greve, T. and Greve, H. R. (2000). "Organizational ecology and job mobility," *Social Forces*, Vol. 79, No. 2, pp547–585.

Hannan, M. T. (1998). "Rethinking age dependence in organizational mortality: Logical formalizations," *American Journal of Sociology*, Vol. 104, No. 1, pp126–164.

Hannan, M. T. and Freeman, J. (1977). "The population ecology of organizations," *American Journal of Sociology*, Vol. 82, No. 3, pp929–964.

Hannan, M. T. and Freeman, J. (1984). "Structural inertia and organizational change," *American Sociological Review*, Vol. 49, No. 1, pp149–164.

Hannan, M. T. and Freeman, J. (1989). *Organizational Ecology*. Harvard University Press, Cambridge, MA.
Hart, S. L. (1995). "A natural resource based view of the firm," *The Academy of Management Review*, Vol. 20, No. 4, pp986–1014.
Haveman, H. A. (1992). "Between a rock and a hard place: Organizational change and performance under conditions of fundamental environmental transformation," *Administrative Science Quarterly*, Vol. 37, No. 1, pp48–75.
Hawley, A. H. (1950). *Human Ecology: A Theory of Community Structure*. Ronald Press Company, New York.
Hawley, A. H. (1986). *Human Ecology: A Theoretical Essay*. University of Chicago Press, Chicago, IL.
Hilborn, R., Walters, C. J. and Ludwig, D. (1995). "Sustainable exploitation of renewable resources," *Annual Review of Ecology and Systematics*, Vol. 26, pp45–67.
Kraatz, M. S. and Zajac, E. J. (2001). "How organizational resources affect strategic change and performance in turbulent environments: Theory and evidence," *Organization Science*, Vol. 12, No. 5, pp632–657.
Marple, D. (1982). "Technological innovation and organizational survival: A population ecology study of nineteenth century American railroads," *The Sociological Quarterly*, Vol. 23, No. 1, pp107–116.
Munck, L. and Borim-de-Souza, R. (2012). "Sustainability and competencies in organizational contexts: A proposal of a model of interaction," *International Journal of Environment & Sustainable Development*, Vol. 11, No. 4, pp394–411.
Nelson, R. R. and Winter, S. G. (1974). "Neoclassical vs. evolutionary theories of economic growth: Critique and prospects," *The Economic Journal*, Vol. 84, No. 336, pp886–905.
Nelson, R. R., Winter, S. G. and Schuette, H. L. (1976). "Technical change in an evolutionary model," *Quarterly Journal of Economics*, Vol. 90, No. 1, pp90–118.
Peukert, H. (2001). "On the origins of modern evolutionary economics: The Veblen legend after 100 years," *Journal of Economic Issues*, Vol. 35, No. 3, pp543–555.
Pfeffer, J. (1985). "Organizational demography: Implications for management," *California Management Review*, Vol. 28, Fall, pp67–81.
Porter, M. E. (1985). *Competitive Advantage*. Macmillan Publishing Co., New York.
Rudel, T. K., Roberts, J. T. and Carmin, J. A. (2011). "Political economy of the environment," *Annual Review of Sociology*, Vol. 37, pp221–238.
Rumelt, R. P. (1974). *Strategy, Structure and Economic Performance*. Harvard University Press, Boston, MA.
Rumelt, R. P. (1982). "Diversification strategy and profitability," *Strategic Management Journal*, Vol. 3, No. 4, pp359–369.
Singh, J. V. and Lundsen, C. J. (1990). "Theory and research in organizational ecology," *Annual Review of Sociology*, Vol. 16, pp161–195.
Sisaye, S. (2006). *The Ecology of Management Accounting and Control Systems: Implications for Managing Teams and Work Groups in Complex Organizations*. Praeger Publications in Business & Economics Series, Greenwood Publishing Group, Greenwich, CT.
Sisaye, S. (2011). "Ecological systems approaches to sustainability and organizational development: Emerging trends in environmental and social accounting reporting systems," *The Leadership & Organization Development Journal*, Vol. 32, No. 4, pp379–396.
Sisaye, S. and Birnberg, J. G. (2014). "Sociological approaches of organizational learning: Applications to process innovations of management accounting systems," *Advances in Management Accounting*, Vol. 23, pp1–43.

Stepp, E. C., Pavao-Zuckerman, M., Casagrande, D. and Zarger, R. K. (2003). "Synthesis: Remarkable properties of human ecosystems," *Conservation Ecology*, Vol. 7, No. 3, Article 11, www.consecol.org/vol7/iss3/art11 (accessed January/February 2015).
Thompson, J. D. (1967). *Organizations in Action*. McGraw-Hill, New York.
Wholey, D. R. and Brittain, J. W. (1986). "Organizational ecology: Findings and implications," *Academy of Management Review*, Vol. 11, No. 3, pp513–533.

2 Population ecology of organizations

The underlying framework in population ecology is that there is a natural selection to populations of organizations in the adaptation process. The approach focuses on those environmental characteristics that select organizational forms which are best suited and adapted to the ecosystem. Organizations are examined in reference to time and space, which explain their survival, growth and decline.

The population and organizational ecology approaches describe selection processes as continuously taking place in organizational change and development. In these processes, organizations selectively replace old forms with new forms that represent the method by which changes take place among populations of organizations. The selection approach to organizational change

> assumes that individual organizations cannot change easily and quickly. When they do change, there are greater risks that are entailed. By this view, when technologies and environments change, some existing organizations fail, while some new organizations also appear. The selective replacement of old forms of organization by the new forms constitute the main way this mechanism accounts for change in the world of organization.
>
> (Barnett and Carroll, 1995: 218; see also Barnett and Hansen, 1996; and Barron, 1999)

The selection process goes through periods of evolution, growth, decline and ecological adaptation. Organizations select their strategies: they adopt an incremental change strategy during periods of stability and a radical/transformational change strategy during periods of crisis and environmental volatility.

Population ecology, selection and organization development and decline: an overview

In general, the population ecology of evolutionary theory is based on the assumption that all organizations go through three stages – variation, selection and retention – over time. Carroll (1984) provided a review of the literature on organizational ecology and the evolutionary theory of organizational change, and suggested that Aldrich's (1979) work on organization and environment contributed much to empirical research in the evolutionary theory of organizations. He stated that

> Aldrich (1979) linked the selection approach to the general literature on organizational theory and fleshed out the evolutionary logic of population ecology … he characterized evolution as a three-stage process consisting of variation, selection and retention. Organizational variation is an essential precondition of selection which could give rise to various organizational forms (p74). On the other hand, in the second stage, selection posits a mechanism for the elimination of certain types of organizations. Elimination can occur through any type of organizational mortality: dissolution, absorption by merger, or radical transformation. The mechanism of elimination is usually an environmental condition.

Lastly,

> the final stage is retention. In formal organizations, retention is not (as in biological organisms) a generation problem – formal organizations can in theory be immortal. Instead, retention is a structural problem. Organizations with advantageous traits must not lose them through incremental change.
>
> (p74)

While the retention stage makes the organizations more adaptive, "inertia now plays a more central role in organizational evolution by providing the basis for selection" (p74; see also Carroll and Barnett, 2004).

Tushman and O'Reilly III (1996) defined the three principles of population ecology – "variation, selection, and retention" – as follows. Organizations "promote variation through strong efforts to decentralize, to eliminate bureaucracy, to encourage individual autonomy and accountability, and to experiment and take risks. They promote wide variations in products, technologies, and markets" (p28). The selection process allows "'winners' in markets and technologies by staying close to their customers, by being quick to respond to market signals, and by having clear mechanisms to 'kill' products and projects" (p29). Finally, the retention process occurs when the market serves as "the ultimate arbiter of the winners and losers" in deciding which of those organizations' "technologies, products, markets, and even senior managers" will be retained (p29).

Tushman and O'Reilly III (1996) found the population ecology adaptation and fitness approach in the evolutionary theory of variation, selection and retention (Aldrich, 1979) to be applicable to study organizational change and development. The organizational ecology approach is useful because it suggests that

> populations of organizations are subject to ecological pressures in which they evolve through periods of incremental adaptation punctuated by

> discontinuities. Variations in organizational strategy and form are more or less suitable for different environmental conditions. These organizations and managers who are most able to adapt to a given market or competitive environment will prosper. Over time, the fittest survive – until there is a major discontinuity. At that point, managers of firms are faced with the challenges of reconstructing their organizations to adjust to the new environment. Managers who try to adapt to discontinuities through incremental adjustment are unlikely to succeed.
>
> (pp12–13)

They found the organizational ecology approach relevant to explain organizational learning and change processes in ambidextrous organizations. They defined ambidextrous organizations as those who are able to align their business to remain competitive by utilizing efficient management techniques to adapt to changes in external and internal environment demands. These organizations are capable of implementing both incremental and revolutionary innovation changes. They extended the ecological approach to study the evolutionary change processes in these organizations.

Selection, age, organizational size and development

The ecological selection approach examines location, technology, geographical boundaries and the social and spatial arrangements of organizational development, and suggests that environmental changes and competitive and adaptive strategies do shape organizational growth and change. For example, theories of the external or environmental control of organizations suggest that there are positive and negative consequences associated with organizational growth. Growth indicates that an organization has been able to acquire the necessary resources that contribute to increased size. In general, organizational growth occurs when management uses resources, goals, priorities and commitments to satisfy customer needs for products and/or services. When growth results in increased size, due to economies of scale, organizations are able to have abundant resources and become competitive, and if they diversify, they are able to spread their risks across several industries, product lines or services. Growth enables organizations to reduce their dependence on the environment and minimize external influence on the organization's activities (Pfeffer and Salancik, 1978).

Hannan (1998) associated age with providing positional advantage in the social and economic structures of organizations built on good relations and reputation. Trust takes time, and older organizations have an advantage over new organizations in building trust and acquiring political influence and market power (pp134, 152). He suggested that mortality declines with age since control of resources and positional power is enhanced with age, which decreases mortality (pp134–138). As organizations age, political friction and conflict diminish collective action for change and increase mortality with age. He implied that mortality hazard among organizations increases with age for organizations that are not resource endowed, while for those resource-endowed organizations, the rate of mortality remained constant. Therefore, "aging can both enhance and diminish capability, depending on the relative strength of the links of age with the cumulation of knowledge and the intensification of internal friction" (p144). If an alignment between organizational capability and the demands of the external environment occurs, the organization has adapted to environmental change, thereby reducing mortality. Otherwise, if the environment changes, the process of inertia makes it harder for the organization to realign with the external environmental changes (pp144–146).

In contrast, there are also dysfunctional consequences of growth that are associated with complexity, rigidity, inefficiency and inaccessibility. Hannan (1998) has noted that size contributes to internal friction, which diminishes the organization's capability of an increased life span (pp139–140). While experience and learning are acquired over time with age, changing and drifting environments create constraints for change by intensifying internal frictions, causing inertia to diminish the capability of change to decline with age (p157).

The ecological selection approach suggests that environmental changes and competitive and adaptive strategies contribute to the development of new organizational policies and procedures, including management accounting control systems. Complexity in accounting systems is commonly associated with organizational growth. As organizations increase in size, profitability and innovation usually diminish with increased size. The organizational learning process focuses more on managing growth through accounting and formal management control systems, resulting in increased communication and coordination activities; bureaucratization of rules and procedures; management hierarchy of offices and positions; and specialization of jobs, all contributing to monotony, repetitiveness and less autonomy, mechanization of work and mass production and job alienation (Whetten, 1987: 341–343). When organizations develop inertia, they tend to resist change. The structural inertia of organizational change assumes that organizations become rigid and resistant to change (inertia) over time as they develop well-established and accepted rules, procedures, functions and structures to conduct their activities. When a change is required because of crisis, market conditions or resource shortages, those sources of inertia are amenable for change and can be overhauled by new rules, regulations and structures (Amburgey et al., 1993; Hannan and Freeman, 1977, 1984, 1989). Accounting rules are subject to change as organizations go through adaptation and change processes.

Since change may result in "winners" and "losers," the implementation of the requisite changes are likely to be met with resistance; this is the case because the inertia embodies the self-interest of some members of the organization. When there is inertia, innovation programs can be successfully implemented only when new structures, strategies and systems are in place. However, accounting changes tend to disrupt existing functions and relationships during the early stage, which affects performance. Over time, as organization members learn and participate in the change program, there is less disruption and the organization is able to improve its current performance. Nevertheless, in a competitive environment, a change program may not necessarily contribute to retention if competition is so intense that the organization is unable to cope with the change. Competition may be one of the most important determining factors that will account for organizational failure along with inertia (Hannan and Freeman, 1984, 1989).

Competition is a destabilizing force in organizations. It increases the likelihood for dissolution if there are too many small firms in the market, there are minimal or no barriers for entry and exit, firms are undifferentiated and products are homogenous (Porter, 1980, 1985; Stigler, 1968). While price is the main form of competition in many merchandising and manufacturing firms, it is less important in service organizations such as auditing firms (Porter, 1980, 1985).

In addition to competition, power and institutional factors affect organizational continuity and dissolution (Baker et al., 1998). Unequal power and exchange relationships increase the likelihood of organizational dissolution. In any exchange relationship, power dictates the terms of exchange. It creates dependency relationships if one party has possession of resources or a commodity valued by the other party (Pfeffer, 1981, 1992). On the other hand, institutional forces create the pressure for conformity and reduce the risk for dissolution.

Baker et al. (1998) argued that competition, power and institutional forces shape organizational dissolution and continuity (meaning uninterrupted long-term market relationships). They suggested that while competition destabilizes market relationships and contributes to dissolution, institutional forces create stability. The balance among competition, power and institutional forces is necessary if market ties are expected to be stable and show continuity (pp153–154). Baker et al.'s (1998: 173) research shows

> that the mortality of market relationships is a function of the institutional rules of exchange created during the emergence of the market, which are supported, reinforced, violated, and transformed over the years by the interplay of competition, power, and institutional forces.

Singh and Lundsen (1990) indicated that if a convergence between ecological and institutional research occurs, researchers will be able to examine the extent to which institutional environment variables have influenced the ecological dynamics of organizational populations, and the role of legitimacy and institutionalization in population dynamics. Institutional variables such as customers, competitors, suppliers and government regulatory agencies have profound effects on vital organizational rates: founding, disbanding, mortality/death or performance change rates. On the other hand, legitimacy or external institutional support reduces selection pressures on organizations. In general, legitimacy in the institutional environment "provides access to resources, which reduces mortality rates" (Singh and Lundsen, 1990: 184). While young organizations lack legitimacy and institutional support due to newness liability assumptions, those organizations that have them have relatively easy access to resources, which reduces their mortality rates. The ecological approaches of sustainability represent the cumulative effects of the institutionalization of environmental programs of organizations in a given population.

The ecological systems approach of populations of organizations has been extended to examine the effect the environment, market forces, technology, natural resources and geographical locations have on sustainable development processes. Similarly, accounting systems, including sustainability accounting reporting, are viewed as populations or groups instead of units or individuals. The organization–environment linkage shapes the evolution of sustainable development and reporting of corporations within the same population or industrial organizations. It assumes that organizational ecology enhances sustainability by linking environmental resources management "to quality, production, service and managerial systems" (Cohen-Rosenthal, 2000; Ehrenfeld, 2000). It promotes organizational learning where employees are trained and made aware of the importance of environmental issues and natural resources conservation. Accordingly, sustainable development and sound environmental management programs comprise the primary components for establishing organizational and anthropological ecological relationships.

In general, ecological studies consider internal and external environmental conditions related to social, economic, cultural and political systems as factors determining organizational forms and structures; growth, maturity and mortality rates; and adaptation and selection strategies. Ecological systems theory follows the deterministic approach to explain the rise and fall of organizations and shapes the conditions that develop homogeneity, diversity, stability, change and growth among them (Astley, 1985: 114).

Ecology as a deterministic approach

The ecological approach puts the emphasis on environmental characteristics and conditions as factors determining organizational evolution and change in organizational structures. Burrell and Morgan (1979) classified the ecological approach under the functionalist paradigm. According to Kuhn (1970), a paradigm has a structure of ideas, principles and propositions; statements are presented in a logical, integrated and systematic manner to provide a coherent set of arguments about the matter of interest in the environment. The ecological approach has sets of rules and propositions that are amenable to incremental change. Any fundamental change requires a shift in paradigm which, in turn, has its own sets of rules and principles that are, in contrast, different from the other paradigm (Walck, 2004: 171–172). According to Walck (2004), the ecology paradigm emphasizes the natural environment, ecological principles and critical limits to natural assets; it favors "ecocentrism" (p171). Ecology thus denotes conservation and environmental protection.

Although the ecological framework concentrated on selection, birth and organizational

> death, it did not exclude from the analysis that adaptation and growth involved both learning and technological changes. It considered technological development as the primary determinant factor in societal transformation processes.

Burrell and Morgan (1979) suggested that the functional assumptions that structures evolved over time, and that these changes fit environmental selection, followed the structural functional (SF) deterministic approach. Child (1977) elaborated that the ecological approach gives little attention to management choice and decisions as factors influencing organizational evolution. Because the ecological approach "considers that units which do not have organizational forms characteristic of their sector – or 'niche' – have a poorer chance of survival," it underscores the role of decision-makers in the organizational adaptation process (Child, 1977: 45). He suggested that because organizations as social systems benefit from learning which results in knowledge creation, they are capable of environmental adaptation. Both Burrell and Morgan (1979) and Child (1977) noted that structures, functions and strategies do play roles in selection, environmental changes and organizational development.

Ecological systems as structural functional views of organizational development

The ecological systems approach studies organizations in relation to contextual environmental factors such as "structure, size, technology, and leadership patterns concerned with articulating patterns of contingent relationships among a collection of variables that appear to figure in organizational survival" (Smirch, 1983: 44). The systems approach views organizations as being composed of several systems that are interdependent, where a change in one or more parts of the system will affect the entire system.

The SF view considers organizations as systems that are functional and purposeful. Systems are assumed to be comprised of individuals, groups/teams, structures, systems and policies (for details, refer to Boulding, 1968; Tracy, 1993; and Von Bertalanffy, 1968, 1975). According to Nadler (1981), the systems model looks at organizations as comprising four major components (subsystems). These include: "the tasks (work to be done in the organization), individuals (who perform the work in the organization), formal organizational arrangements (processes that motivate people to work or achieve organizational goals)," and a set of informal organizational arrangements that deal with "communication, power, influence, values, and norms" (p193). The model assumes the four parts are interrelated, with functional relationships that promote congruence and system maintenance.

The SF approach has focused on the stability of systems relationships, their congruence within organizations and their ability to develop adaptive structures as they interface with environmental changes. Selznick (1969) described the SF analysis as relating organizational structural behavioral characteristics of communication, authority, management relations, social roles and sources of power to the maintenance and continuity of a stable organization (p25). The SF approach to stability and system maintenance constituted the underlying framework for the ecological approach, which laid the foundation for sustainable development and the analysis of complex organizations (Parsons, 1951; Perrow, 1986; Selznick, 1957).

The functional assumption is based on the premise that management generally supports administrative control and accounting information innovations to implement sustainability programs. As change champions, managers continuously revise existing bureaucratic control systems and hierarchical organization rules and procedures that may hinder the formation of collaborative teams/groups to enhance their functional performance. Managers are instrumental in ensuring the availability of required organizational resources to support intra-functional coordination, team collaboration, joint use of resources and consensus decision-making processes (Sisaye and Birnberg, 2014). Greater team cohesion and instrumental cooperation lead to high productivity and output (Etzioni, 1961: 80). When teams function under loose monitoring and control mechanisms, administrative processes encourage taking initiatives in sustainability programs that require risk-taking behaviors (Shane, 1994: 397–421). Managers use their rank and authority strategically to influence teams and individual behaviors for the purpose of creating socio-political processes that support innovative behaviors and the contested changes of sustainability programs in organizations (Deluga and Perry, 1994: 67–86; Maute and Locander, 1994: 161–174; Sisaye, 2006).

The SF approach views ecological and environmental resources management as involving interdependency relationships among ecological living systems. Sustainability defines those acceptable ethical values and mores of social relations within those interdependent living communities (systems). Resource management among humans entails a collective process governed by cultural and social relationships (Thiele, 1999). Accordingly, business organizations are expected to develop growth strategies based on ethical and moral values of sustainability (Sisaye et al., 2004; see also Bansal, 2005; Dilling, 2009; Epstein, 2008; Sahlin-Anderson, 2006). The ecology of sustainable development in business has focused on ethics and corporate social responsibilities (Sisaye, 2011b). A functional synergy developed between environmental ethics and strategic sustainability management which focused on how corporations have integrated sustainability into their strategies with examples of best practice from business corporations.

Ecological sustainability has been influenced by the underlying assumptions of SF to plan and implement improved productivity and conservation management programs. Within this perspective, accounting reporting systems are viewed as functional living organizational ecosystems that are capable of adapting, evolving and growing over time to record and report the production and conservation of ecological resources (Sisaye, 2011a). Ecological sustainability provides an institutional adaptation and selection framework of evolutionary changes in accounting reporting systems necessitated by organizational growth or decline due to age, size and changes or constraints in environmental systems.

Effects of organizational age and size on growth and decline

The failure rates of organizations tend to decline monotonically as a function of size. Size, in turn, is attributed to age. Hannan (1998) noted that as organizations grow over time in size, their mortality declines when compared to young organizations due to advantages of resource endowments. The liability of resource scarcity is higher among young organizations. As resources are depleted, mortality becomes age dependent, as experience and learning matter for survival (pp131–133). Compared to small organizations, large organizations have relatively extensive resources, favorable tax laws and government regulatory agencies, and can exert greater influence over environmental fluctuations, especially competition, either by "monopolizing key environmental resources or by exerting control over their institutional environment" (Ranger-Moore, 1997: 805).

When it comes to aging, "organizations experience a monotonic liability of aging that is reflected in a failure rate that increases at a decreasing rate with age" (Ranger-Moore, 1997: 907). Nevertheless, as organizations go through a learning experience, the failure rates decline monotonically with their age. While older organizations do relatively well in stable environments and their failure rates are low, in dynamic and volatile environments, failure rates for older organizations are higher and lower for younger organizations. This is because inertia forces accumulate with age, resulting in obsolescence, which during environmental turbulence creates panic and uncertainty, contributing to increased mortality or failure rates among older organizations (Ranger-Moore, 1997: 912).

In addition to the failure rates, organizational size has an impact upon growth rates. Growth rates are observed to decline as a function of size, supporting the theory that the accrual of organizational inertia reduces the ability of organizations to capitalize on growth opportunities (Ranger-Moore et al., 1995: 1027). While growing organizations tend to be less adaptable to changing environmental conditions, increased organizational inertia makes these organizations more accountable and reliable, resulting in enhanced performance. In general, environmental periods characterized by government regulatory activities and economic depression or downturn lead to increased mortality rates. On the other hand, economic growth, resource availability and limited competition reduce or decrease organizational death rates. These factors contribute to organizations undergoing an evolutionary process of life-cycle change characterized by growth, decline or death.

Organizational life cycles: staged theory of development

The process of organizational birth, growth, maturity, decline and mortality is based on the theory of organizational life cycles (OLC) and failures. OLC uses a biological analogy to social systems to explain that life-cycle growth is associated with age. Organizations pursue strategies of growth, survival or merger to manage their external environment and competitors. Freeman (1982: 2) referred to the life-cycle process as "patterns over time through which new organizations come into being, change, and disappear."

The theory of OLC involves both incremental and radical changes that occur through longer periods of time. External environmental changes including technologies, markets, government regulations, competitive forces and international conditions bring sudden changes that require discontinuities. Radical changes from one stage to another are the result of discontinuous changes, which result in organizational transformation. According to Barnett and Carroll (1995), the life-cycle theories of organizational change look at the internal factors that contributed to these changes. Most studies are cases which examine the historical growth and transformation of "a few large and successful organizations" (p220).

Whetten (1987) used the life-cycle theory to examine the sequential growth of organizations. The growth stage involved four methods in which organizations can grow. The first method is growth in organizations' existing domains where organizations expand their current activities that they have done well. The second method is through diversification into new domains where organizations spread out their risks across several product lines. The third method is through technological innovation or development. The fourth method is growth through improved managerial techniques that involve the improved efficiency of management administrative processes and turn-around strategies (pp337–349). The role of accounting and sustainability is detrimental to the fourth method of organizational growth.

Incremental and transformational organization development strategies

Organizational development or growth may occur through incremental or transformational change strategies. Incremental growth involves gradual change, while transformational growth is accompanied by revolutionary change. An incremental change involves minor modifications or adjustments in an organization's strategy, policy or structure. Incremental changes are common in organizations' production activities when innovations are undertaken to improve current activities to reduce costs and increase efficiency of production.

On the other hand, transformation involves fundamental changes in strategy (where there is an exit or entry strategy in an industry), structure (reorganization to align functions, change management titles and managers) and power distributions (through turnover) in an organization. Real fundamental transformation requires revolutionary changes that require altering or changing "systems, strategies through short, discontinuous bursts of change over most or all domains of organizational activity" (Romanelli and Tushman, 1994: 1162; see also Tushman et al., 1986). In a true transformational change, there is a punctuated equilibrium, where there is a relative frequency that is high enough to sufficiently effect a change in form or substance for a true overall change in the system to occur (Gould and Eldridge, 1993: 225).

Hailey and Balogun (2002) developed a two-by-two contingency matrix (table) using two dimensions of change. The first dimension, *extent of change*, was defined in terms of transformation and realignment. The second dimension, *speed of change*, was classified as involving incremental and big bang changes. Using these two dimensions of change, they identified four different organizational change typologies: evolution, adaptation, revolution and construction. They suggested that organizations could choose several variations of these different types of changes. Depending on the availability of organizational resources, for example scarce or slack resources, organizations may choose "a stage approach, moving from one change type to another" (p161). While adaptation is an incremental-realignment change strategy, it is "less fundamental change implemented slowly through staged initiatives" (p161). Organizations pursue adaptation strategies to "strengthen their competitive position via some type of realignment," which might involve a rapid reconstruction of a "turnaround, or a slower rationalization of the business portfolio, which then leads into a more revolutionary change" (p162). Realignment may also include mergers, acquisitions, diversifications and integrations of marketing, production and distribution facilities (Balogun and Johnson, 2005).

Innovation and learning are organizational adaptation change strategies that closely parallel Hailey and Balogun's (2002) staged or phased growth strategy. Argyris and Schon (1978) and Lant and Mezias (1992) related organizational learning to incremental change when learning involved first-order (evolutionary) change, and transformational change when learning is followed by second-order (revolutionary) change. Adaptation as an incremental (first-order learning) evolutionary change strategy focuses on formalization, specialization and efficiency in managing organizational operating activities. On the other hand, when organizational change is accompanied by an organizational response to a natural selection process of new forms, it results in transformational second-order change learning.

The strategy becomes revolutionary when organizational learning yields transformational change that is broader in orientation and utilizes organic and dynamic learning. The innovation process becomes entrepreneurial and focuses on new methods to solve problems, search for new market opportunities and product innovations, or seek alternative strategies to respond to environmental uncertainties (Fox-Wolfgramm et al., 1998; see also Morel and Ramanujam, 1988).

Those organizations not implementing radical changes the first time are likely to pursue radical transformations of strategic change following a trial and error period of incremental changes. These radical reorientations have been undertaken primarily for two major reasons: first, due to sustained low performance and, second, because of the need to address major technological, social and environmental changes. It is widely accepted that, in larger organizations, greater structural complexity and interdependence require an emphasis on incremental as opposed to transformational changes. Political, technological and economic conditions of the external environment have also greatly affected the evolution of organizations and their responses to environmental changes (Tushman and Romanelli, 1985: 178, 192, 197, 215; see also Barley, 1986: 78).

Organizational performance can vary due to differences in strategic positions and competitive capabilities. Although organizational learning influences organizational performance, the more organizations face competition in the marketplace, the more likely they are to perform better. However, competition minimizes resource availability and increases organizational dissolution through mergers and acquisitions. For example, according to Barnett et al.,

> having many competitors increases the chances that an organization will not obtain the resources it needs, and so will fail. On the other hand, having many competitors increases the number of potential acquirers in the population, making an organization more likely to disappear through merger or acquisition when its rivals are more numerous.
>
> (1994: 12–13)

Their study of all retail banks operating in Illinois from 1987 to 1993 revealed that competition is a significant issue driving evolution. Organizational evolution and change are caused and then shaped by the strategies and structures of organizations, which enable them to be adaptive to survive regardless of whether or not they learned from their experiences in the market.

Institutional adaptation strategies

Watkins (1998) viewed institutions as having symbiotic relations of interdependence. Symbiotic relations arise from "the product of our cultural inheritance" and "takes the form of institutions." Accordingly, "institutions define the manner in which human beings" cooperate "with one another, based on particular patterns of ideas" (p99). However, ecologically, human beings, like any other living organisms, are governed by forces of nature. They live and abide by forming symbiotic relationships with others. According to Watkins, symbiotic relationships require humans to form cooperative relationships with the natural environment in preserving and using, but not necessarily destroying, environmental resources (p101). According to the evolutionary process of natural selections of institutions, institutions are governed by the principle of the selective adaptation process of survival of the fittest (i.e., only those institutions that are best suited to the environment can survive or adapt).

While organizational responses to environmental changes tend to vary accordingly by age and size, the history or biography of that organization (usually documented through case studies) describes the organization's selective and adaptive processes to environmental changes. For example, Fox-Wolfgramm et al. (1998) suggested that organizations have biographies that describe their responses or reactions to change. These biographies are unique and distinct to organizations, describing identities that reflect their prior successes, and are used to reinforce their identities during periods of crisis. Organizational identity and envisioned image help to sustain organizational change, provide a common ideology to organization members, and reinforce common strategic orientations among members. These orientations reflect those ideas, ideologies, values and beliefs that the organization has or aspires to have. While an organizational biography reinforces image and identity, it does not necessarily imply that those images and identity are in conformity with institutional environmental changes, and in some cases, those identities may inhibit or deter change. On the other hand, those biographies that are conducive to change become positive forces that enhance institutionalization and organizational visibility.

The ecological approach view of institutions as having symbiotic relationships and selective adaptation mechanisms has implications for strategic and management control systems. Seal (1990) indicated that the institutional approach examines "the internal organization of the firm with a particular reference to management control mechanism" (p68). In this context, control is related to the structural arrangements of functions and work-related activities (jobs) that allow managers to observe and monitor employees'/people's behavior to ensure compliance and conformity with both company and government regulations.

The institutional view assumes that firms have to meet certain social requirements and norms of acceptable business behavior to gain legitimacy and be competitive. Institutional norms enforce conformity and enable access to resources and the business community. Institutional adherence conveys commitment to sustainable development through observation of shared values and belief systems and norms of acceptable behavior. Bansal (2005) suggested that institutional pressures on firms through regulations, public opinions, business norms or coercive sanctions through "fines and penalties" influence the diffusion of "corporate sustainable development practices" among firms (p202). Moreover, firms over time are more likely to "mimic" or imitate those corporate sustainable development practices that are visible and considered to be successful among competitive firms to avoid sanctions and penalties and to convey a positive image and gain legitimacy.

Moreover, the media has altered corporate behavior by exposing unacceptable practices, and this can result in legitimate behavior. Media coverage encourages active participation from environmental interest groups and others to shape corporate policies. Media publicity – both positive and negative – influences corporate sustainable development policies. These institutional pressures are instrumental in shaping early corporate sustainable development practices (Bansal, 2005: 203). As these business-acceptable behaviors become institutionalized as corporate sustainable development practices, they are more likely to be diffused as common acceptable business practices. Over time, these practices develop into shared industry-setting standards and behaviors.

It is evident that those organizations that have legitimacy and institutionalization enjoy high visibility and attract increased attention and regulation from governmental agencies. These regulations shape organizational policies and strategies to meet regulatory requirements. Accordingly, regulatory requirements arising from national and state regulations lead to conformity and inertia. That is, legislations enacted to promote and limit competition, norms and values, and cognitive models of divergent change, will have direct effects on organizational change. For example, D'Aunno et al. (2000) found that "organizations that meet regulatory requirements in their fields are less likely to make divergent changes," whereas "organizations that are members of multidivisional firms are more likely to make divergent changes" (pp682–686). In large and complex organizations with multi-divisionalized structures, performance of divisions or branches will decline after a core organizational change takes place when compared to small and unitary organizations (Greve, 1999: 591–592). These organizations are likely to face a multitude of government regulations because of their size and complexity of institutional structures.

Lounsbury (2001) discussed the institutional structural differences in terms of temporal and/or spatial variations that contribute to the diffusion and adoption of organizational practices, which eventually become institutionalized as rules and organizational procedures. In his study of the staffing practices for the management of recycling programs in universities, Lounsbury found that the creation of a full-time recycling manager or addition to an existing staff either in full-time or part-time capacity contributed to additional responsibility of recycling programs. Institutionalization of recycling programs reduced the normative pressures from national student organizations, social movements and environmental coalitions, including students. In larger, more selective universities, full-time recycling managers/coordinators were employed because student environmental groups were active and lobbied for the creation of these positions. Comparatively, those universities "that staffed their recycling programs through role accretion tended to be public, smaller and were importantly influenced by social comparison processes among schools of similar selectivity" (Lounsbury, 2001: 49; see also Stone et al., 2004). The study revealed that organizational stratification, which is determined by size, played a role in the diffusion of organizational practices and their institutionalization over time.

As the organizational adaptation process implies, crisis created the need for institutional development and the conditions for strategic change. Universities were pressurized to create institutional mechanisms to handle environmental and recycling programs by external parties and interest groups, including students and environmental coalition groups. The groups' successful lobbying efforts resulted in strategic changes that brought organizational changes, either in full-time or part-time staff additions, to institutionalize the recycling program. Management control mechanisms were put into place to balance and check the administrative mechanisms of the recycling programs. While there was institutional variation in organizational practices or recycling programs, the institutional adaptation process effectively provides legitimacy and visibility to those organizations that have fully diffused and adopted those environmental organizational practices. This institutionalization of environmental practices documents how universities and colleges are able to adapt to the changes in their external environment.

Ecology and adaptation approaches to organization development

Whether the changes in the external environment are minimal or significant, the adaptation process shows differences in organizational approaches and responses to environmental change. To this effect, Damanpour and Evan (1984: 395) suggest that: "The organization-adapting function requires that as the environment changes, the structure or processes of the organization undergo change to meet the new environmental conditions."

They focused on administrative innovations as enabling changes in organizational structures. In this context, sustainable development can be considered as an administrative innovation in which the outcomes are ambiguous and unknown (Bansal, 2005: 198). The administrative innovations in sustainable development include policy changes and initiatives whose outcomes are not easily observable. They tend to become broad in orientation, covering a wide range of areas related to environmental resources management and conservative policies.

The question of sustaining and/or improving current performance thus becomes of paramount importance for organizations that face environmental changes and uncertainty. The mix between strategy and structure influences the ability of the organization to adapt to environmental changes. According to Lant and Mezias (1992: 55), "organizations with an adaptive strategy search for information that reveals the relationship between organizational characteristics and performance. That is, they determine which mix of organizational characteristics is associated with the highest performance and adopt those characteristics." In other words, performance is dependent upon whether or not there exists a close relationship between current environmental changes and the ability of the organization to handle and process these changes (Lawrence and Lorsch, 1969). Adaptive organizations thus develop networks of relationships that are open, dynamic and capable of learning and handling situations that are of "ambiguity and uncertainty" (Bate, 1990: 100). Organizations use networks to exchange ideas among them. They can foster cultural change to modify or alter network and organizational relationships that tend to be innovative. The success of an organization depends on the ability of the organization to sustain and maintain continuous change.

According to Barnett and Carroll (1995: 217–218), the adaptive organizational change process "assumes that change in the world of organizations occurs mainly through the adaptive responses of existing individual organizations to prior changes in technology, environment or whatever." They classified contingency theory, resource dependence theory and institutional theory in the adaptive change process framework. Moreover, the effects of organizational transactions on organizational change involve the adaptation strategies of economic resources.

The transaction cost approach: an extension of the functional and population ecology of organizations

Williamson (1987) introduced transaction cost economic analysis to the study of organizations and change. He provided an alternative view of the organization based on economic choice and cost efficiency. The transaction cost approach assumes that there are differences among organizations "because transactions differ so greatly and efficiency is realized only if governance structures are tailored to the specific needs of each type of transaction" (p568). Transaction then becomes the unit of analysis. He noted that transaction costs are critical because they constitute "the crucial importance of organizations for economizing on such costs. This brings organization theory to the fore, since choice of an appropriate governance structure is preeminently an organization theory issue" (p568).

Williamson (1987) suggested the transaction cost approach has similarity to the population ecology model of Hannan and Freeman (1977), Aldrich (1979) and Carroll (1984) because of its concern about an organization's ability to adapt to environmental changes. In order to answer the question of which organizations have better characteristics to fit and adapt, the transaction cost approach addresses whether "both product and capital market competition are the sources of natural selection pressures" (Williamson, 1987: 568).

Transaction costs extended the population ecology approach to examine organizational adaptation and inertia processes. It assumed organizations with better transaction costs could adapt and survive while others with poor transaction costs fail or disintegrate. For Williamson (1987), the transaction cost approach is based on the principle that organizations with

> governance structures that have better transaction cost economizing properties will eventually displace those that have worse, ceteris paribus. The *cetera*, however, are not always *paria*, where the governance implications of transaction costs analysis will be incompletely realized in noncommercial enterprises in which transaction cost economizing entails the sacrifice of other valued objectives (of which power will often be one); the study of these tradeoffs is an important topic on the future research agenda.
>
> (p574; italics in original)

This proposition assumes that organizations that are functional–purposive operate under the population ecology principle of natural selection forces. In essence, Williamson (1987) applied the transaction cost approach to explain both the functional and population ecology theories of organizations. Organizations, as systems, are not only functional and selective in their adaptation processes, but also pay attention to transaction costs associated with technology, production, distribution and the delivery of products and services.

Williamson (1987) indicated that "transaction cost analysis supplements the usual preoccupation with technology and steady-state production (or distribution) expenses with an examination of the comparative costs of planning, adapting, and monitoring task completion under alternative governance structures" (pp552–553). He noted that transaction cost has two behavioral assumptions. These are "(1) the recognition that human agents are subject to bounded rationality and (2) the assumption that at least some agents are given to opportunism" (p553). Bounded rationality could lead to incomplete contracting in economic exchanges that are based on contracts (Simon, 1957).

Van de Ven (1986) extended the transaction cost approach to study innovation processes in organizations. He viewed the "management of the innovation process ... as managing increasing bundles of transactions over time. Transactions are 'deals' or exchanges which tie people together within an institutional framework." Transactions more often go through "trial-and-error cycles of renegotiations, recommitment, and re-administration of transactions" (p597). Transactions usually occur among people who

> know, trust, and with whom they have had successful experiences. As a consequence, what may start as an interim solution to an immediate problem often proliferates over time into a web of complex and interdependent transactions among the parties involved.
>
> (p598)

Van de Ven made a connection between transactions and organizational structures and systems. He formulated that

> transactions are the micro elements of macro organizational arrangements. Just as the development of an innovation might be viewed as a bundle of proliferating transactions over time, so also, is there proliferation of functions and roles to manage this complex and interdependent bundle of transactions in the institution that houses the innovation.
>
> (p598)

Hence, organizational systems having interdependent functions are preoccupied with the management of transaction costs.

Organizations go through staged cycles of growth and transactions to maintain functional relationships of organizational change and process innovation in management control systems. Accordingly, organizations experience several stages or cycles of growth, maturity, decline, retention and downsizing to manage transaction costs, adapt to their environmental surroundings, and institute sustainable environmental management programs.

The ecology of sustainability and institutionalization of environmental programs

The ecological framework has argued that environmental concerns and responsibilities have become part of the institutionalization process of organizations. Recently, organizations have prepared and issued reports of environmental audits and performance indicators such as the consumption and management of water, energy, toxic materials and assets (Füssel and Georg, 2000). The amount of space an organization allocates to environmental issues on annual and/or other accounting reports indicates the level of commitment an organization has on environmental management systems. The support and commitment of management and the participation of employees in the design and management of environmental programs makes the process of institutionalization of environmental concerns and issues a continuous and an ongoing process. Since environmental concerns are of interest and concern to employees and are more likely to arouse public emotions and desires, recognizing the importance of environmental management programs as mechanisms in resolving the various contending issues among interest groups shapes organizational policies and accounting systems. Accordingly, it can be inferred that environmental management can become part of management's best organizational practices that prevail in socially responsible organizations.

The ecological framework has integrated sustainability with the institutionalization of the environmental conservation policies of organizations (Sisaye, 2006). Federal, state and local governmental institutions have enforced sustainability programs through promulgations of new legislations and by empowering existing regulatory agencies with enhanced policies and regulations to monitor business development and production activities. Environmental interest groups have mobilized their resources to lobby for legislations to minimize the impact of business and industrial growth on the environment and natural resources.

For example, Rudel et al. (2011) noted that business organizations are pursuing a policy of ecological modernization to counterbalance the environmental mobilization of interest groups and the government policies of protection and conservation. The ecological modernization policies integrate ecological and environmental issues as part of the strategic planning and operating decisions of the business practices. These ecological policies are reflected at both the national and international levels, particularly in the European countries. In both the United States and Europe, these activist groups, including "green consumers," have shaped industrial policies concerning products and services (p230). Their efforts have received a high-profile media campaign and coverage which has intensified the importance of green products and services. These efforts have contributed to the certification and labeling of green products. Rudel et al. argued that, in the long run, environmental policies occur in a series of steps over time, and the legislation of these policies requires a long timeframe.

It is evident that there is a growing interest among customers, employees and shareholders of business organizations whose products and services support sustainable development. For example, Epstein and Young (1999) have suggested that economic value added (EVA) measures can be incorporated to develop profitable investment decisions in line with responsible environmental management policies (pp45–49). Customers who are considered to be socially conscious have shown preferences to invest in companies whose investment portfolios included sustainable ecological conservation and development policies. They tend to purchase products and services from companies with reputable environmental programs. In response to the needs of environmentally conscious customers, small and medium-sized firms have taken the lead in innovation by producing products that sustain environmental protection. For example, paper and bottle recycling companies are advancing social and environmental causes by collaborating with not-for-profit organizations (NFPs). They are placing garbage collection facilities in parks, and providing sanitation training to public and NFP employees. They work closely with service-sector organizations – for example, hotels and restaurants – to promote water conservation and marketing of green-based products (Nelson, 2004). These reform efforts also have been supported by governmental policies and international organizations' resource allocations to advance the development of environmentally sound technological innovations.

In other words, these studies suggest that there is a positive relationship between a balanced pro-growth environmentally responsible management program and improved organizational performance. Florida and Davison (2001) have also indicated that an environmental management system (EMS) program serves as a formal system for gathering information and making choices among programs that balance environmental and green management with an overall business strategy for managing balanced manufacturing growth and improved business performance. They suggested that green management is not an alternative concern, but rather balanced pro-growth and environmental management programs where performance, productivity and profit motivations go together with environmental management programs that reduce waste, pollution and emissions, as well as conserve natural resources (pp37–50).

The cumulative effect of investors, customers, public interest groups, regulatory agencies and international development and donor organizations has shaped business organizations' industrial growth to conform with national and international environmental protection policies. Business organizations have prepared financial accounting reports that disclose quantitative and qualitative information of their ecological, environmental and social programs. Sustainability has been accepted by business organizations as a green management program to protect and sustain the environment and its natural resources.

Competing approaches of sustainability

Sustainable development has attracted several interpretations, including the ecological environmental, humanistic, ethical and managerial reformist view as well as the stakeholder view. The concepts of sustainability and sustainable development have received considerable attention since their introduction to the public by the Brundtland Report, *Our Common Future* (WCED, 1987). The report defined sustainability as "the ability to meet the needs of present generations without compromising the ability of future generations to meet their own needs." The report also challenged the world to envision a future in which the threats of environmental destruction are minimized and the people of the world enjoy economic stability and social equity between and within generations. It made humans aware of their dependency on the environment to meet their needs and well-being. The report highlighted that both ecology and economy are mutually dependent and interrelated in local, regional, national and international communities. Even if humans don't need to dominate or exploit resources, they are dependent on the environment for their security, well-being, and current and future growth. If natural resources are not properly managed, there will be environmental degradation. This will exacerbate existing poverty problems, which can threaten people's health, livelihood and survival for now and future generations (pp39–40). The report caused social scientists to turn their attention towards practices and behavior that are more sustainable than others.

Anthropologists have extended this view of sustainability to address development issues that encompass economic goals, social justice/equity, survival, responsibility, environmental management, and cultural development (Bozzoli, 2000; Morse, 2008). For them, sustainability is a holistic approach that promotes economic growth and prosperity to meet current demands but without sacrificing future generations' needs and priorities (Kottack, 1999). Sustainability is a goal that has regional, national and global ramifications. Sustainability encourages the exchange of information (ideas) and transfer of resources and materials from the well-endowed countries to those societies and countries that need aid and assistance. International donor organizations' economic aid assistance, when trickled, is expected to contribute to sustainable development and to social equity among the recipient countries. Before sustainability became the focus of international development organizations, foreign aid industrial growth policies increased the gap between the rich and the poor in quality of life and consumption of goods and services (Sisaye, 1981). The forces of nature, such as climatic changes, and wastes of natural resources, have also devastated ecological systems.

Sustainability has embedded key futuristic ideals and principles of conservation and development that are based on equity and social justice focusing on inter-organizational, geographical as well as biodiversity equity. An evolutionary ecological analysis integrates sustainability with communities' development plans, resources management, geographical locations and boundaries. This approach is consistent with the view that business organizations as living systems are in a constant sustenance mode of operations to adapt their economic growth strategies with communities' social well-being and cultural development programs.

Ecological anthropologists have argued that sustainability should be adapted to local conditions and cultures. Stone (2003) noted that the absence of common agreement and understanding on the notion of sustainability and sustainable development has resulted in definitions and practices that underestimate cultural, political and economic systems. She highlighted that the simplistic notion of people and landscapes led to some misguided models that resulted in land degradation or desertification, and livestock overstocking in certain parts of the world, where common sense and tradition that led and sustained them through centuries, and in difficult times, were substituted by modernization and economic exploitation. In general, the process of economic globalization and speed of cultural integration and local sustainability are fundamentally hostile to sustainability. In other words, the homogenizing process of production is in contradiction to the need to preserve social and ecological diversity for sustainable development.

From an anthropological perspective, sustainability cannot be developed and imposed on a community by someone outside that community. Outside development experts can provide assistance at crucial points, or help to move the development process along with local, national and international development organizations (Hoben, 1982). It needs to be developed and implemented by the community itself or it will not work. It requires educating and assisting communities to understand and measure how well they meet the needs and expectations of their current and future members. People in the community are the experts on their community, and these community members need to be the driving force to achieve a sustainable quality of life for all members, current and future. Sustainability has to be integrated alongside the quality of life of a community, and whether the economic, social and environmental systems that make up the community are providing a healthy, productive and meaningful life for all its residents, present and future. For example, Bozzoli (2000) and Stone (2003) saw sustainability as advancing long-term development programs. They suggested that in order for a community to make real and positive progress and create a sustainable environment, the links and associations of the interconnected economic, social and environmental factors must be sought and analyzed. Sustainability does not only address quality of life, but understands the interconnections and need for balance among the social, economic and environmental elements of a community.

Zairi (2002) claimed that sustainability is crucial to a company's performance. The organizational goal describes where the organization is headed based upon the business environment and must be consistent with the corporate vision. Organizational growth, prosperity and survival can be sustained at the present time, and in the future as well, only when business interests are in line with community and local development interests suggested by ecological anthropologists and sociologists.

Hopwood et al. (2005: 38) indicated that sustainable development broadly encompasses efforts to balance environmental concerns with socio-economic growth. Proponents of sustainability changed the view of the environment from external to humanity that can be used and exploited, to that of central for humanity's survival and livelihood to be conserved with the planned management of natural resources. The Brundtland Report (WCED, 1987), *Our Common Future*, made the reader aware of the dependency of humans on the environment to meet their needs and well-being and that ecology and economy are mutually dependent and interrelated at the local, regional, national and international level. Humans depend on the environment for security, well-being and growth, now and in the future. Environmental mismanagement can lead to degradation of the environment with associated poverty, threatening people's health, livelihood and survival (pp39–40). Accordingly, sustainability has key futuristic principles based on equity and social justice: inter-organizational, geographical as well as biodiversity equity.

The social, ethical and managerial reformist view of business has reinforced the status quo argument that policy-makers and consumers will align their interests with businesses that practice corporate citizenship and ethical business practices to achieve sustainable development. On the other hand, if necessary, reform through government policies and international organizations are implemented to introduce environmentally sound technological changes. Environmental interest groups and organizations also lobby government and business for policy changes. Recently, some of these interest groups (e.g., the Sierra Club) have moved from grassroots activism to political lobbying by making alliances with other environmental and social justice movements.

Parker (2005) argued that the ethical and managerial perspective of social and environmental accounting falls under the general framework of stakeholder theory. The approach incorporates social responsibility within corporate strategies that are accountable to an organization's stakeholder groups. It provides an explanation for social and environmental disclosure as part of the corporate voluntary disclosure and responsiveness to the interests/demands of stakeholders. It states that profitability goals require a tradeoff between social–environmental and economic objectives (pp845–846). In essence, corporate citizenship – responsibility and accountability – is justified in terms of responsiveness of corporate disclosure to the influential stakeholders (i.e., financial stakeholders).

The stakeholder approach is embedded in institutionalization/legitimization theory as part of a corporation's role to educate the public on environmental issues that affect society. The legitimacy theory is focused on ensuring that the social, political and economic systems are in balance and that accountability entails the institutional duty to provide a report or account on the actions that the organization/entity is held responsible. Accordingly, moral and ethical dimensions are incorporated to justify social responsibility for preserving and conserving environmental resources. In the process, the future prospects for growth and survival of all levels of species are linked to current ecological and sustainability efforts to maintain reasonable living standards by protecting the environment.

In this book, I apply the sociological and anthropological ecological view of sustainability that recognizes the collaborative joint interests of business, government and communities to work together to plan and implement sustainability programs to conserve and sustain environmental resources. In other words, ecology has a transformational view of sustainability that suggests that addressing environmental issues requires the joint effort and collaboration of business, government and community-based organizations and environmental interest groups working within the existing social, economic and political structures (Hopwood et al., 2005). To this effect, Hopwood et al. (2005) employed the transformation view to suggest that environmental problems are rooted in society and addressing them requires strong commitment to social equity and justice. Inequality and poverty can be addressed and dealt only when there is "access to livelihood, good health, resources, and economic and political decision making are connected" (p48). Although Hopwood et al. have indicated that the transformation view calls for these "changes to occur through political action working both in and outside the existing structures" (p48), the transformational argument to work within existing structures is consistent with the managerial–reformist view. There are examples from participatory sustainable development programs that have employed existing local structures to implement process-oriented programs consistent with the reformist view of social change.

Sustainable development as a sociological and anthropological approach to change is based on continuous learning and adaptation that can be used to guide policies, technological innovations and institutions. It is a continuous process, not a one-time improvement or action program advocating specific policy or program – rather, it is integrated with other policies in a continuous process of learning and continuous innovations of social change addressing structural problems

(Mog, 2004: 2140). It is also known that sustainable development efforts cannot be achieved without broad-based community participation and involvement where local people have accepted the process as a catalyst for change and are involved in identifying and solving problems.

Sustainability requires efforts by communities to organize and create locally controlled institutions that are decentralized where locals have the ability to set up goals, make decisions, evaluate outcomes and assume responsibility and accountability to these programs in order to make them everlasting. When locals are empowered to plan and implement and are educated to institute long-term social and structural changes, sustainability becomes a continuous process with "sociopolitical impacts," including those that have "cultural acceptability, policy support, facilitate learning and knowledge sharing, facilitate a process of social change, minimize local growth in human population and the consumption of non-renewable resources" (Mog, 2004: 2151). The organization and mobilization of local resources become critical for the success of sustainable development programs. According to Mog (2004), desired ecological impacts from the efforts include the maintenance of "ecological integrity," protection and possibly growth in "biological and genetic diversity (particularly of indigenous species) and the prevention of land degradation" (p2152). Chapter 3 elaborates on ecological, anthropological and economic rationales from industrial ecology and organizations and institutional adaptation strategies to document the theoretical background and practical implications of sustainability for governmental, bilateral and multilateral international development organizations.

References

Aldrich, H. E. (1979). *Organizations and Environments*. Prentice-Hall, Englewood Cliffs, NJ.

Amburgey, T. L., Kelly, D. and Barnett, W. P. (1993). "Resetting the clock: The dynamics of organizational change and failure," *Administrative Science Quarterly*, Vol. 38, No. 1, pp51–73.

Argyris, C. and Schon, D. A. (1978). *Organizational Learning: A Theory of Action Perspective*. Addison-Wesley, Reading, MA.

Astley, W. G. (1985). "The two ecologies: Population and community perspectives on organizational evolution," *Administrative Science Quarterly*, Vol. 30, No. 2, pp224–241.

Baker, W. E., Faulkner, R. R. and Fisher, G. A. (1998). "Hazards of the market: The continuity and dissolution of inter-organizational market relationships," *American Sociological Review*, Vol. 63, No. 2, pp147–177.

Balogun, J. and Johnson, G. (2005). "From intended strategies to unintended outcomes: The impact of change recipient sensemaking," *Organization Studies*, Vol. 26, No. 1, pp1573–1601.

Bansal, P. (2005). "Evolving sustainability: A longitudinal study of corporate sustainable development," *Strategic Management Journal*, Vol. 26, No. 3, pp197–218.

Barley, S. R. (1986). "Technology as an occasion for structuring: Evidence from observations of CT scanners and the social order of radiology departments," *Administrative Science Quarterly*, Vol. 31, No. 1, pp78–108.

Barnett, W. P. and Carroll, G. R. (1995). "Modeling internal organizational change," *Annual Review of Sociology*, Vol. 21, pp217–236.

Barnett, W. P. and Hansen, M. T. (1996). "The red queen in organizational evolution," *Strategic Management Journal*, Vol. 17 (Special Issue, Summer), No. 1, pp139–157.

Barnett, W. P., Greve, H. R. and Park, D. Y. (1994). "An evolutionary model of organizational performance," *Strategic Management Journal*, Vol. 15 (Special Issue, Winter), No. 1, pp11–28.

Barron, D. (1999). "The structuring of organizational populations," *American Sociological Review*, Vol. 64, No. 3, pp421–445.

Bate, P. (1990). "Using the culture concept in an organization development setting," *The Journal of Applied Behavioral Science*, Vol. 26, No. 1, pp83–106.

Boulding, K. L. (1968). "General systems theory: The skeleton of science," in *Modern Systems Research for the Behavioral Scientist*, ed. W. Buckley, pp1–10. Aldine, Chicago, IL.

Bozzoli, M. E. (2000). "A role for anthropology in sustainable development in Costa Rica," *Human Organization*, Vol. 59, No. 3, pp275–279.

Burrell, G. and Morgan, G. (1979). *Sociological Paradigms: Organizational Analysis*. Heinemann, Portsmouth, NH.

Carroll, G. R. (1984). "Organizational ecology," *Annual Review of Sociology*, Vol. 10, pp71–93.

Carroll, G. R. and Barnett, W. P. (2004). "Organizational ecology: An introduction," *Industrial and Corporate Change*, Vol. 13, p1.

Child, J. (1977). "Strategic choice in the analysis of action, structure, organizations and environment: Retrospect and prospect," *Organization Studies*, Vol. 18, No. 1, pp43–76.

Cohen-Rosenthal, E. (2000). "A walk on the human side of industrial ecology," *American Behavioral Scientist*, Vol. 44, No. 2, pp245–264.

Damanpour, F. and Evan, W. M. (1984). "Organizational innovation and performance: The problem of 'organizational lag,'" *Administrative Science Quarterly*, Vol. 29, No. 3, pp392–409.

D'Aunno, T., Succi, M. and Alexander, J. A. (2000). "The role of institutional and market forces in divergent organizational change," *Administrative Science Quarterly*, Vol. 45, No. 4, pp679–703.

Deluga, R. J. and Perry, J. T. (1994). "The role of subordinate performance and ingratiation in leader–member exchanges," *Group & Organization Management*, Vol. 19, No. 1, pp67–86.

Dilling, P. F. A. (2009). "Sustainability reporting in a global context: What are the characteristics of corporations that provide high quality sustainable reports – an empirical study?," *International Business & Economics Research Journal*, Vol. 9, No. 1, pp19–30.

Ehrenfeld, J. R. (2000). "Industrial ecology: Paradigm shift or normal science?," *American Behavioral Scientist*, Vol. 44, No. 2, pp229–244.

Epstein, M. J. (2008). *Making Sustainability Work: Best Practices in Managing and Measuring Corporate Social, Environmental and Economic Impacts*. Greenleaf Publishing and Berrett-Koehler Publishers, Sheffield, UK, and San Francisco, CA.

Epstein, M. J. and Young, S. D. (1999). "'Greening' with EVA," *Management Accounting*, Vol. 80, No. 1, pp45–49.

Etzioni, A. (1961). *A Comparative Analysis of Complex Organizations: In Power, Involvement, and Their Correlates*. The Free Press, New York.

Florida, R. and Davison, D. (2001). "Gaining from green management: Environmental management systems inside and outside the factory," *California Management Review*, Vol. 43, No. 1, pp64–84.

Fox-Wolfgramm, S. J., Boal, K. B. and Hunt, J. G. (1998). "Organizational adaptation to institutional change: A comparative study of first-order change in prospector and defender banks," *Administrative Science Quarterly*, Vol. 43, No. 1, pp87–126.

Freeman, J. (1982). "Organizational life cycles and natural selection processes," *Research in Organizational Behavior*, Vol. 4, pp1–32.

Füssel, L. and Georg, S. (2000). "The institutionalization of environmental concerns: Making the environment perform," *International Studies of Management and Organization*, Vol. 30, No. 3, pp41–58.

Gould, S. J. and Eldridge, N. (1993). "Review article: Punctuated equilibrium comes of age," *Nature*, Vol. 36, No. 3, pp223–227.

Greve, H. R. (1999). "The effect of core change on performance: Inertia and regression toward the mean," *Administrative Science Quarterly*, Vol. 44, No. 3, pp590–614.

Hailey, V. H. and Balogun, J. (2002). "Devising context sensitive approaches to change: The example of Glaxo Wellcome," *Long Range Planning*, Vol. 35, No. 1, pp153–178.

Hannan, M. T. (1998). "Rethinking age dependence in organizational mortality: Logical formalizations," *American Journal of Sociology*, Vol. 104, No. 1, pp126–164.

Hannan, M. T. and Freeman, J. (1977). "The population ecology of organizations," *American Journal of Sociology*, Vol. 82, No. 3, pp929–964.

Hannan, M. T. and Freeman, J. (1984). "Structural inertia and organizational change," *American Sociological Review*, Vol. 49, No. 2, pp149–164.

Hannan, M. T. and Freeman, J. (1989). *Organizational Ecology*. Harvard University Press, Boston, MA.

Hoben, A. (1982). "Anthropologists and development," *Annual Review of Anthropology*, Vol. 11, pp349–375.

Hopwood, B., Mellor, M. and O'Brien, G. (2005). "Sustainable development: Mapping different approaches," *Sustainable Development*, Vol. 13, No. 1, pp38–52.

Kottack, C. P. (1999). "The new ecological anthropology," *American Anthropologist*, Vol. 101, No. 1, pp23–35.

Kuhn, T. S. (1970). *The Structure of Scientific Revolutions*. University of Chicago Press, Chicago, IL.

Lant, T. K. and Mezias, S. J. (1992). "An organizational learning model of convergence and reorientation," *Organizational Science*, Vol. 31, No. 1, pp47–71.

Lawrence, P. R. and Lorsch, J. W. (1969). *Organization and Environment*. Richard D. Irwin, Inc., Homewood, IL.

Lounsbury, M. (2001). "Institutional sources of practice variation: Staffing college and university recycling programs," *Administrative Science Quarterly*, Vol. 46, No. 1, pp29–56.

Maute, M. F. and Locander, W. B. (1994). "Innovation as a socio-political process," *Journal of Business Research*, Vol. 30, No. 2, pp161–174.

Mog, J. M. (2004). "Struggling with sustainability – a comparative framework for evaluating sustainable development programs," *World Development*, Vol. 32, No. 12, pp2139–2160.

Morel, B. and Ramanujam, R. (1988). "Through the looking glass of complexity: The dynamics of organizations as adaptive and evolving systems," *Organization Science*, Vol. 10, No. 3, pp278–293.

Morse, S. (2008). "Post-sustainable development," *Sustainable Development*, Vol. 16, No. 5, pp341–352.

Nadler, D. A. (1981). "Managing organizational change: An integrative approach," *Journal of Applied Behavioral Science*, Vol. 17, No. 2, pp191–211.

Nelson, K. (2004). "How small firms innovate sustainability," *In Business*, Vol. 26, No. 6, pp24–26.

Parker, L. D. (2005). "Social and environmental accountability research: A view from the commentary box," *Accounting, Auditing & Accountability Journal*, Vol. 18, No. 6, pp842–860.

Parsons, T. (1951). *The Social Systems*. The Free Press, New York.

Perrow, C. (1986). *Complex Organizations*, 3rd ed. Random House, New York.

Pfeffer, J. (1981). *Power in Organizations*. Pitman Publishing Inc., Marshfield, MA.

Pfeffer, J. (1992). *Managing with Power: Politics and Influence in Organizations*. Harvard Business School Press, Boston, MA.

Pfeffer, J. and Salancik, G. R. (1978). *The External Control of Organizations*. Harper & Row, New York.

Porter, M. E. (1980). *Competitive Strategy*. Macmillan Publishing Co., New York.

Porter, M. E. (1985). *Competitive Advantage*. Macmillan Publishing Co., New York.

Ranger-Moore, J. (1997). "Bigger may be better. But is older wiser? Organizational age and size in the New York life insurance industry," *American Sociological Review*, Vol. 62, No. 6, pp903–920.

Ranger-Moore, J., Breckenridge, R. S. and Jones, D. L. (1995). "Patterns of growth and size-localized competition in the New York state life insurance industry, 1860–1985," *Social Forces*, Vol. 73, No. 3, pp1027–1049.

Romanelli, E. and Tushman, M. L. (1994). "Organizational transformation as punctuated equilibrium: An empirical test," *Academy of Management Journal*, Vol. 37, No. 5, pp1141–1166.

Rudel, T. K., Roberts, J. T. and Carmin, J. A. (2011). "Political economy of the environment," *Annual Review of Sociology*, Vol. 37, pp221–238.

Sahlin-Anderson, K. (2006). "Corporate social responsibility: A trend and a movement, but of what and for what?," *Corporate Governance*, Vol. 6, No. 5, pp595–608.

Seal, W. B. (1990). "De-industrialization and business organization: An institutionalist critique of the natural selection analogy," *Cambridge Journal of Economics*, Vol. 14, No. 3, pp267–275.

Selznick, P. (1957). *Leadership in Administration: A Sociological Interpretation*. Row, Peterson & Co., Evanston, IL.

Selznick, P. (1969). "Foundations of the theory of organizations," in *A Sociological Reader on Complex Organizations*, 2nd ed., ed. A. Etzioni, pp19–32. Holt, Rinehart and Winston, Inc., New York.

Shane, S. A. (1994). "Are champions different from non-champions?," *Journal of Business Venturing*, Vol. 9, No. 5, pp397–421.

Simon, H. A. (1957). *Models of Man*. Wiley and Sons, New York.

Singh, J. V. and Lundsen, C. J. (1990). "Theory and research in organizational ecology," *Annual Review of Sociology*, Vol. 16, pp161–195.

Sisaye, S. (1981). "Theory and practice of international development assistance in third world countries," *India Quarterly*, Vol. 37, No. 4, pp566–582.

Sisaye, S. (2006). *The Ecology of Management Accounting and Control Systems: Implications for Managing Teams and Work Groups in Complex Organizations*, Praeger Publications in Business & Economics Series. Greenwood Publishing Group, Greenwich, CT.

Sisaye, S. (2011a). "Ecological systems approaches to sustainability and organizational development: Emerging trends in environmental and social accounting reporting systems," *The Leadership & Organization Development Journal*, Vol. 32, No. 4, pp379–396.

Sisaye, S. (2011b). "The functional–institutional and consequential–conflictual sociological approaches to accounting ethics education: Integration from sustainability and ecological resources management literature," *Managerial Auditing Journal*, Vol. 26, No. 3, pp263–294.

Sisaye, S. and Birnberg, J. G. (2014). "Sociological approaches of organizational learning: Applications to process innovations of management accounting systems," *Advances in Management Accounting*, Vol. 23, pp1–43.

Sisaye, S., Bodnar, G. H. and Christofi, P. (2004). "Total quality management and sustainability reporting: Lessons from Social Soundness Analysis," *Internal Auditing*, Vol. 19, No. 5, pp32–39.

Smirch, L. (1983). "Concepts of culture and organizational analysis," *Administrative Science Quarterly*, Vol. 28, No. 3, pp339–358.

Stigler, G. J. (1968). *The Organization of Industry*. Irwin, Homewood, IL.

Stone, G., Joseph, M. and Blodgett, J. (2004). "Toward the creation of an eco-oriented corporate culture: A proposed model of internal and external antecedents leading to industrial firm eco-orientation," *The Journal of Business and Industrial Marketing*, Vol. 19, No. 1, pp68–84.

Stone, M. (2003). "Is sustainability for development anthropologists?," *Human Organization*, Vol. 62, No. 2, pp93–99.

Thiele, L. P. (1999). "Evolutionary narratives and ecological ethics," *Political Theory*, Vol. 27, No. 1, pp6–38.

Tracy, L. (1993). "Applications of living systems theory to the study of management and organizational behavior," *Behavioral Science*, Vol. 38, No. 3, pp218–230.

Tushman, M. L. and O'Reilly III, C. A. (1996). "Ambidextrous organizations: Managing evolutionary and revolutionary change," *California Management Review*, Vol. 38, No. 4, pp8–30.

Tushman, M. L. and Romanelli, E. (1985). "Organizational evolution: A metamorphosis model of convergence and reorientation," *Research in Organizational Behavior*, Vol. 7, pp171–222.

Tushman, M. L., Newman, W. H. and Romanelli, E. (1986). "Convergence and upheaval: Managing the unsteady pace of organizational evolution," *California Management Review*, Vol. 29, No. 1, pp29–44.

Van de Ven, A. H. (1986). "Central problems in the management of innovation," *Management Science*, Vol. 32, No. 5, pp590–607.

Von Bertalanffy, L. (1968). *General Systems Theory*. George Brazuller, New York.

Von Bertalanffy, L. (1975). *Perspectives on General System Theory: Scientific Philosophical Studies*, ed. E. Taschdjian. George Brazuller, New York.

Walck, C. (2004). "Healing the divided mind: Land as an integrating concept for organizations and the natural environment," *Organization and the Environment*, Vol. 17, No. 2, pp170–194.

Watkins, J. P. (1998). "Towards a reconsideration of social evolution: Symbiosis and its implications for economics," *Journal of Economic Issues*, Vol. 32, No. 1, pp87–105.

WCED (World Commission on Environment and Development) (1987). *Our Common Future*, The Brundtland Report. World Commission on Environment and Development (WCED) and Oxford University Press, New York.

Whetten, D. A. (1987). "Organizational growth and decline processes," *Annual Review of Sociology*, Vol. 13, pp335–358.

Williamson, O. E. (1987). "The economics of organization: The transaction cost approach," *American Journal of Sociology*, Vol. 87, No. 3, pp548–577.

Zairi, M. (2002). "Beyond TQM implementation: The new paradigm of TQM sustainability," *Total Quality Management*, Vol. 13, No. 8, pp1161–1172.

3 Ecological anthropology and sustainable development

Evolution of social science approaches in integrating ecology in community and national development programs

Organizational ecology and sociology have addressed the process of environmental and structural changes and social change and adaptations. They viewed organizations as continually changing and developing. Within the ecological framework, organizational change and development are related to those environmental, technological and geographical factors that affect sustainable development and reporting in organizations. Sociological and anthropological research has focused on internal and external processes such as those driving the concern about sustainability that necessitate organizational change and development.

Organizational ecology has enhanced sustainability by linking environmental resources management to quality, production, service and managerial systems (Cohen-Rosenthal, 2000; Ehrenfeld, 2000). Environmental resource management has an evolutionary focus for addressing sustainability, conservation and industrial growth as well as population problems. This is because both population and industrial growth are potential threats for environmental destruction. At the same time, people within and outside the organization are also concerned for environmental conservation and attempt to limit industrial growth by focusing on natural resource conservation (Penn, 2003). As a result, sustainability management is a continuous, ongoing process, not a one-time improvement or action program advocating specific government legislation, policy or program. In this context, sustainable development and sound environmental management constitute the primary components for establishing organizational and anthropological ecological relationships.

An evolutionary ecological analysis integrates sustainability with other activities including community development plans, resource management, geographical locations, and boundaries (Wilbanks, 1994). This approach is consistent with the view that business organizations as living ecological systems are in a constant sustenance mode of operation in order to adapt their economic growth and industrial development strategies with community social well-being and cultural development programs. This concern arises due to self-interest and concern to align their business activities with the welfare of external parties. Accordingly, strategy, competition and cultural adaptations (i.e., both organizational and anthropological ecological practices) are intertwined to form the basic foundation for sustainable development.

While both sociology and anthropology share the community and societal perspectives that sustainability has for community and national development programs, ecological anthropology specifically examines the influence of national and local organizational and political systems and their subsequent influences on culture, people and socio-cultural systems. Both industrial ecology and ecological anthropology suggest that business sustainability interfaces with society's community development and social well-being.

An integrated approach of industrial ecology and ecological anthropology frameworks of sustainable development

This section presents the two contrasting industrial ecology and ecological anthropology approaches to sustainable development that have impacted upon the development programs and initiatives of international donor organizations in developing economies, as well as in the industrialized economies of the United States and European countries. While both approaches stress the importance of sustainability and the need for the conservation of natural resources and protection of the environment, their differences are in their foci: industrial ecology focuses more on industrial sectors and an organizational emphasis on sustainability; on the other hand, ecological anthropology addresses the balance between economic growth, cultural and local development, and the promotion of sustainability in developing economies (Sisaye, 2012a, 2012b). Thus, they complement each other.

Industrial ecology and sustainable development

Industrial ecology has normative assumptions about human behavior that involve cooperation, competition, conflict and interdependence in managing sustainable development. Interdependence involves exchanges that are relational and dependent on human and mutually integrated community relationships. It views adaptation and sustainability as a continuous process.

Ehrenfeld (2000) laid the basic foundation and underlying principles of ecology, industrial ecology and sustainable development connections as follows: "Ecology is fundamentally a science of living systems. Ecology focuses on the inter-connections and community character of a system and seeks to identify and characterize the web of energy and natural flow that maintain its health." Industrial ecology attempts "to understand the intricate web of energy and material flows and discover the rules that govern robustness and resiliency in such systems" of industrial societies. This knowledge becomes instrumental "for designing more effective technologies and institutional structures" to adapt organizational technologies to societal growth and development (p239).

The industrial ecology assumptions of organizations

Industrial ecology thus deals with organizational and human connections in both business and organizational development and in commerce and industry in a sustainable manner where energy materials and natural resources flow between businesses and their communities. Industrial ecology as a humanistic and social interventionist approach promotes the integration of a balanced management between resource exploitation and the better use of resources to protect the environment. According to Cohen-Rosenthal (2000: 250), "industrial ecology is an intervention at the organizational and social level." There is human intervention in natural ecology to ensure that technological innovations are used to explore new connections, create new possibilities, and enable managers to make responsible choices in sustainable ways. Thus, in industrial ecology, the notion of exchange and interconnection of economic benefits between industrial development and environmental management is important. When synergies exist between economic growth and sustainable development, organizations can improve resource utilization and conservation that would encourage competition and social responsibility (Sisaye, 2006).

Cohen-Rosenthal (2000) described the relationship between business organizations and the community/environment as follows:

> Social aspects of industrial ecology stretch beyond the inter-organizational relationships within a symbiotic connection or eco-industrial cluster. The environment in which industrial ecology operates includes the larger community and social context. These factors can be enabling or inhibiting to achieving broad goals for industrial ecology.
>
> (p251)

Thus, it can be inferred that strategies which enhance industrial performance/profitability can be linked to global welfare in broader terms. Accordingly, "profit-maximizing strategies are linked to strategies that improve public welfare." The use of social processes where the broader communities are involved can become "essential for effective strategy development and implementation" (Cohen-Rosenthal, 2000: 252). It seems to me that there is a link, but it can be positive or negative. While the objective of industrial ecology is to shape a positive relationship between business profitability and sustainable development, there are also situations where the relationship is not positive. This arises because of the presence or absence of goal congruence, although the goal of industrial ecology is to achieve goal congruence (i.e., bring about business behavior to achieve both economic and sustainable performances).

Industrial ecological systems approaches and sustainable development

The interrelationships among environmental management, industrial growth, community development and societal changes have been described by Bailey (1982: 423) as open and interactive systems, whereby

> society inevitably transforms its environment while adapting to it, just as the environment transforms the society. Thus, each stage in the cycle of

> societal–environmental relations sees successive transformation of both the society and environment. The society, as it develops, can transform the environment (positively as well as negatively), and in turn the transformed environment has further impact on society – in reality, the cumulative effect results in a changed society.

In an open system, the boundary of a society is defined by a political border that defines the internal resources including land, water and all available natural resources (Bailey, 1982: 423). When communities interact outside the political border, they exchange and trade their internal resources to obtain external resources that are not available within their political boundaries. Communities can sustain economic development and minimize dependency of external resources through technological innovation and industrial growth.

The unit of interest in industrial ecology is the organization and not society. While there are potential differences between organizational and societal interests, there are similarities and common interests when both organization and society work in sustainable development programs. Accordingly, industrial ecology's goals of community growth, social welfare and environmental management can be linked to sustainable development and cultural change. Both industrial ecology and ecological anthropology assume that sustainable development is an evolutionary process that transforms societal development over time. Accordingly, they both incorporate the study of cultural and economic development and industrial and business growth to the social systems adaptation process. These social systems include populations and their surrounding natural environmental resources. Ecological anthropology specifically addresses political systems, culture, language, beliefs and religion as being part of the social and political systems. Technology, organization systems and accounting information systems constitute human and industrial ecology systems having subsequent influence to shape sustainable development.

Ecological anthropology approaches to community and sustainable development

Ecological anthropology examines the influence of national and local organizational and political systems and their subsequent influences on culture, people and, in general, socio-cultural systems. Ecological anthropologists have primarily studied the economies and political systems of emerging societies in developing nations. They have long recognized the role of politics in societies and communities as governing agricultural land use, farming practices, pastoral herding activities and population migration movements. These are issues of sustainability concerns for emerging economies.

The ecological anthropological literature suggests that national and local politics govern human land relations and interactions with the natural and social environments. At the same time, organizational systems influence the formation and operations of class and economic structures to regulate social and political order as well as environmental resource management. The process of natural selection influences social behavior and interactions among groups, physical and psychological adaptations, and the social structure of organizations (Gray, 2000; Pierce and White, 1999; see also Dietz and Burns, 1992; Feldman, 1986, 1988; Haenn, 2000; Kottack, 1999; Mog, 2004). Anthropologists have been concerned with the role of political institutions in the management of environmental and structural changes, and how politics shape the process of social change and adaptation strategies involving culture, people and, in general, socio-cultural systems.

Political systems' influence on ecology and social structures

Ecological anthropologists have long recognized the role of politics among tribal and ethnic groups to explain agricultural land use, farming practices, pastoral herding activities and population migration movements. Politics governed human land relations and interactions with the natural and social environment. In these ecological relations, class and economic structures regulate social and political order and environmental resources management (Pierce and White, 1999). Political evolution and systems cannot be separated from the process of natural selection and sequential adaptation to the environment involving both physical and psychological adaptation.

The political systems of many developing countries do not have the institutional structural arrangements to support agricultural development. A study of sustainable development programs in Burkina Faso, West Africa, by Kaminski et al. (2010) highlighted the importance of institutional change and arrangement for sustainable agricultural growth and development. They found that agricultural cooperatives and unions organized by central and local government officials and powerful landlords can become corrupt and less accountable. This raises questions about whether these institutions effectively represent the interests of cotton farmers in the area. While farmers have benefited from the development program through participation in the extension of education and local/regional agricultural credit programs and subsidies and higher cotton prices, there was a lack of accountability of cooperatives and union leaders, which led to corrupt practices. This affected the sustainable development programs of international donors, the French Development Agency (AFD) and the World Bank (Kaminski et al., 2010: 1470–1471).

Kaminski et al. (2010) suggested that unless current agricultural practices lead to conservation, land cultivation and degradation, climate change could hamper sustainable development. If institutions exist and farmers are not able to implement improved farming methods without conservation practices, it would affect sustainable development practices (p1472; see also Andersson et al., 2011). The political institutions in developing countries do not have the infrastructures to promote and support conservation and preservation policies that are necessary for sustainable development farming practices.

The link between culture, political systems and sustainable development has been recognized by the proponents of economic development. Clark (1995), for example, perceived that culture and ecological preservation are related, as ecosystems may be affected by community/local ecological culture and political systems. In other words, without democratic government structures, "environmental destruction will persist" (p236). Sustainable development can be effective only in a society with a democratic governmental system that values ecology, social justice and scientific and technological development that promotes conservation. If society possesses these values, but has no (political) power to implement and enforce them, the values are moot and questionable.

Technological changes and their impacts upon local development practices

In general, ecological anthropology examines human adaptation, cultural change and development in relation to environmental and technological changes. In doing so, it recognizes the role of culture as providing a distinctive set of values and norms among groups. Culture, in essence, becomes the main force behind human adaptation to the environment. In other words, cultural practices contribute to differences in local and regional organizational systems, although, to a large extent, information technology and communication have spread across cultural and social boundaries and have minimized cultural barriers among groups of populations (Dietz and Burns, 1992; Feldman, 1986, 1988; Haenn, 2000; Kottack, 1999).

Technological development has eroded cultural differences and has altered the quality of life and the way of living among differing cultural and population groups. Issues such as deforestation, irrigation, commercial farming, business development and population growth have changed local living conditions and, in some cases, have contributed to cross-political and cultural boundary environmental degradation (Mog, 2004).

Holzman (2012) cited the Harvard School of Public Health Study to describe the disturbing negative effects that technological developments for dams, irrigation systems and deforestation have on the ecosystem. What was particularly noticeable was the impact upon the local population's health (e.g., increases in diarrhea, malaria and other environmentally related diseases), thus making it difficult to quantify the economic costs and benefits of technological changes in developing societies (p155). If technology affects the environment, climate change may occur that "magnifies all these ecological uncertainties." For example, deforestation may affect the relationship of hunters and gatherers to their environment and their subsistence to "sustainable access to wildlife and their children's nutritional needs" (p157). This suggests that the impact of technological development upon the sustainability of ecological resources is more likely to be significant in subsistence developing economies where preservation and conservation of natural resources are not local and national priorities.

Local planning and sustainability

When technological development affected local populations and communities in their dependence for natural resources for their livelihood, planning sustainability discourse was used to find alternative approaches for economic development. Hanna (2005) gave an example from two small towns in the Canadian Northwest, Tofino and Unclear on Western Vancouver Islands, who used sustainability to shift the towns' economic base of timber and fishing. Sustainability-facilitated dialogue and discourse helped to change the core social and economic activities, and aimed to respond to these changes in livelihood and within the community. Planning has become inclusive in various interest groups (stakeholders) and has provided a medium of communication/information with technical details, allowing for negotiation and revision of plans to adjust to local conditions. In the process, "each town began to think of a locally based planning capacity as not only an essential aspect of civic governance, but one that had to be controlled at the community level" (p31). The process of dialogue and interaction involved the community deciding on how sustainability could eventually allow for discourse, community survival and growth, enabling them to respond to environmental changes, and be able to manage growth consistent with local and community values. Sustainability was defined based on personal experience, and the desire to maintain resources that the community can sustain and "grow in a healthy way from land use but not at the expense of its future" was the common theme expressed among participants (p33).

According to Hanna (2005), sustainability facilitated a local development initiative to preserve community lifestyle and to manage the environment, seeking avenues for economic development that benefited the community, increased employment opportunities for the young population, and created a climate for sustaining business growth. Sustainability became a regional concept and formed a local identity to spur economic growth while maintaining the ecological balance of the community. The process enabled local governments to take an integrative step towards sustainable development planning based on social, environmental and economic objectives.

Hanna (2005) suggested that, "for planners, sustainability is useful as an organizing theme in planning a community's response to change." The planning process helped "to develop a sustainability discourse that helped each town to identify what it values most and what qualities it seeks to maintain and endorse" (p38). Hanna affirmed that planning for sustainability is a viable approach for managing the economy of communities that are based on natural environmental resources, as is the case in Canada for the two Western Vancouver Islands whose natural resources include timber and fishing.

Management of natural resources

The economic development focus on the production of goods and services, exploitation of resources and the effect of industrialization and commercialization has given priority to sustainable development. The publication of the Brundtland Report (WCED, 1987) linked sustainable development to interdependent ecological, social and economic objectives. Lamberton (2005) elaborated on sustainable development and sufficiency using the Buddhist perspective, where the concept of sustainable sufficiency ensures that natural resources are preserved and the welfare of the individual local community as well as the international community are sustained. This approach links self-sufficiency to sustainability where the "concept of sustainable sufficiency imports a version of economics based on Buddhist principles that is consistent with ecological preservation and social welfare" (p66).

Sustainability self-sufficiency is dependent on the availability of scarce resources such as land and water. In developing countries, arable land is not only scarce, but is sacred and worshipped. When land is scarce, competition intensifies conflict.

LAND AND FARMING RESOURCES

Arable (farming) land is one of the scarcest natural resources in developing countries, where agriculture accounts for the majority of the people's income and subsistence, as well as their export commodities. Villarreal (2004) viewed the "competition for arable land" in terms of human ecology where competition exists among humans for geographical and spatial distribution. This is predominant in rural areas where "land is seen as a resource necessary for subsistence and not simply as a place of residence." There is conflict over land, because the loss or ownership of land affects the "livelihood of the peasant" or survival (p315). Because migration in rural areas is restricted due to cultural, ethnic and linguistic bondage to a locality, arable land competition aggravates land conflict among kin and neighbors. There are limited opportunities for land expansion once forests are depleted for agricultural farming, which increases violence/conflict because of scarcity over arable landownership (p315). Scarcity of land weakens social bonds because of competition for scarce/limited resources. "Insufficient arable land" weakens social bond and cohesion, increases mistrust, and increases the ability of the community to control crime or violence (p316).

According to Villarreal (2004), "conflict over land may result not only from scarcity, but also when property rights over plots are not clear, are not well enforced, or are contingent" (p317). In situations where rights are insecure and not clearly defined, conflict and violence arise over property rights and their distribution/transfer to the next generation (p318).

When a commodity is scarce, it becomes something sacred that is worshipped. According to Walck (2004), land is a sacred commodity. Land embodies food, ecosystems and community, and includes water, plants and animals, soil, minerals and other types of natural resources (p177). Thus, the concept of land requires an examination of the relationships that humans have to the environment. Land ethics raises human's relationship to the Earth and brings ethical (land ethics) identity and a duty of care and respect when developing land (economy and ecology principles). The transaction between land and humans raises the concern as to the availability of land to support the whole community in which the principles of economy and ecology can co-exist.

Walck's (2004) notion of land is based on several writers' constructs that include the themes of land based on community, beauty, ethics, locality, property, markets and political power relations in land use for human purposes that has to be balanced with conservation and preservation for stability and integrity for future generations (pp177–178). There are limitations to what can be done to land; development and conservation are interdependent and lay the foundation for well-being. If terrestrial ecosystems have been degraded, there is a resultant loss of biodiversity, as well as scarcity of water and natural resources. These concerns put limits on the use of land and call for the preservation of natural resources to minimize the threat for land integrity and stability (Walck, 2004: 183).

In developing economies, land is the basic natural and environmental resource: its scarcity and/or abundance determines local and community livelihoods, creates an unequal distribution of resources, and creates potential for conflict among locals for ownership and control of fertile/arable land. Walck (2004) articulated the importance of the land perspective as an integrative framework to view both ecological and economic approaches for the management and use of land resources in the communities. A land perspective uses sustainability tools such as environmental systems management and product life-cycle analysis, among others, to document the impact that development and organizations' actions have upon managing those sustainability concerns to preserve land health by integrating workplace and residence habitat into one land community.

If managers formulate the land perspective in their administrative policies, decisions can be improved in development plans where priority is put on preserving land integrity and stability in order to maintain land health. Managers can learn about "specific landscape forms" when making development decisions (Walck, 2004: 181). These decisions promote land ethics and health for natural resource preservation since the use of land determines the future. Accordingly, "land and its health (ecology) will determine our human possibilities (economy); as we impoverish the land, so too do we ultimately impoverish ourselves" (p190). Land-use planning and management constitutes the core of the ecology of natural and environmental resource conservation and preservation.

WATER

Another example of a natural resource that is scarce and non-substitutable is water. The management of water in both the industrialized and the developing countries has called for sustainability approaches as climatic changes, land erosion and human consumption have diminished the supply of water. Orlove and Caton (2010) suggested "integrated water resource management (IWRM)" to promote the sustainable development practices of water management (p408). For them, IWRM can be used to legitimize, implement or provide a paradigm to manage water resources. Since water is a scarce resource and there are competing demands on the use of water from households (domestic use), industries, agriculture and other business activities, integrated sustainable management practices are needed to ensure the availability and conservative use of water resources. They approached IWRM not only as an economic tool to manage water, but also as part of the social system. Water is an economic resource that is diminishing over time, and cannot be left solely to the market to manage, but is an economic commodity that has social ownership and requires the equitable distribution of water among all sectors, including the poor. It needs to be managed as an integrated resource that is coordinated and embedded in social equality, economic growth, resource conservation and environmental sustainability. Collectively, water is a world resource that requires coordination with international policies to manage and conserve water (pp408–410).

In 2013, a study by the World Resources Institute (WRI) in conjunction with the U.S. Environmental Protection Agency (EPA) was conducted to study natural water infrastructure and the impact that investment in forested landscapes could have on protecting water resources in the United States. The report noted that U.S. water infrastructure is aging, and that increased demand, continued changes in land use for housing development and agriculture and extreme weather events such as drought, rain and snow have contributed to the increased costs of water management in the United States. The study suggested the importance of investing in integrated water management strategies to develop engineered "natural infrastructure" solutions from water-related functions of networks of forests and other ecosystems that can reduce costs, enhance services and provide long-term benefits for communities and the environment (WRI, 2013).

For example, Holzman (2012) stated that "healthy ecosystems provide us with fertile soil, clean water, timber and food. They reduce the spread of diseases. They protect against flooding. Worldwide, they regulate atmospheric concentrations of oxygen and carbon dioxide. They moderate climate." Without these and other "ecosystem services, we all perish" (p153). However, increased use of ecosystems for agriculture development brought the realization that ecosystems can be properly managed through cultural as well as regulating services.

Economically, Holzman (2012) suggested assigning monetary values to intangible benefits from nature. It means that cost/benefit analyses can be more easily included to assign monetary values in these planning decisions. If dollar values are assigned to denote the value that nature provides to humans, these monetary values can be derived from "existing prices in the market place" to develop accounting measures for nature's benefits (p154). Accordingly, management of the ecosystem, including water, land and other natural resources, is essential in sustainable development.

OTHER NATURAL RESOURCE STOCKS

Ecosystems have resource stocks which include land, water and air as well as animal species. Stern (1997) suggested that natural resource stocks can be used as indicators of sustainability. This may include, "for example, the concentration of carbon dioxide in the atmosphere, the depth of agricultural soil, or the area and fragmentation of the range of an endangered species" (p161). A recent article in the *New York Times* raised the possibility that ecological and climatic changes may contribute to the mass extinction of animals, endangered species and vegetation in sea water and oceans (Zimmer, 2015).

The management of natural resource stocks is dependent on the availability of technological and economic development programs that employ efficient utilization of existing resources as well as their substitutions with alternative resources. Although industrial ecology recognizes the limits to economic development and growth, it suggests that the prospects for long-term growth is dependent on sustainable development programs that balance the interactions between the ecology/environment through the preservation of natural resources and sound industrial development policies.

Ecological ethics

From an ecological anthropology perspective, sustainability has economic, technological as well as market development dimensions and social components to safeguard and protect the environment and natural resources. Therefore, sustainability is embedded in ecological ethics, which suggests that those who are in positions of power and influence have the responsibility not to harm the environment, but to use it in a manner that morally and equitably shares the ecological resources for the survival of humans and other species today and in the future (Sisaye, 2011a, 2011b). There is a consciously intended social aim to use resources morally and responsibly in order to manage and sustain long-living systems. Accordingly, sustainable development and sound environmental management constitute the primary components for establishing organizational and anthropological ecological relationships.

In developing countries, ethics in agricultural sustainability assumes that land and water resources, among others, are available to sustain livelihoods. However, the danger is that as resources such as water, air and soil become scarce, the attempt to monopolize these scarce resources is intensified, particularly by business interests. The provision of access to these resources assumes equity in resource distribution. Equity and sustainability are basic ecological principles that are consonant with "ethical values of conservation" (Clark, 1995: 242). Clark (1995) suggests that there has to be collaboration among historians, ecologists and development specialists to work together to nurture economic development, conservation and the preservation of natural resources and sustainability.

Ecological anthropology, Social Soundness Analysis and sustainable development

Ecological anthropology has sought to integrate conservation policies with local land management and farming practices. The social soundness approach to sustainable development programs focused on how the needs of the people can be aligned with technological developments to minimize the effect of technology on altering/changing indigenous/local modes of living and social life.

Kottack (1999) has related the Social Soundness Analysis (SSA) approach to "sustainable development aims at culturally appropriate, ecologically sensitive, self-regenerating change" (p26). SSA has implications in the development and preparation of management accounting sustainability reports that promote environmental resource conservation (Sisaye et al., 2004). The contribution of ecological anthropology to sustainable development is that the level of acceptance of sustainability programs depends on how well these programs can best promote and support economic development programs that are compatible with existing cultural practices (Bozzoli, 2000; Stone, 2003).

If sustainable development is to balance the present and future needs of both present and future generations according to the Brundtland Report (WCED, 1987), Custance and Hillier (1998) suggest that there is a need for the development of social indicators. These indicators are primarily ecological and environmental and are related to land, soil, water, air and other natural resources that are not substitutable (p283). They elaborated that

> economic growth does not merely cause pressures on the environment. It brings benefits – income, employment and goods and services which people need and improve their welfare. One may argue about the relative merits of sustaining economic growth and improving environmental quality. But a balanced assessment of sustainable development must report on both aspects – not just the pressures caused by economic growth, but also the benefits that it brings. The model now also needs to incorporate the social aspects of welfare. (p284)

Custance and Hillier (1998) proposed that a balanced indicator that utilizes social, economic, environmental and ecological resources needs to be developed. The targets at both the local and national-scale levels are specified and data are available for all sectors of the economy – environment, transport, energy and industry, among others. These are pertinent to sustainable development when developed using the "standard definitions and classifications" used by the United Nations (UN), the Organisation for Economic Co-operation and Development (OECD), and other international development organizations (p286). The ecological anthropological approach of SSA has been used by many international donor organizations to develop both quantitative and qualitative indicators of sustainable development to manage and fund agricultural and industrial development projects in developing countries.

Industrial ecology and anthropology influences on sustainable development

Both industrial ecology and ecological anthropology address conservation and natural resources management issues in sustainable development. Ecological anthropology specifically addresses the issue that the level of acceptance of sustainability programs depends on how well economic and accounting indicators can best promote and support economic development programs that are compatible with existing national and local cultural practices, customs and mores (Bozzoli, 2000; Hoben, 1982; Stone, 2003).

As social science disciplines, both industrial ecology and ecological anthropology address sustainability within the context of organizations and the broader environment – community, nation, ecosystem and planet. These are organizational ecological issues addressing the imbalance from pollution, environmental degradation and damage to the ecosystem. The industrial ecology and ecological anthropology approaches to growth, development and interdependencies are embedded in several social, agricultural and biological sciences disciplines – for example, in economics (agricultural and resource economics), sociology (rural sociology and human ecology), geography and organization management studies (population ecology) (refer to Aldrich, 1979; Astley, 1985; Batie, 1989; Bozzoli, 2000; Carroll, 1984; Cohen-Rosenthal, 2000; Ehrenfeld, 2000; Pierce and White, 1999; Singh and Lundsen, 1990; Stone, 2003; Vondal, 1988; Wilbanks, 1994). Sustainable development became an integrated subject of study from various social disciplines, including economics. The multidisciplinary approach from sociology, anthropology and economics to sustainability growth has thus been incorporated into various reports and programs advocated by international development organizations.

Sustainability has thus emerged as an important subject area of research and teaching in the business education curriculum (Sisaye, 2011b). In accounting, there is a growing interest in sustainability as the demand for the voluntary uniform disclosure of sustainability and environmental data by business and governmental organizations has increased over the years. If there is a lack of fit, where existing accounting indicators of sustainable development do not have relevance, they are deemed to fail and die. The ecological assumption is that when existing methods are not consistent with emerging trends in sustainable development, this will necessitate the replacement of old assumptions with new ones, contributing to a new birth of accounting indicators and/or rules. It implies that over time, due to legitimacy and institutionalization, this could contribute to a new birth and/or breed of population of sustainability accounting rules. In this context, the subject of sustainability accounting and reporting is an emerging phenomenon and can be best addressed through integration within the resource-based view of organizations – that is, the ecological approaches of sociology, anthropology and economics.

Sustainable development: the ecology of sociology, anthropology and economic development

Sustainable development is based on ecology and economic development. Sociology, anthropology and economics argue that natural resources should be ecologically utilized to protect the environment and that economic development can simultaneously occur with ecologically based sustainable development approaches (Sisaye, 2012a, 2012b). Clark (1995) suggested that while sustainability may imply limits to growth for biodiversity among human and animal populations, as well as economic development, ecological sustainability promotes harmony among living organisms and natural habitat (pp230–231). The sociological and anthropological views of sustainability are based on the assumption that both economic development and the sustenance of natural and environmental resources are necessary to preserve human and animal populations, natural resources and society at large.

While sustainability has its roots in the agricultural sciences, including rural sociology and ecological anthropology in the study of subsistence agriculture in agrarian societies in the developing economies, it received prominence with the publication of the Meadows et al. report *The Limits to Growth* (1972, 1974). While Clark (1995) suggested that sustainability has its origin in ecological economics, the subject of sustainability dates back prior to the 1970s during the agricultural technological development era of the green revolution technology of high-yield fertilizers for seeds in the 1960s. Rural sociologists and ecological anthropologists advocated the need for sustainable agriculture development strategies through integrated national governmental agricultural organizational infrastructures to balance economic growth and national (local) community-based sustainable agriculture (Sisaye and Stommes, 1985). The Meadows et al. report (1972, 1974, 1992, 2004; Meadows, 2007) has brought to the forefront the need for family planning programs to reduce population growth and to manage future economic growth due to scarcity and the limited availability of natural resources (for a review, see Turner, 2008). Sustainable development is thus based on an ecological framework to balance the long-term objectives of economic development to improve human standards of living, welfare and social progress with the simultaneous objectives of maintaining balance with natural and environmental conservation policies.

Accordingly, sustainability denotes both futuristic (White, 2013) and spiritual (Custance and Hillier, 1998) aspirations to address the relationships among economic growth, social development and environmental management. It seeks to promote an integrated balance amongst human actions, environment and economic development where equitable distribution and the efficient allocation of resources as well as environmental protection and resource conservation are maintained. White (2013) noted that sustainability has inter-related objectives to balance environmental, social and economic development to reduce growth imbalances amongst societies and communities. Similarly, Walck (2004) viewed sustainability as integrating the competing approaches of economic development and ecology/conservation policies by forging a middle ground for economy and ecology to link development to natural resources and conservation to promote a sustainable economy and ecology, where the negative impacts of growth and development are mitigated through the principles of ecological economies (pp174–175). In addition, regulation, competition, triple bottom line (TBL) accounting and humanistic ethical values are used to balance the conflicts between economy and ecology principles through sustainable development.

It should also be noted that sustainability has not been fully accepted as a developmental strategy to balance ecological and economic growth. For example, Davidson (2011) criticized sustainability and sustainable development from a radical/critical perspective by equating it to sustainable economic growth that assumed substitution and replacement of resources that are attainable, but cannot be realized in the long term. The criticism was directed against the Brundtland Report (WCED, 1987). His argument was that the Brundtland definition of sustainability did not recognize the long-term implication of sustainability where equity and redistribution goals as well as preservation of natural resources might not be achievable. He saw the limitation of the report as putting too much emphasis on growth and expressed less concern on environmental resources and conservation.

On the other hand, proponents of the Brundtland Report (WCED, 1987) put forward both economic growth and resource conservation on the same agenda (Clark, 1995; Shirvastava, 1995; Stern, 1997). For example, Stern (1997) highlighted the economic and ecological implications of the Brundtland Report by noting that the report has policy-making implications since it advocates for equity among generations in the use of resources. There is the implication that the rights of future generations need to be protected by the current generation in the form of a "social contract" that is binding and enforceable to protect the interests of future generations (p163).

Clark (1995) suggested that sustainable development encompassed "ecological health and social welfare" as well as "ecology and equity" (p226). While the Brundtland Report (WCED, 1987) argued that planned economic development and growth can be attained through sustainable development programs that support environmental protection and conservation, it also noted that both developed and less developed societies may not fully embrace the policy. In developing countries where poverty and a low standard of living resulted in the over-exploitation of resources, environmental degradation and hazardous waste, sustainability cannot be realized without political changes. If there are no "functional democratic societies" where "social justice is embedded," sustainability as an economic development policy for environmental protection, preservation and ecological health will not be achievable (Clark, 1995: 236). Sustainability is embedded in ecological principles, social justice and environmental ethics where ecological welfare and quality of life are pursued in conjunction with economic growth.

Shrivastava (1995) described how the Brundtland Report (WCED, 1987) put forward the prominence of "ecologically sustainable development" to address the issues of economic growth and its impact upon the ecological system. Ecologically sustainable development (ESD) focuses on resource preservation and natural resource management. The focus is to reduce resource depletion, maintaining biodiversity and balancing the impact of growth and technology on climate change and global warming. He viewed ESD "as a comprehensive strategy for global development" that can address the concerns expressed in *The Limits to Growth* (Meadows et al., 1972, 1974) and the Brundtland Report (WCED, 1987). Shrivastava (1995) viewed the strategies of the WCED (1987) in terms of an ESD focus on ecosystems. Ecosystems address the environment and the impact that population growth and technology has on existing natural ecosystem resources, ensuring adequate worldwide food resources, sustainable economies and competitive strategies, managing ecosystem resources and sustainable industrialization and growth (p939).

The management of ecosystems, as Shrivastava (1995) noted, depends on maintaining the "long-term variability" of resources: avoiding deforestation and degradation of ecosystems, "conserving nonrenewable natural resources," and managing the diversity of resources (pp939–940). In terms of strategy, when ecosystem preservation is used in conjunction with ecological sustainability, it can create a "competitive advantage" that can be used as a "public relations" tool for enhancing "corporate image" (pp954–955).

Moreover, Custance and Hillier (1998) summarized that sustainable development fostered the balancing of three broad objectives. They include "maintenance of economic growth, protection of the environment and prudent use of natural resources, and social progress which recognizes the needs of everyone" (p281). Sustainable development and consumption gained acceptance to address environmental crisis and natural resources management (Rudel et al., 2011). Sustainability thus broadly addressed both internal and external factors. Ecology has addressed these factors as determining economic development, community well-being, social welfare and environmental resources management.

In essence, sustainability is based on ecology and equity where local political power is utilized to control and manage resources (Clark, 1995: 226–232). Ecological sustainability advanced the management of ecosystems, the importance of land ethics, respecting the rights and livelihood of indigenous populations, enacting legislation for the conservation of resources, and the need to have a politically stable government at the local, regional and national levels to manage environmental programs. The coalitions of several interest groups are lobbying governmental regulatory organizations to implement environmental legislation and monitor industrial growth so that it does not come at the cost of sustainable development.

Feltnote (1997) explained the risks associated with the externalities involved – government, local, regional and community stakeholders whose reliance on natural resources involved externalities in costs and accounting issues associated with environmental pollution and resource utilization. However, there are practical issues associated with the implementation of accounting for sustainable development because the costs and benefits cannot easily be determined, and there is lack of support for perceived benefits. On the other hand, if implemented, it shows organizations' commitment and willingness to practice voluntary self-regulation.

Accounting theory and practice can facilitate the realignment of organizational ecological resources to advance learning and knowledge system development related to sustainability management, resource conservation and environmental management, and their integration within an organization's activities to improve operational performance. Sustainable development and reporting can thus become one of the differentiating competitive strategies amongst organizations. From a strategic point of view, the ecology of sustainability has become one of the most important resources available to manage the discontinuity of changes in the environment, market forces, technology, natural resources and geographical locations. Sustainability accounting has become a byproduct of ecological economics, industrial ecology, ecological anthropology and organizational ecology (sociology).

The coevolution of the ecology of sustainability in sociology and anthropology and their implications for sustainability accounting and reporting systems

Ecological studies consider internal and external environmental conditions related to social, economic, cultural and political systems as factors determining organizational forms and structures; growth, maturity and mortality rates; and adaptation and selection strategies. Wolf (1999) suggested that there are cognized models that represent the conceptions and understandings of the environment by the people who live, act and interact with the environment. For these people, the environment guides their actions, beliefs, cultures and rituals. The environment molds the changes, compositions and relationships among them and their entities (Wolf, 1999: 19). These cognized models also explain the actions and strategies that organizations adopt to manage their environment. They are expected to vary depending on the condition of the environment (dynamic or stable) and resource availability (slack or scarcity). When resource conditions are slack, environmental conditions are favorable to support growth. In contrast, when organizational resources are scarce, organizations adopt retrenchment strategies that enhance the organization's goal for survival and adaptability to environmental changes.

Ecology views organizations as communities having interdependency relationships among multiple and diverse populations (Astley, 1985). Similarly, accounting systems, including sustainability accounting reporting, are considered part of ecological systems that belong to populations or groups or units (instead of individuals). Organizations' coevolution involves competition, growth, decline and death. Learning and innovation support the prerequisite for organizations' evolution and growth (Sisaye, 2011a).

Industrial ecology and ecological anthropology approaches are embedded in evolutionary economics and the resource-based view of the firm which views the development of sustainability accounting and reporting as a strategic management process that is evolutionary by following a staged growth development process in the preparation and disclosure of social and environmental information in financial (external) and managerial (internal) accounting reports. In accounting, the disclosure of economic, social and environmental reports is broadly classified as triple bottom line (TBL) reports which are included in external accounting reports.

TBL reports containing sustainability information on social and environmental issues are considered voluntary information. Nevertheless, the accounting profession has emphasized the importance of including standardized sustainability information in annual reports (such as the American Institute of Certified Public Accountants, AICPA, reports). The big four accounting firms have developed guidelines for sustainability and corporate social reporting (CSR) (Lusher, 2012). It has now become part of business practice to report social and environmental information, when necessary, at the discretion of the organization, either in footnotes, appendices or supplements to the annual reports. However, the information reported is not uniform: it is either included in the introduction of the annual report as part of the overall report provided by the president or the chief executive officer (CEO), included in a footnote as supplementary information in the annual report, or provided in a separate publication prepared for external constituencies.

Sustainability reporting has been recognized as one of the most important recent developments in accounting theory and research. While natural resource extracting industries (e.g., petroleum producers) are required to provide estimates of their petroleum reserves in annual reports, the information is considered important for external users. However, this trend was required for manufacturing industries who extract non-renewable natural resources. It was not commonly practiced for other industries. Sustainability reporting has now been given credence by many manufacturing industries, particularly those that are operating in environmentally sensitive areas; they provide environmental reports of their activities. The reports reflect the concerns that ecological anthropologists and industrial ecologists have expressed for accountability and transparency within manufacturing organizations.

Ecological anthropology has laid the foundation for the most widely used social soundness approach to sustainable development programs that links economic growth with sustained improvement of the community development needs of the people. Kottack (1999) has related the Social Soundness Analysis (SSA) approach to "sustainable development aims at culturally appropriate, ecologically sensitive, self-regenerating change" (p26). In accounting, Sisaye et al. (2004) suggested that SSA has implications in the development and preparation of sustainability accounting reports that promote the conservation of environmental resources.

Nordhaus and Kokkelenberg (2000) developed guidelines for management accounting systems that incorporate environmental information systems associated with renewable and environmental resources related to agriculture, forestry, recreation, land, timber and fisheries, as well as livestock and grain, and non-renewable resources of oil and natural resources. They recommended that organizations prepare environmental reports that focus on pollution, global warming and sustainable resources, to determine their costs, if any, and their effect on financial performance, as well as to report on natural resources such as air, oceans, water and lakes that are of interest to the general public and to governmental regulatory agencies such as the Environmental Protection Agency (EPA) as well as state, local and municipal governments (see also Howes, 1999: 32–33). For example, the EPA has conducted several studies on the effects of carbon and petroleum emission from agriculture and dairy products. A good example of this study describes petroleum and dairy productions in San Joaquin Valley, California, to understand the emission and air quality impacts from oil/gas operations. The report outlined those ground sites and aircraft measurements that were used in the project to determine the sources contributing to gas-phase organic carbon emissions (EPA, 2013b).

Similarly, in economics, the national income and product accounts have been extended to include non-market accounts – for example, air and water quality beyond consumer products with market accounts. This has the potential for the development of parallel indicators for non-market accounts similar to near-market accounts. Accordingly, these innovative changes in environmental management and accounting reporting systems become one of the main core competencies of socially responsible organizations, particularly in technology and manufacturing firms, characterized by a highly competitive environment. To remain competitive, these organizations continuously adopt policies that support the development and reinvention of new products and services to enhance continuous changes and adaptation in environmental and natural resource management. In this context, sustainable accounting can provide the systematic recording and reporting of assets and production activities associated with natural resources and the environment. Ecological anthropology and organizational ecology which focused on the broader environment – community, nation, ecosystem and the planet – broadened these issues by suggesting that the imbalances from pollution, environmental degradation and damages to the ecosystem could be addressed better at the local and community levels.

For example, Burritt (1999) proposed that environmental and ecological issues could be best handled at local and regional government levels. Ecologically sustainable development (ESD) is an important concern that can be addressed effectively at the local and municipal government levels. Local expenditures on environmental projects are handled well by local governments to satisfy the voluntary disclosure of funds and contending stakeholder interests, and to fulfill communication, reporting, independence and accountability requirements. Although ESD is based on the principle of local autonomy, the program objectives cannot be fully realized unless there is interagency cooperation of governmental agencies at the local, state and federal government levels on environmental data collection, design and reporting (pp57–60; see also Nordhaus and Kokkelenberg, 1999: 50–65; and Wood, 2000: 161).

Recently, the National Research Council (NRC) (2000) recommended that environmental indicators should be included in the national accounting system. That is, the NRC calls for a systematic development of green accounting that will include assets and production activities associated with natural resources and the environment. In other words, the national income and product accounts (NIPA) would be extended to include non-market accounts – for example, air and water quality – with near-market accounts/activities such as cooking hot dogs at home or consumer products such as televisions or cameras. By developing parallel indicators for non-market accounts similar to near-market accounts, the NRC puts forward that protecting the environment (e.g., air and water quality) contributes to the growth of gross domestic product (GDP).

Along similar lines, Holzman (2012) advocated replacement cost to estimate the value of "the cost of the least expensive technical fix as a replacement for an ecosystem service" (p155). In terms of ecosystem preservation, the suggestion was for paying farmers/landowners to employ better farming management/watershed practices that prevent fertilizer and animal waste from washing into the waterways. For example, New York City paid over U.S.$1 billion to farmers to improve their management practices to maintain clean water, realizing that "the value of clean water is much higher" than the cost since there are millions of residents that are served by the water (p156).

NIPA and replacement cost accounting are quantitative measures that can be used to account for intangible and non-renewable resources. When they are developed, these indicators will increase voluntary environmental disclosures and reporting on environmental policies, expenditures and audits. GDP indicators and processes can include benefits from environmental products and related details on sustainable and renewable resources as well as the limitations that companies in the chemical, forestry, paper, utilities and related sectors face in managing environmental resources. The EPA has noted that the potential growth from renewable sources of energy is substantial. In its 2013 report, the agency included information on non-hydroelectric renewable energy sources of electricity supplied from solar, geothermal, biomass, landfill gas and wind. Although installation of these renewable energy resources is growing, non-hydro renewable energy currently accounts for less than 2 percent of the electricity generation in the United States and its usage varies by states depending on the availability of these energy resources (EPA, 2013a).

Ecologically sustainable development has shaped the development policies and programs of many multilateral and bilateral international development organizations, including the World Bank and USAID, as well as business organizations and multinational corporations (MNCs). There has been an internationalization of sustainability across all sectors of the economy.

Most corporations used the USAID Social Soundness Analysis and World Bank Social Impact Assessment (SIA) sociological and anthropological models in their approaches to business interventions in developing countries. Although initiated in emerging economies to promote social and economic development for community growth, sustainability has also become central to business development in industrially developed countries, particularly in North America and Western Europe. These countries have instituted measures that go beyond economic performance in that they also include social and environmental accomplishments. These are voluntarily reported in annual reports and company publications and are publicized in various media outlets. Chapter 4 documents how sustainable development initiatives from USAID, the World Bank, international donor organizations and the U.S. federal government have influenced the incorporation of sustainability into business management policies and practices.

References

Aldrich, H. E. (1979). *Organizations and Environments*. Prentice-Hall, Englewood Cliffs, NJ.

Andersson, E., Brogaard, S. and Olsson, L. (2011). "The political ecology of land degradation," *Annual Review of Environment and Resources*, Vol. 36, August, pp295–319.

Astley, W. G. (1985). "The two ecologies: Population and community perspectives on organizational evolution," *Administrative Science Quarterly*, Vol. 30, No. 2, pp224–241.

Bailey, K. D. (1982). "Post-functional social systems analysis," *The Sociological Quarterly*, Vol. 23, No. 4, pp509–526.

Batie, S. S. (1989). "Sustainable development: Challenges to the profession of agricultural economics," *Proceedings of the American Agricultural Economics Association*, Vol. 71, No. 5, pp1083–1101.

Bozzoli, M. E. (2000). "A role for anthropology in sustainable development in Costa Rica," *Human Organization*, Vol. 59, No. 3, pp275–279.

Burritt, R. (1999). "Thinking local: Towards an environmental standard," *Australian CPA*, Vol. 69, No. 3, pp57–60.

Carroll, G. R. (1984). "Organizational ecology," *Annual Review of Sociology*, Vol. 10, pp71–93.

Clark, J. G. (1995). "Economic development vs. sustainable societies: Reflections on the players in a crucial contest," *Annual Review of Ecology and Systematics*, Vol. 26, pp225–248.

Cohen-Rosenthal, E. (2000). "A walk on the human side of industrial ecology," *American Behavioral Scientist*, Vol. 44, No. 2, pp245–264.

Custance, J. and Hillier, H. (1998). "Statistical issues in developing indicators of sustainable development," *Journal of the Royal Statistical Society. Series A (Statistics in Society)*, Vol. 161, No. 3, pp281–290.

Davidson, K. M. (2011). "Reporting systems for sustainability: What are they measuring?," *Social Indicators Research*, Vol. 100, No. 2, pp351–365.

Dietz, T. and Burns, T. R. (1992). "Human agency and the evolutionary dynamics of culture," *Acta Sociologica*, Vol. 35, No. 3, pp187–200.

Ehrenfeld, J. R. (2000). "Industrial ecology: Paradigm shift or normal science?," *American Behavioral Scientist*, Vol. 44, No. 2, pp229–244.

EPA (U.S. Government, Environmental Protection Agency) (2013a). *Clean Energy: Non-Hydroelectric Renewable Energy*, www.epa.gov/cleanenergy/energy-and-you/affect/non-hydro.html (accessed February 10, 2015).

EPA (2013b). *Climate Change Research Products in the Science Inventory*, http://cfpub.epa.gov/si/si_public_record_report.cfm?dirEntryId=278577&subject=Climate%20Change%20Research&showCriteria=0&searchAll=Climate%20and%20Air%20quality&actType=Product&TIMSType=JOURNAL&sortBy=revisionDate (accessed February 10, 2015).

Feldman, S. (1986). "Management in context: An essay on the relevance of culture to the understanding of organizational change," *Journal of Management Studies*, Vol. 23, No. 6, pp587–607.

Feldman, S. (1988). "How organizational culture can affect innovation," *Organizational Dynamics*, Vol. 17, No. 1, pp57–68.

Feltnote, B. W. (1997). "Making sustainable development a corporate reality," *CMA Magazine*, Vol. 71, No. 2, pp9–16.

Gray, S. J. (2000). "A memory loss: Ecological politics, local history, and the evolution of Karimojong violence," *Human Organization*, Vol. 59, No. 4, pp401–418.

Haenn, N. (2000). "Review article: Renovating ecology," *American Anthropologist*, Vol. 27, No. 3, pp736–745.

Hanna, K. S. (2005). "Planning for sustainability: Experiences in two contrasting communities," *Journal of American Planning Association*, Vol. 71, No. 1, pp27–40.

Hoben, A. (1982). "Anthropologists and development," *Annual Review of Anthropology*, Vol. 11, pp349–375.

Holzman, D. C. (2012). "Accounting for nature's benefits: The dollar value of ecosystem services," *Environmental Health Perspectives*, Vol. 120, No. 4 (April), ppA153–A157.

Howes, R. (1999). "Accounting for environmentally sustainable profits," *Management Accounting*, Vol. 77, No. 11, pp32–33.

Kaminski, J., Headley, D. and Bernard, T. (2010). "The Burkinabe cotton story 1992–2007: Sustainable success or sub-Saharan mirage?," *World Development*, Vol. 19, No. 8, pp1460–1495.

Kottack, C. P. (1999). "The new ecological anthropology," *American Anthropologist*, Vol. 101, No. 1, pp23–35.

Lamberton, G. (2005). "Sustainable sufficiency – An internally consistent version of sustainability," *Sustainable Development*, Vol. 13, No. 1, pp53–68.

Lusher, A. L. (2012). "What is the accounting profession's role in accountability of economic, social, and environmental issues?," *International Journal of Business and Social Science*, Vol. 3, No. 15, pp14–19.

Meadows, D. L. (2007). "Evaluating past forecasts: Reflections on one critique of the limits to growth," pp399–415 in Costanza, R., Grqumlich, L. and Steffen, W. (eds) *Sustainability or Collapse: An Integrated History and Future of People on Earth.* MIT Press, Cambridge, MA.

Meadows, D. L., Behrens III, W. W., Meadows, D. H., Naill, R. F., Randers, J. and Zahn, E. K. O. (1974). *Dynamics of Growth in a Finite World.* Wright-Allen Press, Inc., Boston, MA.

Meadows, D. L., Meadows, D. H. and Randers, J. (1992). *Beyond the Limits: Global Collapse or a Sustainable Future*. Earthscan Publications Ltd., London.

Meadows, D. L., Meadows, D. H. and Randers, J. (2004). *Limits to Growth: The 30-Year Update.* Chelsea Green Publishing Co., White River Junction, VT.

Meadows, D. L., Meadows, D. H., Randers, J. and Behrens III, W. W. (1972). *Limits to Growth: A Report for the Club of Rome's Project on the Predicament of Mankind.* Universe Books, New York.

Mog, J. M. (2004). "Struggling with sustainability – A comparative framework for evaluating sustainable development programs," *World Development*, Vol. 32, No. 12, pp2139–2160.

National Research Council (NRC) (2000). "Nature's numbers: Expanding the national economic accounts to include the environment," National Academy Press, Washington, DC, Mimeo.

Nordhaus, W. D. and Kokkelenberg, E. C. (1999). "Overall appraisal of environmental accounting in the United States," *Survey of Current Business*, Vol. 79, November, pp50–65.

Nordhaus, W. D. and Kokkelenberg, E. C. (2000). "Accounting for renewable and environmental resources," *Survey of Current Business*, Vol. 80, March, pp26–51.

Orlove, B. and Caton, S. C. (2010). "Water sustainability: Anthropological approaches and prospects," *Annual Review of Anthropology*, Vol. 39, pp401–415.

Penn, D. J. (2003). "The evolutionary roots of our environmental problems: Toward a Darwinian ecology," *The Quarterly Review of Biology*, Vol. 78, No. 3, pp275–301.

Pierce, B. D. and White, R. (1999). "The evolution of social structure: Why evolution matters," *Academy of Management Review*, Vol. 24, No. 4, pp843–853.

Rudel, T. K., Roberts, J. T. and Carmin, J. A. (2011). "Political economy of the environment," *Annual Review of Sociology*, Vol. 37, pp221–238.

Shrivastava, P. (1995). "The role of corporations in achieving ecological sustainability," *The Academy of Management Review*, Vol. 20, No. 4, pp936–960.

Singh, J. V. and Lundsen, C. J. (1990). "Theory and research in organizational ecology," *Annual Review of Sociology*, Vol. 16, pp161–195.

Sisaye, S. (2006). *The Ecology of Management Accounting and Control Systems: Implications for Managing Teams and Work Groups in Complex Organizations*. Praeger Publications in Business & Economics Series, Greenwood Publishing Group, Greenwich, CT.

Sisaye, S. (2011a). "Ecological systems approaches to sustainability and organizational development: Emerging trends in environmental and social accounting reporting systems," *The Leadership & Organization Development Journal*, Vol. 32, No. 4, pp379–396.

Sisaye, S. (2011b). "The functional–institutional and consequential–conflictual sociological approaches to accounting ethics education: Integration from sustainability and ecological resources management literature," *Managerial Auditing Journal*, Vol. 26, No. 3, pp263–294.

Sisaye, S. (2012a). "An ecological approach for the integration of sustainability into the accounting education and professional practice," *Advances in Management Accounting*, Vol. 20, pp47–73.

Sisaye, S. (2012b). "An ecological analysis of four competing approaches to sustainability development: Integration of industrial ecology and ecological anthropology literature," *World Journal of Entrepreneurship, Management and Sustainable Development*, Vol. 8, No. 1, pp18–35.

Sisaye, S. and Stommes, E. (1985). "Green revolution as a planned intervention strategy for agricultural development: A systems perspective," *Public Administration and Development*, Vol. 5, No. 1, pp39–55.

Sisaye, S., Bodnar, G. H. and Christofi, P. (2004). "Total quality management and sustainability reporting: Lessons from Social Soundness Analysis," *Internal Auditing*, Vol. 19, No. 5, pp32–39.

Stern, D. I. (1997). "The capital approach to sustainability: A critical appraisal," *Journal of Economic Issues*, Vol. 31, No. 1, pp145–173.

Stone, M. (2003). "Is sustainability for development anthropologists?," *Human Organization*, Vol. 62, No. 2, pp93–99.

Turner, G. (2008). *A Comparison of the Limits to Growth with Thirty Years of Reality*. Socioeconomics and the Environment in Discussion, CSIRO Working Paper Series 2008–09, March.

Villarreal, A. (2004). "The social ecology of rural violence: Land scarcity, the organization of agricultural production, and the presence of the state," *American Journal of Sociology*, Vol. 110, No. 2, pp313–348.

Vondal, P. J. (1988). "Social and institutional analysis in agriculture and natural resources management project assistance: Suggestions for improvement from Africa Bureau experience," USAID, Bureau of Africa: Social/Institutional Analysis Working Paper No. 2, Office of Development Planning, March.

Walck, C. (2004). "Healing the divided mind: Land as an integrating concept for organizations and the natural environment," *Organization and the Environment*, Vol. 17, No. 2, pp170–194.

WCED (World Commission on Environment and Development) (1987). *Our Common Future*, The Brundtland Report. World Commission on Environment and Development (WCED) and Oxford University Press, New York.

White, M. A. (2013). "Commentary and sustainability: I know when I see it," *Ecological Economics*, Vol. 86, February, pp213–217.

Wilbanks, T. J. (1994). "'Sustainable development' in geographic perspective," *Annals of the Association of American Geographers*, Vol. 84, No. 4, pp541–556.

Wolf, E. R. (1999). "Cognizing 'cognized models,'" *American Anthropologist*, Vol. 101, No. 1, pp19–22.

Wood, W. W. (2000). "Environmental accounting: The new bottom line," *Ground Water*, Vol. 38, No. 2, p161.

WRI (World Resources Institute) (2013). *Natural Infrastructure: Investing in Forested Landscapes for Source Water Protection in the United States*, www.wri.org/sites/default/files/wri13_report_4c_naturalinfrastructure_v2.pdf (accessed February 14, 2015).

Zimmer, C. (2015). "Ocean Life Faces Mass Extinction, Broad Study Says," *New York Times*, January 15, www.nytimes.com/2015/01/16/science/earth/study-raises-alarm-for-health-of-ocean-life.html?smid=nytcore-ipad-share&smprod=nytcore-ipad (accessed January 17, 2015).

4 Application of the ecological framework to the U.S. federal government and bilateral and multilateral development organizations

Ecology and sustainable development received prominence in the early 1970s when economists suggested that existing natural resources create potential limits to growth. A group of economists from the Massachusetts Institute of Technology (MIT) argued that the current rate of population growth could adversely affect food and industrial production, the environment (pollution), climatic conditions and geographical location (Meadows et al., 1972, 1974, 1992, 2004). The Meadows et al. (1972, 1974) report suggested the need for sustained economic growth by reducing population growth due to limited resources availability (see also Meadows, 2007). Sustainable development came as a reaction to limits to growth, and the environmental movement which followed advocated for governmental regulations to control environmental degradation (Castro, 2004). Conservation and sustainability called for regulation and planned development.

There came the realization that there was a need for conservation and carefully managing non-renewable resources, and strategies that enabled developing alternative renewable resources (Gray, 2006: 802). Organizational ecology which focused on the broader environment – community, nation, ecosystem and planet – expanded the limits to growth by addressing the imbalances from pollution, environmental degradation and damages to the ecosystem in relation to local and community development. Sustainability was propagated in the 1970s and 1980s as a guiding framework to balance the impact of economic growth upon the environment.

The foundation of sustainability in national and international development programs

Sustainability emerged as an ecological framework to guide government and business organizations to be involved in community development for sustained economic growth. It focused "on the broader environment – community, nation, ecosystem and planet" (Hansen, 2004: 66). Sustainability was accepted by social scientists and policy-makers to redress the imbalance from pollution, environmental degradation and damages to the ecosystem. However, implementing the goals of sustainability would require active involvement by individuals, groups, communities, businesses and public/governmental organizations (Hussey et al., 2001).

For example, Mog (2004) suggested that local, regional and national development efforts have substantiated that sustainability is a continuous change process with "sociopolitical impacts," including cultural acceptability and policy support to "facilitate learning and knowledge sharing." The social change programs support sustainability to "minimize local growth in human population and the consumption of non-renewable resources" (p2151). The organization and mobilization of local resources become critical for the success of sustainable development programs. Accordingly, the focus of sustainability is broader, addressing ecological and natural resource preservation and management, and is not limited only to economic growth and development. It also includes reforms aimed at the conservation of resources for economic purposes such as consumption, and an attempt to redirect economic gains to social concerns for disadvantaged members of society. These elements of sustainability include social justice, land and environmental ethics, ecological conservation and management of natural resources (Sisaye, 2011).

Sustainability evolved in the social sciences to advance the developmental needs of low-income countries, particularly their practices of sustainable agriculture and rural development (Sisaye, 2012). It addressed a wide range of developmental issues in

> an attempt to combine growing concerns about a range of environmental issues with socioeconomic issues ... It concentrates on long-term environmental sustainability which requires a strong basis in principles that link the social and environmental concerns to human equity ... with the potential to address fundamental challenges for humanity, now and into the future.
>
> (Hopwood et al., 2005: 38)

Sustainability was popularized by the 1987 publication of the Brundtland Report under the title *Our Common Future*. The report will be discussed in detail later in the chapter. It is briefly introduced here as the approach that has had a significant impact upon the U.S. federal government agencies that oversee environmental management and natural resource conservation.

The Brundtland Report defined sustainability as "the ability to meet the needs of present generations without compromising the ability of future generations to meet their own needs" (WCED, 1987: 8). The report also challenged the world to envision a future in which the threats of environmental destruction are minimized and the people of the world enjoy economic stability and social equity between and within generations. It recognized that humans are dependent on the environment to meet their needs, and the well-being of society is linked to the balance between ecology and economic growth. The report emphasized that human activities and existence depended on the balance between exploitation of resources and environmental protection and conservation. It formulated that environmental problems are best handled when economic and environmental issues are jointly addressed in decision making.

In general, the Brundtland Report (WCED, 1987) increased the awareness of world leaders and development experts of the importance of ecological resources and human beings' dependency on the environment to meet their needs and well-being. It suggested a balanced economic approach to utilize or exploit resources by considering the impact of development upon the environment and for human beings' security, well-being and current and future growth. It argued that if natural resources are not properly managed, there will be environmental degradation, which will exacerbate existing poverty problems and threaten people's health, livelihood and survival for now and future generations (pp39–40). To mitigate both anticipated and unanticipated consequences, it articulated a long-term sustainability management development effort that is continuous, not a one-time improvement or action program advocating specific policies or changes.

The Brundtland Report's (WCED, 1987) political and philosophical outlooks of growth are based on humanitarian principles where access to resources is fundamentally necessary for the survival, livelihood and well-being of society (Hopwood et al., 2005). The Brundtland Report was well received by both industrialized and developing countries and international bilateral and multilateral development organizations. They developed guidelines, which are discussed below, to expand development and humanitarian efforts in developing countries (Sisaye, 2012).

The evolution of sustainability in U.S. federal governmental organizations

The environmental movement in the United States not only addressed environmental concerns, but also brought other reform movements in sustainability and ecological systems management – water, natural resource management, and conservation and pollution control, among others. The economic-oriented production approach was challenged by the conservation movement, which argued that industrial growth would undermine the natural resource base that supports growth, and called for protection of the environment and conservation of natural resources. This followed the passage of laws and regulations to protect the environment and adopt a climate policy among nations to limit global warming (Rudel et al., 2011: 226–227).

The environmental movement in the United States has contributed to the legitimization and institutionalization of environmental resource conservation concerns within the U.S. federal government agencies (McLaughlin and Khawaja, 2000). The most notable government agency that has regulatory power over business development practices which could affect the environment, including pollution, hazardous waste and other environmental resources, is the Environmental Protection Agency (EPA). The EPA was established by the Nixon administration in the early 1970s in response to the call for natural resource conservation and protection of the environment. The federal government also passed the clean water act legislation and programs to address environmental issues and concerns (Rudel et al., 2011). The U.S. federal government, which was at the forefront of environmental management as early as the 1960s with the establishment of the EPA, has incorporated the Brundtland Report into the management of environmental programs associated with industrial growth in the country.

The U.S. Environmental Protection Agency

The EPA received regulatory power to enforce conservation and environmental protection and promote sustainable development. The 1969 National Environmental Policy Act enforced by the EPA stressed the need to "create and maintain conditions under which [humans] and nature can exist in productive harmony, and fulfill the social, economic, and other requirements of present and future generations of Americans" (U.S. Government, EPA, 2009). The federal government has issued several environmental regulations, including the Resource Conservation and Recovery Act (RCRA) of 1976 and the Comprehensive Environmental Response, Compensation Liability Act of 1980 (Superfund) to balance the impact of business innovation and growth with the management of and conservation of natural resources. These regulations enforced by the EPA have contributed to the development of accounting standards – namely, SFAS No. 5, Accounting for Contingencies – to recognize and report corporations' environmental liabilities associated with business innovations and growth.

Over time, the EPA policies expanded beyond regulatory enforcement to promoting sustainability programs to manage and conserve environmental and natural resources. A study by Grossarth and Hecht (2007) discussed the evolution of the EPA from a regulatory agency that was created to monitor pollution control to that of an organization that is responsible for the formulation and development of sustainability issues that encompassed population increases, urbanization and global economic growth. They suggest that "EPA can enhance its role in promoting sustainability by redefining relationships with the regulated community, defining and measuring sustainable outcomes, using science to support sustainable decision-making, and promoting stewardship and collaborative problem solving" (p1).

The EPA delineated sustainability as the ability to achieve continuing economic prosperity while protecting the natural systems of the planet and providing a high quality of life for its people (U.S. Government, EPA, 2010). As is manifested in the EPA's sustainability definition, the concept of sustainability has been broadened to include social, environmental and ecological issues that affect the well-being and standard of living of American citizens and the world population at large. Following the EPA, other federal government agencies were given regulatory power to administer national natural and environmental resources.

The U.S. Department of Commerce

The U.S. Department of Commerce is a federal government agency that administers fisheries and manages the Malcolm Baldrige award. It has adopted Social

Impact Analysis (SIA) to assess the management of development programs and their social impact upon various stakeholders, such as employees, customers, organizations and communities. It used these sustainability measures to develop programs to improve the standard of living and to protect the environment.

Similarly, the U.S. Department of Commerce's National Oceanic and Atmospheric Administration (NOAA) Fisheries Service has programs that promote habitat conservation and the sustenance of marine services, and also support oil exploration as well as protection of the local sustainable economy: fisheries and related development (U.S. Government, Department of Commerce, 2010a, 2010b).

The U.S. Department of Commerce has several agencies that have used social assessment techniques to evaluate the impact of business development programs upon the nation's natural and environmental resources. The most visible is the U.S. Department of Commerce's Malcolm Baldrige Award, which recognizes organizations that have achieved excellence in the delivery of their products and services. The award has recently established the *Community Impact Assessment Report* (CIAR) that noted sustainable development as one of the criteria to be included in the quality award. The quality award has extended beyond business organizations. Recently, the winners have included not-for-profit organizations (NFPs), including colleges and universities that have met the award's criterion of excellence in service and products, but also in sustainable development efforts that support local, regional and self-help community development programs (U.S. Government, Department of Commerce, 2010b).

The Technology Innovation Program (TIP) of the National Institute of Standards and Technology (NIST) Division of the Department of Commerce prepared a report in 2011 called *Energy: Green Data Centers for Sustainability* to make policy-makers aware of the importance of green energy data centers to the global sustainability transition. The report stressed the need to

> create energy efficient data centers heading towards a greener and more sustainable environment. A corresponding research goal is the development of a Decision Support System (DSS) that will allow data center professionals to make better management decisions for server and other information technology (IT) systems while balancing energy efficiency with various functionality demands.
>
> (U.S. Government, Department of Commerce, 2011: 1)

The Department of Commerce sustainable development programs have encompassed many areas, ranging from the development of national standardization criteria to select and award meritorious business organizations that exceed its quality standards, to the creation of energy data centers, to managing nonrenewable natural habitats. In terms of natural habitat management, the NOAA Fisheries Service has programs that promote habitat conservation and the sustenance of marine services, support oil exploration, and protect the local sustainable economy: fisheries and related development (U.S. Government, Department of Commerce, 2010a). The United States National Marine Fisheries Service (USNMFS) Agency is within the NOAA and uses Social Impact Assessment (SIA) as "a method of gauging the social and cultural consequences of alternative fishery management actions or policies" (U.S. Government, Department of Commerce, 2001).

The USNMFS uses SIA to determine the social and cultural conditions in areas where human populations are more likely to be affected by the projects. The USNMFS uses SIA to estimate the social and cultural impacts that the fishery projects have at local, regional and national scales. Social impacts have been defined as the "consequence to human populations of any public or private actions that alter the ways in which people live, work, and play, relate to one another, organize to meet their needs, and generally cope as members of society." The term also includes cultural impacts involving "changes to the norms, values, and beliefs that guide and rationalize their cognition of themselves and their society" (U.S. Government, Department of Commerce, 2001: 1).

The objective of SIA is to assist the organization in preparing an assessment report before the project is initiated (i.e., at the planning stage) so that improvements can be made to address the required social and cultural issues that would interfere in the successful implementation of the project. Since 1994, the USNMFS has prepared SIA reports for projects that it has either sponsored or authorized. The SIA has been used as an avenue to involve stakeholders in the design and delivery of government-sponsored projects.

Accordingly, the USNMFS has applied ten steps in the SIA process:

1 Develop plans to involve stakeholders.
2 Identify any alternative if there are proposed changes or plans.
3 Describe the relevant environment/area of influence.
4 Prepare a technical report that is comprehensive and addresses the concerns or issues of stakeholders.
5 Investigate the impact of the proposed project.
6 Determine how the affected people will respond to the project.
7 Estimate the long-term impacts of the project.
8 Develop guidelines that address changes in alternatives when they arise.
9 Develop plans that can mitigate the adverse impacts of these projects.
10 Develop a monitoring program that can identify actions when unanticipated problems arise.

(U.S. Government, Department of Commerce, 2001: 11–17)

Building on the notion of continuous improvement, an essential ingredient of total quality management (TQM), DiBella (1997) reported that many practitioners had been focusing on creating learning organizations over the past 10 to 15 years. He suggested that social learning requires having staff take part directly in learning interventions because of the potential contributions of each and every individual, and the collective effort of all individuals working in groups to define and solve problems. Shapiro (2002), in one of her studies on the effects of change intervention on employee attitudes, found out that participation in a TQM intervention can enhance the development of employees' orientation to continuous improvement. In other words, she suggests that employee-perceived fairness of profit-sharing and perceived ability to contribute to the profitability of a site are significantly associated with continuous improvement intervention programs such as TQM. Indeed, this is the heart of the SIA, where continuous improvement is achieved no longer through some external, expert-generated model of organizational learning, but instead through the involvement and participation of the affected (targeted) population in the process of problem identification and solution, sub-activity selection and design, implementation and evaluation. As firms and organizations adopt and adapt to TQM and its continuous improvement philosophy of environmental management, they create the need of staff training in organizational learning while concurrently emphasizing staff participation to achieve those improvement programs.

Other U.S. federal government regulatory agencies

In addition to the EPA, there are also other federal-level government agencies that have oversight in the management and sustainability of natural and environmental resources. The United States federal government has instituted sustainability and environmental management initiatives among its several departments and agencies to regulate and conserve the natural resources administered by the federal government. These agencies have provided oversight and passed legislation and accounting rules to regulate business activities in conformance with governmental environmental and natural resource conservation policies in both the United States and abroad.

For example, the U.S. Departments of Agriculture and Interior have been authorized with oversight responsibilities for forestry, parks, recreation centers, wildlife and fisheries management. The state governments have their own agricultural and environmental agencies that have jurisdictions over state-owned lands, parks, forests and other natural resource programs independent from those owned and administered by the federal (national) government agencies and departments. Both the federal and state governments did recognize the fact that the best strategy for a balanced sustainability management program depended on the effective coordination of these federal and state-level agency programs for the preservation and conservation of these natural and ecological resources.

There are several federal government agencies that are involved in sustainability and natural resource management programs. For example, the United States Department of Agriculture has an agency that is involved in natural resources conservation and sustainable development. The U.S. Forest Service (U.S. Government, Forest Service, 2010) is involved in natural resource management programs that sustain parks, forests, vegetation and recreational centers

– camps, trails and other natural recreation centers. The U.S. Forest Service, like other federal government agencies involved in sustainable development and the natural preservation of forests, has used Social Impact Analysis (SIA) to evaluate the feasibility and impact of its sponsored projects on national forests. The U.S. Forest Service uses SIA to determine the economic, social and cultural impacts of development projects on the local economy, as well as the environmental consequences and impact upon the preservation of natural forests (Turnley, 2002; U.S. Government, Forest Service, 2001). Several United States federal government agencies conduct *Social Impact Assessment Reports* (SIARs) to evaluate the impact of business development programs on ecological resources, including the environment.

Internationally, the Department of State has handled federal government foreign policy and international development initiatives. Most recently, the Department of State has conducted an environmental impact evaluation of the Keystone XL Pipeline project because it involved a neighboring country, Canada. The department conducts a sustainability impact assessment when development projects involve neighboring countries. It is also responsible for the administration and implementation of a sustainability framework to manage the U.S. government's international development programs. Through the Global Climate Change Initiative (GCCI) and other climate-related United States government programs, the Department of State is integrating climate change considerations into relevant foreign assistance through the full range of bilateral, multilateral and private donor and aid organizations to foster low-carbon growth, promote sustainable and resilient societies, and reduce emissions from deforestation and land degradation. The department is working with these organizations to provide incentives for national government leaders to make climate financing efficient, effective and innovative, based on country-wide plans, and focused on achieving long-term, measurable results (U.S. Government, USAID, 2010a).

The agency that is responsible for international development assistance is the United States Agency for International Development (USAID), which developed Social Soundness Analysis (SSA), together with the World Bank's Social Assessment Analysis (SAA) or SIA frameworks and guidelines – to formulate development assistance programs in the least developed countries (LDCs).

International development assistance and social assessment of programs in the U.S. federal government agencies: USAID

The most important bilateral organization that has significantly influenced sustainable development is USAID (U.S. Government, USAID, 2002, 2010b). USAID laid the foundation of sustainable development in its SSA report that was prepared by anthropologists to guide agricultural and industrial development efforts in developing countries (see Hoben, 1982; Hoben et al., 1996; Mog, 2004; Vondal, 1988). They argued that social and cultural development in development assistance programs can become successful and impact progress when local populations are directly involved in the planning and administration of these development programs.

The SSA framework of sustainable development is a subject where social and ecological anthropologists address development issues as encompassing economic goals, social justice/equity, survival, responsible environmental management, and cultural development (Bozzoli, 2000; Kottack, 1999; Stone, 2003). SSA is a general framework used by social scientists to assess the management of development programs and its social impact upon stakeholders – employees, customers and organizations as well as communities. The underlying framework of SSA takes on the planning and implementation of projects and services with the participation and full involvement of stakeholders. SSA is based on the principles of the continuous improvement of projects so that the information is disseminated and becomes part of the operating activities of those organizations that sponsored the projects.

USAID has applied SSA, sometimes referred to as Social Assessment Analysis (SAA), Social Impact Assessment (SIA) or Social Impact Measurement (SIM), to assess the design and delivery of programs with social and cultural consequences. SSA and SIA, as discussed above, have been used by the Departments of Commerce and Agriculture to assess the impact of economic development programs on the various stakeholders. USAID (U.S. Government, USAID, 2002: 1) stated that the agency's SSA policy is "to ensure the wide and significant participation of the poor (the targeted population) in the development process." USAID viewed involvement or participation as sharing the economic benefits and contribution of resources, but it also included involvement in the processes of problem identification and solution, sub-activity selection and design, implementation and evaluation. The agency's SSA is composed of three distinct but related aspects:

1 the compatibility of the activity with the socio-cultural environment in which it is to be introduced;
2 the likelihood that the new practices or institutions introduced among the initial activity target population will be diffused among other groups; and
3 the social impact or distribution of benefits and burdens among different groups, both within the initial activity population and beyond.

(U.S. Government, USAID, 2002: 1)

The objective of SSA is to commit resources for recruiting and hiring, as well as the training of technical specialists in SSA objectives, so that the experts are able to carry out the agency's objectives through systematic consultation with stakeholders, local business leaders and government officials. The technical experts used SSA's report to redesign the agency's operations so that the objectives of the project addressed the needs of the stakeholders. Government provided data, fundraising and institutional support to disseminate the results of the project. After SSA's objectives were communicated, government agencies, at both the local and central levels, supported the project and were able to minimize bottlenecks that would hamper the success of the projects.

It is assumed that if SSA's approach for improving the welfare of the community is not followed, the local ethno-ecologies are being challenged, transformed and replaced. To maximize the likelihood of success, the project's social design for change needs to consider and rely on local cooperation and participation. The most effective development projects have been planned conservation strategies that pay particular attention to the needs and wishes of the people living in the target area (Hoben, 1982; Hoben et al., 1996). An SSA-designed project takes a proactive approach in evaluating both the economic and the social consequences of development programs. SSA provides a balanced approach – a socio-political, economic-based approach – to analyze any proposed program when that program is planned and implemented, with the objective of bettering and improving a given population in a specified locality or region in a given country. The World Bank and other bilateral and multilateral organizations were influenced by USAID's SSA approach to local and national development programs.

Sustainability within the context of international bilateral and multilateral development organizations

There are several international bilateral and multilateral organizations besides USAID who are involved in international development assistance programs. International development has become a cumulative effort by both bilateral (USAID and OECD) and multilateral organizations to support economic development in LDCs.

The Organisation for Economic Co-operation and Development

An international bilateral organization that is comparable to that of USAID in its effort of sustainable development in LDCs is that of a European international development organization. The highly industrialized countries of Europe formed the Organisation for Economic Co-operation and Development (OECD) after World War II. The OECD, which is based in Paris, has 34 member countries including the United States, Canada and Japan (OECD, 2010).

The OECD has continued its historical foundation of reconstructing Europe under the Marshall Plan following World War II by extending the European Commission organization's expertise in conducting most of the work that supports sustainable economic development. It has supported and assisted economic development programs in many LDCs. The OECD has published several reports on sustainable development focusing on economic growth and sustainable development indicators (SDIs). The report prepared for the National Round Table on the Environment and the Economy's (NRTEE's) Environment and Sustainable Development Indicators (ESDIs) Initiative provided an overall framework for the establishment of sustainable development indicators centered on the concept of capital and wealth creation to support employment, provision of consumer goods and services, and management of environmental and natural resources that benefit the economy and society at large (OECD, 2001).

The use of global-level environmental indicators at the international level was advanced by the OECD. It suggested that the European Union member countries use these indicators as a benchmark for their sustainable development policies. Following the OECD, many international organizations including the United Nations Environment Programme (UNEP), the United Nations Development Programme (UNDP) and the World Resources Institute (WRI) publish an Environmental Sustainability Index (ESI), a Well-Being Index (WI), an Ecological Footprint (EF) and a Living Planet Index (LPI) (Moldan et al., 2004).

In 2008, the OECD published a book entitled *Sustainable Development: Linking Economy, Society, Environment*, which provided a historical perspective of the environmental, developmental and security challenges facing the world now and in the future. The book elaborated upon the role of the OECD in promoting sustainable and equitable growth focusing on economic growth in developing countries, managing production and consumption, promoting corporate social responsibility, supporting government and civil society, and mitigating the impact of climate change (OECD, 2008).

In addition to the OECD, there are several other international multilateral development organizations whose work has influenced the theoretical and practical approaches of sustainability in evaluating development assistance and business programs in LDCs. Some of these organizations include the International Bank for Reconstruction and Development (referred as the World Bank), the UNDP, the Food and Agriculture Organization (FAO) of the United Nations, and the International Labour Organization (ILO).

The International Bank for Reconstruction and Development (World Bank)

The World Bank (WB) is an example of an international development multilateral agency that has incorporated sustainability within the context of Social Assessment Analysis (SAA) guidelines (World Bank, 2003). The WB uses SAA as a general framework like USAID's SSA framework, where the bank consults with social anthropologists to assess the management of a development program and its social impacts upon stakeholders – target groups/people, government employees, local business customers and organizations, as well as a community's inhabitants. The WB has used SAA as a tool to incorporate social analysis and the participation of local people into project and analytical work. SAA combines systematic procedures to analyze socio-economic variables and processes with the purpose of assessing impacts and risks, mitigating adverse impacts, enhancing positive impacts, and developing the institutional conditions for social change and development (Sisaye et al., 2004).

The WB's SAA examined the impact of WB-supported economic operations on 42 social assessment factors. Their reports addressed beneficiary assessment, including the identification and design of development activities, feedback on interventions, and constraints on project implementation of the targeted client population, particularly the poor. The WB's SAA looked at the economic livelihood of the people and the institutional arrangements that provided the service, as well as the effect that the project had on gender and diversity. SAA guidelines not only provided a "framework for information dissemination, consultation and participation," but also allowed the bank to use SAA "as a vehicle for gaining stakeholders' commitment, and for improving sustainability of development interventions" (World Bank, 1995: 2). It focused on how the WB-supported economic projects can incorporate social soundness, quality and sustainability of bank operations as reflected in the bank's SAA guidelines.

Sustainability within the context of other international multilateral development organizations

This section introduces the sustainable development programs of several international multilateral development organizations. These multilateral organizations include the UNDP, the FAO and the ILO.

The United Nations Development Programme

The UNDP is an international development agency that parallels the development objectives of the World Bank (UNDP, 2010). The UNDP, which is headquartered in New York City, supported the World Commission on Environment and Development (WCED)'s report, *Our Common Future*, published in 1987. The report, commonly referred to as the Brundtland Report, is the most noted sustainability report which gave credence to the importance and recognition of sustainability growth and development in LDCs. It defined sustainability as "the ability to meet the needs of present generations without compromising the ability of future generations to meet their own needs" (p8).

The Brundtland Report (WCED, 1987) broadly approached sustainability as "a process of change in which the exploitation of resources, directions of investments, orientation of technological development, and institutional change are made consistent with future as well as present needs" (p9). According to Banerjee (2002), the report emphasized balanced growth – economic, social and environmental, the equitable use of resources in the present without sacrificing future needs, social justice, environmental management and social responsibility. The implication for corporations and business organizations is that business growth and development cannot occur in isolation, and that these core inter-relationships have implications for environmental and social well-being in sustainable development (Banerjee, 2002: 106–107). The links between sustainability, ecologically sustainable organizations and balanced economic development provided the broad objectives of the Brundtland Report (WCED, 1987). It integrated economic development with ecological conservation and environmental resources management.

The WCED (1987) report sets out a framework for an environmentally sustainable society that focuses on economic growth, responsible use of natural resources, environmental management and transfer of technology from the well-developed to the less-developed countries. By combating poverty, the WCED report argued that the problem of environmental degradation and crisis can be managed if it is coupled with control of population growth and that science and technology are the key to sustainable development. Economic growth that addresses solutions to poverty, which is the cause of environmental degradation, thus contributes to sustainable development (Castro, 2004; Clark, 1995; Morrison-Saunders and Retief, 2012; Stern, 1997).

The WCED (1987) view of sustainable development is broader and includes both the industrially developed and developing economies. It outlined an ecological and economic rationale which has worldwide implications. Stern (1997) articulated the economic rationale when suggesting that there is a common agreement among economists "that sustainability implies that certain indicators of welfare or development are non-declining over the very long term; that is, development is sustained," and that there exists the capacity "of maintaining a capital stock as a prerequisite for sustainable development" (p145). Stern extended the argument that the capital theory approach of sustainability is based upon the premise that developed countries can contribute to "degrading the environment" (p146). When poverty is combined with population growth, it leads to overconsumption and depletion of resources and "environmental degradation, but degradation would also undermine development and lead to the perpetuation of poverty" (p146). While the capital theory approach assumes that there are contradictions between economic growth and environmental quality, the WECD report expanded the approach globally to mean that sustainable development becomes a goal for both developing nations and industrialized countries as well (Stern, 1997: 146–147; WCED, 1987: 4).

The WCED (1987) report advocated for an inclusive approach to sustainability that has humanistic, economic and cultural dimensions internationally. It made policy-makers and practitioners aware that the global ecosystem is interconnected and that nations work together to achieve "social and environmental goals," equity and the "fair distribution of resources," safeguarding and protecting natural resources, guaranteeing secure and healthy lifestyles and "quality of life," and allowing social and political liberty in the participation of the democratic government (Gladwin et al., 1995: 879–880). The WCED (1987) report broadened sustainability beyond economic development to include environmental, ecological and social systems.

White (2013) expanded sustainable development to include three interrelated relationships in economic and social development and environmental management. The economic aspect addresses efficiency in resource use and allocation, while social issues are concerned with equity and the redistribution of resources among segments of society to alleviate poverty. It addresses the need for "reducing economic disparity" while addressing poverty by promoting economic development that conserves resources for future generations (p215). The environmental management objectives centered on conservation policies and control of pollution and environmental degradation, and reduction of imbalances in environmental, social and economic growth among communities, societies, nations and the world at large (pp216–217).

The management of sustainability's economic, environmental and social performance depends upon social responsibility and accountability. Elkington (1977), as described in triple bottom line (TBL) reporting, suggested that the Brundtland Report (WCED, 1987) embedded three components of accountability: social–ethical, environmental and economic (or financial) accountability. However, the report has not developed an integrated framework for accounting sustainability. Beckett and Jonker (2012) and Elkington (1977) framed the accounting of sustainability emerging from researchers and practitioners who incorporated a number of complementary concepts/ideas from quality and environmental management as well as social responsibility into measures of financial/economic performance.

For example, Burritt and Schaltegger (2010) have listed four indicators – compliance reports, compliance, decision-making and disclosure/reports – that make sustainability environmental performance reporting part of the integrated business enterprise system. They suggested that this approach can be used to develop sustainability scorecard performance indicators, which is integrative to address the business interests and the stakeholder relations of organizations (pp842–843). In other words, they are inferring that the sustainability scorecard can be adapted to the indicators developed in the balanced score card (BSC) formats. The TBL approach, which encompasses sustainability, has been referred to as an extension of BSC, which integrates accounting indicators into the marketing, production and human resources functions of the organization. Mitchell et al. (2012) indicated that if TBL is used in conjunction with BSC, BSC can be incorporated incrementally to modify and adapt sustainability accounting principles to business performances.

The economic growth approach equates both business financial and economic performance as promoting sustainable development. It is assumed that as business organizations accumulate wealth over time and are profitable, it is in their best interests to pursue sustainability. Sustainability is based on the notion of sharing accumulated wealth with the community, society and various stakeholders. As wealth increases over time, leading to more production and industrial development, economic growth and development will create the need for sustainability to maintain the current standard of living and to pursue further economic growth with conservation and future planning. The business growth and accountability approach attempts to mitigate the conflicting goals of productivity and the ecological limits to growth hypothesis.

Although the WCED (1987) report recognized the existence of environmental and natural resource limitations to economic growth, it saw sustainability as providing changes in the direction of economic development that will sustain social equity and improved standards of living for current and future generations. Bansal (2005) interpreted the WCED (1987) report as comprising three principles of sustainable development – environmental integrity, social equity and economic prosperity – that support economic development. The principle of environmental integrity focused on ecosystem preservation, natural resources management, sustaining non-renewable resources, biodiversity, forestry management, pollution control, waste management, natural resource preservation and the management of "air, water, and food" quality to sustain human and animal life for now and in the future (p198). The second principle, social equity, is based on having "equal accesos to resources and opportunities" as well as on the redistribution of wealth for improved standards of living (p198). Equity raises social and economic well-being for current and future generations. The third principle, economic prosperity, is based on a better quality of life and improved standard of living, where wealth creation, innovation, business growth and government policies promote economic prosperity, improved healthcare services, agricultural management and forestry programs (pp198–199).

The Brundtland Report (WCED, 1987) saw equity as having two dimensions – social and economic equity – and focused on both objectives. Bansal (2005) saw social equity in terms of access to economic resources, which is similar to Orlove and Caton's (2010) view of equity within the broader social and economic equity of sustainable development. For them, sustainability implies equity in terms of access and distribution of resources, management philosophy (organization and rules) and the governance (politics) of natural resources including water. These policies require an understanding of indigenous culture, values and political systems (pp404–405). Sustainability has provided an integrative approach to handle natural, biological and environmental resources at the local, national and international levels. It has achieved legitimacy by government, community and society at large. Business organizations embraced sustainability as a long-term solution for the availability of resources for business expansion and growth consistent with local and national development priorities (Joshi and Krishnan, 2010). In 2003, *World Resources, 2002–2004* was issued as the collaborative report of four international organizations: the United Nations Development Programme, the United Nations Environment Programme, the World Bank and the World Resources Institute. The report focused on the importance of good environmental governance by exploring how citizens, government leaders and business managers can work together to foster balanced environmental decisions to manage ecosystems and natural and environmental resources to promote redistributive economic growth and social equity at the local, national and international levels (WRI, 2003).

In general, the Brundtland Report (WCED, 1987) advised policy-makers and international donor organizations to envision a future in which the threats of environmental destruction are minimized, where all people of the world enjoy economic stability and social equity (redistribution) between and within generations. This approach implied that, at the international level, the UN would support a democratic political system. Stern (1997) used the analogy of a "global democracy" for the institutionalization of independent organizations that can help national governments institute organizational infrastructures to enable the economy and environment to work together mutually to support democratic governments (p164). For example, Clark (1995) viewed the Brundtland Report as a general framework to promote "business interests, government affiliation around the world, powerful international institutions such as the World Bank, the International Monetary Fund, UN Food and Agricultural organizations" as well as national political elites who work together to promote sustainable development (p232). National governments supported the redistribution of economic development programs across the board as long as these changes maintained social and political orders. The United Nations development agencies, the FAO and ILO, embarked on implementing the WCED's (1987) sustainable development programs in developing countries.

The Food and Agriculture Organization

The FAO is one of the United Nations' international development organizations (FAO, 2010). It is located in Rome, Italy. The FAO's international efforts have focused on eliminating hunger and food shortage. It serves both developed and developing countries by providing a forum to negotiate agreements and debate food policies. The FAO assists developing countries in modernizing and improving agriculture, forestry and fisheries practices that support sustainable development.

The FAO has outlined that its

> three main goals are: the eradication of hunger, food insecurity and malnutrition; the elimination of poverty and the driving forward of economic and social progress for all; and the sustainable management and utilization of natural resources, including land, water, air, climate and genetic resources for the benefit of present and future generations.
>
> (FAO, 2013a)

The FAO has followed the guidelines of the Brundtland Report in its agricultural development policies in LDCs. Its policies and plans promote sustainable agricultural development in the developing countries by supporting high-yield variety crops, fertilizers, agriculture credit, expert advice and extension programs directed at rural development.

In line with its sustainable development policy, the FAO has conducted several studies on the impact of agricultural technology and food wastages upon the environment. In 2013, the FAO issued the *Food Wastage Footprint: Impacts on Natural Resources* summary report. The report outlined "a worldwide account of the environmental footprint of food wastage along the food supply chain, focusing on impacts on climate, water, land and biodiversity, as well as an economic quantification based on producer prices." The FAO developed the Food Wastage

Footprint (FWF) model to document "the impacts of food wastage on natural resources" and their sources. The report summarized "the wastage footprint by regions, commodities or phases of the food supply chain in order to identify 'environmental hotspots' and thus, point towards action areas to reduce food wastage" (FAO, 2013b). The FAO has pursued policies that support agricultural development and preserve environmental and natural resource sustainability.

The International Labour Organization

The ILO, which is headquartered in The Hague, the Netherlands, advocated the International Fair Practice Employment and Labour Standards as part of its sustainable development efforts for child labor protection and equal pay for equal work initiatives in the developing world. It supported the United Nations Global Compact (UNGC, 2009), which is a strategic policy initiative for businesses committed to aligning their operations and strategies around four sustainability objectives. They are the:

- Universal Declaration of Human Rights;
- International Labour Organization's Declaration of Fundamental Principles and Rights at Work;
- Rio Declaration on Environment and Development;
- United Nations Convention against Corruption.

The ILO supported the International Organization for Standardization (ISO) (i.e., the ISO 9000 certification), which developed a set of procedures, guidelines and standards for multinational corporations (MNCs) to adhere to certain standards dealing with improved labor standards and protection, equal pay and workers' rights (child labor and safe working conditions) and the anti-corruption act (ILO, 2006, 2007). It required that companies provide documentation showing that they have developed record-keeping systems required for ISO certification. The certification became the standard for recognition of quality products and services.

The ILO later revised and introduced ISO 14000 for environmental management system documentation, which addressed the world's depletion of natural resources and the environmental risks associated with industrialization. It required participating companies to keep track of raw materials usage, the generation, treatment and disposal of their hazardous wastes, emission control and continuous improvement plans. It set guidelines on pollution emissions and for companies to prepare ongoing improvement plans in their environmental performance.

The ISO 14001 certifications that followed elaborated upon the advantages of sustainability as ranging from a corporate mandate, to regulatory considerations, and subsequently to environmental benefits. It provided a framework for members' business organizations to satisfy and fulfill external requirements related to customers, improved relationship with governmental agencies, improved stakeholder responsibility, positive publicity, competitive advantage and reduced insurance premiums.

Implications of international development assistance programs on the sustainability policies of business organizations: an overview

In general, sustainable development efforts have been accepted and implemented by the international bilateral and multilateral organizations and by the United States federal agencies and departments. Social Soundness Analysis, which sometimes has been referred to as Social Assessment Analysis or Social Impact Assessment, and which has been applied to assess the design and delivery of USAID and World Bank operations (see World Bank, 1995), has influenced the international development assistance programs of the UN and the OECD. These two assessment studies, the SSA and SIA, were particularly notable because they focused on those identified stakeholders and ensured that the overall project objectives and benefits were fully understood and accepted by the participants (Sisaye, 2012). The business stakeholder approach to sustainability is grounded in USAID and World Bank international development assistance programs. It has influenced MNCs, financial institutions and manufacturing/industrial organizations' sustainability business programs in LDCs.

The stakeholder approach to the business view of sustainability recognizes that there are risks associated with external parties: customers, the government at national and local levels, the community and regional and organized interest groups – labor and environmental associations, among others – when businesses are involved in sustainable development programs. Feltnote (1997) noted that the risks associated with externalities have to be part of accounting for externalities; a good example is the cost associated with environmental pollution (pp13–14). It became apparent that external costs associated with development and growth are to be incorporated into sustainability accounting.

Atkinson (2012) noted that sustainability accounting is based on the triple bottom line objectives of the economic, environmental and social performance of business organizations. It integrates profit and concerns for human welfare to improve quality of life. In terms of environmental performance, Atkinson suggested quantifiable indicators that "may include a decrease in raw materials wastage, improved power efficiency and decreased fuel consumption" (p32). These indicators not only conserve environmental and natural resources, but they are also intended to improve quality of life and sustain the long-term financial and economic profitability of business organizations.

Business policies that link sustainability to community well-being and values enhance the legitimacy of business organizations. Lopez et al. (2007) noted that sustainable development among European countries focuses on proactive policies to protect and preserve environmental resources and discloses sustainability performance information to the public. Sustainable business strategies are implemented to shape future economic policies and environmental performance for long-term value creation for business organizations (see also Orlove and Caton, 2010). These studies suggest that business sustainable development and subsequent accounting policies have been derived from the sustainability practices of international bilateral and multilateral development organizations as well as United States federal government regulatory agencies.

Chapter 5 discusses the impacts that the sustainable development programs of the U.S. federal government and the international bilateral and multilateral development organizations have on the recent developments of sustainability approaches in business organization programs. It details the subsequent evolution of the integration and documentation of corporate environmental and resource management performances into sustainability accounting and reporting.

References

Atkinson, M. (2012). "No nonsense sustainability: Organizations can create more value by increasing sustainability," *Chartered Accountants Journal* (New Zealand), July, p32.

Banerjee, S. B. (2002). "Corporate environmentalism: The construct and its measurement," *Journal of Business Research*, Vol. 55, No. 3, pp177–192.

Bansal, P. (2005). "Evolving sustainably: A longitudinal study of corporate sustainable development," *Strategic Management Journal*, Vol. 26, No. 3, pp197–218.

Beckett, R. and Jonker, J. (2012). "AccountAbility 1000: A new social standard for building sustainability," *Managerial Auditing Journal*, Vol. 17, Nos. 1–2, pp36–42.

Bozzoli, M. E. (2000). "A role for anthropology in sustainable development in Costa Rica," *Human Organization*, Vol. 59, No. 3, pp275–279.

Burritt, R. L. and Schaltegger, S. (2010). "Sustainability accounting and reporting: Fad or trend?," *Accounting, Auditing & Accountability Journal*, Vol. 23, No. 7, pp829–846.

Castro, C. J. (2004). "Sustainable development: Mainstream and critical perspectives," *Organization and Environment*, Vol. 17, No. 2, pp195–225.

Clark, J. G. (1995). "Economic development vs. sustainable societies: Reflections on the players in a crucial contest," *Annual Review of Ecology and Systematics*, Vol. 26, pp225–248.

DiBella, A. J. (1997). "Organizational learning and participatory assessments gearing up to become a learning organization," *The Journal for Quality and Participation*, Vol. 20, No. 3, pp2–14.

Elkington, J. (1977). *Cannibals with Forks: The Triple-Bottom Line of the 21st Century Business*. Capstone, Oxford, UK.

FAO (Food and Agriculture Organization of the United Nations) (2010). *Natural Resources and Environment*. Publications and Newsletters, Rome, www.fao.org (accessed January/February 2015).

FAO (2013a). *About FAO*, www.fao.org/about/en (accessed February 14, 2015).

FAO (2013b). *Food Wastage Footprint: Impacts on Natural Resources*, www.fao.org/docrep/018/i3347e/i3347e.pdf (accessed February 14, 2015).

Feltnote, B. W. (1997). "Making sustainable development a corporate reality," CMA *Magazine*, Vol. 71, No. 2, pp9–16.

Gladwin, T. N., Kennelly, J. J. and Krause, T.-S. (1995). "Shifting paradigms for sustainable development: Implications for management theory and research," *The Academy of Management Review*, Vol. 20, No. 4, pp874–907.

Gray, R. (2006). "Social, environmental and sustainability reporting and organizational value creation? Whose value? Whose creation?," *Accounting, Auditing & Accountability Journal*, Vol. 19, No. 6, pp793–819.

Grossarth, S. K. and Hecht, A. D. (2007). "Sustainability at the U.S. Environmental Protection Agency: 1970-2-20," *Ecological Engineering*, Vol. 30, No. 1, pp1–8.

Hansen, S. (2004). "Resilience and sustainability," *Chartered Accountants Journal of New Zealand*, Vol. 83, No. 9, pp66–67.

Hoben, A. (1982). "Anthropologists and development," *Annual Review of Anthropology*, Vol. 11, pp349–375.

Hoben, A., Peters, P. and Rocheleau, D. (1996). "Participation and development assistance in Africa." Washington, DC: A joint initiative of the U.S. Agency for International Development and World Resources Institute Policy Brief No. 3, September, mimeo.

Hopwood, B., Mellor, M. and O'Brien, G. (2005). "Sustainable development: Mapping different approaches," *Sustainable Development*, Vol. 13, No. 1, pp38–52.

Hussey, D. M., Kirsop, P. L. and Meissen, R. E. (2001). "Global reporting initiative guidelines: An evaluation of sustainable development metrics for industry," *Environmental Quality Management*, Vol. 11, No. 1, pp1–20.

ILO (International Labour Organization) (2006). "Socially sustainable development and participatory governance: Legal and political aspects," by K. Papadakos. International Institute for Labour Studies, Geneva.

ILO (2007). *Decent Work for Sustainable Development: The Challenge of Climatic Change*. Report by Working Party on the Social Dimension of Globalization. Geneva, www.ilo.org/empent/Publications/WCMS_093969/lang--en/index.htm (accessed January/February 2015).

Joshi, S. and Krishnan, R. (2010). "Sustainability accounting systems with management decision focus," *Cost Management*, Vol. 24, No. 6, pp20–30.

Kottack, C. P. (1999). "The new ecological anthropology," *American Anthropologist*, Vol. 101, No. 1, pp23–35.

Lopez, M. V., Garcia, A. and Rodriguez, L. (2007). "Sustainable development and corporate performance: A study based on the Dow Jones sustainability index," *Journal of Business Ethics*, Vol. 75, No. 3, pp285–300.

McLaughlin, P. and Khawaja, M. (2000). "The organizational dynamics of the U.S. environmental movement: Legitimation, resource mobilization, and political opportunity," *Rural Sociology*, Vol. 65, No. 3, pp422–439.

Meadows, D. L. (2007). "Evaluating past forecasts: Reflections on one critique of the limits to growth," pp399–415 in Costanza, R., Grqumlich, L. and Steffen, W. (eds) *In Sustainability or Collapse: An Integrated History and Future of People on Earth*. MIT Press, Cambridge, MA.

Meadows, D. L., Behrens III, W. W., Meadows, D. H., Naill, R. F., Randers, J. and Zahn, E. K. O. (1974). *Dynamics of Growth in a Finite World*. Wright-Allen Press, Inc., Boston, MA.

Meadows, D. L., Meadows, D. H. and Randers, J. (1992). *Beyond the Limits: Global Collapse or a Sustainable Future?* Earthscan Publications Ltd., London.

Meadows, D. L., Meadows, D. H. and Randers, J. (2004). *Limits to Growth: The 30-Year Update*. Chelsea Green Publishing Co., White River Junction, VT.

Meadows, D. L., Meadows, D. H., Randers, J. and Behrens III, W. W. (1972). *Limits to Growth: A Report for the Club of Rome's Project on the Predicament of Mankind*. Universe Books: New York.

Mitchell, M., Curtis, A. and Davidson, P. (2012). "Can triple bottom line reporting become a cycle for 'double loop' learning and radical change?," *Accounting, Auditing & Accountability Journal*, Vol. 25, No. 6, pp1048–1068.

Mog, J. M. (2004). "Struggling with sustainability – a comparative framework for evaluating sustainable development programs," *World Development*, Vol. 32, No. 12, pp2139–2160.

Moldan, B., Hak, T., Kovanda, J., Havranek, M. and Kuskova, P. (2004). *Composite Indicators of Environmental Sustainability*, *OECD*, www.oecd.org/site/worldforum/33829383.doc (accessed February 8, 2015).

Morrison-Saunders, A. and Retief, F. (2012). "Walking the sustainability assessment talk – progressing the practice of environmental impact assessment (EIA)," *Environmental Impact Assessment Review*, Vol. 36, No. 1, pp34–41.

OECD (Organisation for Economic Co-operation and Development) (2001). *A Proposed Approach to Environment and Sustainable Development Indicators Based on Capital*, www.oecd.org/site/worldforum/33626361.pdf (accessed February 8, 2015).

OECD (2008). *Sustainable Development: Linking Economy, Society, Environment*, www.oecd.org/insights/sustainabledevelopmentlinkingeconomysocietyenvironment.htm (accessed February 8, 2015).

OECD (2010). OECD publications on sustainable development. OECD Publications Service, Paris, www.oecd.org/home/0,2987,en_2649_201185_1_1_1_1_1,00.html (accessed January/February 2015).

Orlove, B. and Caton, S. C. (2010). "Water sustainability: Anthropological approaches and prospects," *Annual Review of Anthropology*, Vol. 39, pp401–415.

Rudel, T. K., Roberts, J. T. and Carmin, J. A. (2011). "Political economy of the environment," *Annual Review of Sociology*, Vol. 37, pp221–238.

Shapiro, J. A. M. C. (2002). "Changing employee attitudes: The independent effects of TQM and profit sharing on continuous improvement orientation," *The Journal of Applied Behavioral Science*, Vol. 38, No. 1, pp57–77.

Sisaye, S. (2011). "Ecological systems approaches to sustainability and organizational development: Emerging trends in environmental and social accounting reporting systems," *The Leadership & Organization Development Journal*, Vol. 32, No. 4, pp379–396.

Sisaye, S. (2012). "An ecological analysis of four competing approaches to sustainability development: Integration of industrial ecology and ecological anthropology literature," *World Journal of Entrepreneurship, Management and Sustainable Development*, Vol. 8, No. 1, pp18–35.

Sisaye, S., Bodnar, G. H. and Christofi, P. (2004). "Total quality management and sustainability reporting: Lessons from Social Soundness Analysis," *Internal Auditing*, Vol. 19, No. 5, pp32–39.

Stern, D. I. (1997). "The capital approach to sustainability: A critical appraisal," *Journal of Economic Issues*, Vol. 31, No. 1, pp. 145–173.

Stone, M. (2003). "Is sustainability for development anthropologists?," *Human Organization*, Vol. 62, No. 2, pp93–99.

Turnley, J. G. (2002). *Social, Cultural, Economic Impact Assessments: A Literature Review*. Prepared for The Office of Emergency and Remedial Response, US Environmental Protection Agency, Mimeo, October.

UNDP (United Nations Development Programme) (2010). Publications on sustainable development, www.undp.org (accessed January/February 2015).

UNGC (United Nations Global Compact) (2009). *Overview of the UN Global Compact*, www.unglobalcompact.org/AboutTheGC/index.html (accessed January/February 2015).

U.S. Government, Department of Commerce (2001). *Guidelines and Principles for Social Impact Assessment*. National Oceanic and Atmospheric Administration, National Marine Fisheries Service, Mimeo, Revised March 2001.

U.S. Government, Department of Commerce (2010a). *NOAA Strategic Plan*, /www.ppi.noaa.gov/PPI_Capabilities/Documents (accessed January/February 2015).

U.S. Government, Department of Commerce (2010b). *2011–2012 Criteria for Performance Excellence*. Baldrige Performance Excellence Program, Mimeo, www.nist.gov/baldrige (accessed January/February 2015).

U.S. Government, Department of Commerce (2011). *Energy: Green Data Centers for Sustainability*, Technology Innovation Program (TIP), National Institute of Standards and Technology (NIST), www.nist.gov/tip/wp/pswp/upload/261_green_data_centers_for_sustainability1.pdf (accessed February 14, 2015).

U.S. Government, EPA (Environmental Protection Agency) (2009). *Sustainability*, www.epa.gov/sustainability/basicinfo.htm (accessed January/February 2015).

U.S. Government, EPA (Environmental Protection Agency) (2010). *Sustainable development*, Washington, DC, www.epa.gov/ebtpages/pollsustainabledevelopment (accessed January/February 2015).

U.S. Government, Forest Service (2001). *National Forest Systems Road Management Strategy*. Washington, DC, Mimeo, January.

U.S. Government, Forest Service (2010). *Sustainable Operations*, www.fs.fed.us (accessed January/February 2015).

U.S. Government, USAID (Agency for International Development) (2002). *Social Soundness Analysis*. Washington, DC, Mimeo.

U.S. Government, USAID (Agency for International Development) (2010a). *President Obama's Development Policy and the Global Climate Change Initiative*, www.usaid.gov/climate/us-gcci (accessed February 10, 2015).

U.S. Government, USAID (Agency for International Development) (2010b). *What We Do*, www.usaid.gov (accessed January/February 2015).

Vondal, P. J. (1988). "Social and institutional analysis in agriculture and natural resources management project assistance: Suggestions for improvement from Africa Bureau experience," USAID, Bureau of Africa: Social/Institutional Analysis Working Paper No. 2, Office of Development Planning, March.

WCED (World Commission on Environment and Development) (1987). *Our Common Future*, The Brundtland Report. World Commission on Environment and Development (WCED) and Oxford University Press, New York.

White, M. A. (2013). "Commentary and sustainability: I know when I see it," *Ecological Economics*, Vol. 86, February, pp213–217.

World Bank (1995). "Social assessment structured learning preliminary findings," *Social Development Notes*, No. 14 (September), pp1–4.

World Bank (2003). *Social Analysis Sourcebook*, www.worldbank.org/socialanalysis (accessed January/February 2015).

WRI (World Resources Institute) (2003). *World Resources, 2002–2004: Decisions for the Earth*, www.wri.org/sites/default/files/pdf/wr2002_fullreport.pdf (accessed February 14, 2015).

5 Ecology of business sustainability

The business management approach to sustainability has been largely shaped by the sustainability programs and policies of international development organizations, federal, state and local governmental regulatory organizations, consumer advocacy groups, as well as organized bodies and other environmental private organizations who have lobbied for legislation and government oversight of business activities. In the United States, there are several federal governmental agencies, under the Departments of Agriculture and Commerce, and in particular the Environmental Protection Agency (EPA), who have regulatory control over business activities to enforce natural and resource conservation policies to support sustainability programs. In particular, the EPA has enforced environmental regulations and legislations that require business organizations to meet governmental standards of pollution control and to institute programs that prohibit the exploitation and use of natural resources (EPA, 2010). In addition, as discussed in Chapter 4, the international development policies of bilateral and multilateral development organizations have influenced the directions and approaches of business organizations' sustainability programs.

In most parts, business development efforts have focused on environmental preservation and resource conservation issues. Sustainability planning has evolved as an ecological resources endowment approach to provide organizations with ecosystem advantages or opportunities to manage their business development programs consistent with environmental protection and resource conservation management policies. Ecologically, environmental issues have shaped market (new and emerging) strategies among corporations to promote long-term sustainability visions and missions for many business organizations. It can be argued that corporations that have linked sustainability with corporate strategy have embraced the ecological anthropological view of sustainability. This implies that there exists joint ownership or claims to corporate resources by all stakeholders, including not only shareholders, but also the community at large.

Measuring and reporting sustainability initiatives: an overview of external reporting guidelines

Many corporations voluntarily include sustainability information as part of their external financial reports providing information on social and environmental accomplishments. They also disclose sustainability data in annual reports and company publications, and publicize them in the mass media and newspaper publications. In the last few decades, the issuance of sustainability reports has become a mainstay in business practices. The Brundtland Commission created the overall concept of sustainable development in 1987 (WCED, 1987; see also Dilling, 2009: 19). Following the Brundtland Report, international organizations such as the Global Reporting Initiative (GRI) have established sustainability reporting guidelines on how to document and prepare a company's economic, environmental and social performance. Corporate social responsibility (CSR) is part of sustainability reporting which is prepared to document "the continuing commitment by business to behave ethically and contribute to economic development while improving the quality of life of the workforce and their families as well as of the local community and society at large" (Moir, 2001: 18). Many corporations have prepared corporate social reports to communicate their social and environmental programs to their stakeholders.

Moreover, the Dow Jones Sustainability Index (DJSI) and the Morgan Stanley Capital International Index (MSCI) address sustainability in social and environmental programs in their choice of corporations for inclusion in their list of sustainable companies' investment portfolios. Other guidelines in the United States are under review by the Financial Accounting Standards Board (FASB) as part of the development of, for example, Generally Accepted Accounting Principles (GAAP) on sustainability reporting. At present, the Sarbanes-Oxley Act (SOX) of 2002 does provide a general framework and approach for the sustainability of business reports. All of these initiatives have been influenced and shaped by the Brundtland Report (WCED, 1987).

The Brundtland Report: the foundation for sustainability and CSR reporting

During the late 1980s, the World Commission on Environment and Development (WCED) was formed to report on the accelerating deterioration of the human environment and natural resources, and the consequences of that deterioration for economic and social development. After three years of work, the commission produced a report entitled *Our Common Future*, referred to as the Brundtland Report. The report defined "sustainability" as "the ability of the present generation to meet its needs without compromising the ability of future generations to meet their own needs" (WCED, 1987: 8). The Brundtland Report for the first time framed the importance of sustainable development for the future well-being of society and natural resources management. The report tied the United States government's United States Agency for International Development (USAID) report on Social Soundness Analysis (SSA) and the World Bank's Social Impact Assessment (SIA) guidelines of sustainability into the future well-being of society and natural resources management (Sisaye, 2012b).

The Brundtland Report (WCED, 1987) recognized that humans' reliance on the environment to meet their needs and the well-being of society depends on a balance between ecology and economic growth. It suggested that human activities and existence depended on the balance between exploitation of resources and environmental protection and conservation, and that environmental problems are not local and regional, but national and international issues. The report emphasized increased global trade and industry growth models that focus on merging economic and environmental issues in decision-making, human involvement and participation in economic development, with an emphasis on equity and social justice.

Sustainable development was promoted as having a broader transformational view of society with a commitment to social equity goals (Mog, 2004). The political and philosophical approaches of sustainability are based on humanitarian principles where access to resources is fundamentally necessary for the survival, livelihood and well-being of society (Hopwood et al., 2005: 39–46). These concepts formed the underlying economic concepts of productivity and growth in the advancement of social and environmental welfare.

The publication of the Brundtland Report (WCED, 1987) brought sustainability and sustainable development to the attention of the international community, particularly the international development organizations, such as USAID, the World Bank, the United Nations Development Programme (UNDP), the World Health Organization (WHO), the Food and Agriculture Organization (FAO) and the Organisation for Economic Co-operation and Development (OECD). The report challenged the international organizations/communities to envision a future in which the threats of environmental destruction are minimized and the people of the world benefit from economic stability and social equity for present and future generations.

Following the Brundtland Report, both USAID and the World Bank (WB) have used SSA and SIA, respectively, to study the feasibility of economic development programs which they funded or supported in these countries (Sisaye et al., 2004; USAID, 2002, 2010; Vondal, 1988; World Bank Group, 2003). If the projects proposed are not supported by these analyses, the strategy is to revise and/or modify the project so that it can become sustainable or, otherwise, to abandon it in favor of other proposed project sites. Their approaches have influenced corporations by stressing the importance of sustainability and continued economic growth in business ventures.

The Brundtland Commission favored a "macro" or national/international approach–solution to the world economic, social and environmental challenges of the twenty-first century, which gave rise to sustainable development. While the concept of sustainability had been around for some time, the publication of the report gave prominence to sustainability, environmental management and conservation. International organizations captured the essence of the report and diffused them in their development projects in the least developed countries (LDCs).

The Brundtland Report brought the importance of supporting corporate social reporting (CSR) and sustainability by multinational corporations (MNCs) that operate globally, particularly those businesses whose products and services have a direct bearing and impact upon natural and environmental resources. Business organizations were challenged to envision a future in which the threats of environmental destruction are minimized and the people of the world benefit from economic stability and social equity for present and future generations (Sisaye, 2012b).

The Brundtland Report (WCED, 1987) publicized the importance of sustainability in environmental management and conservation. The general guidelines and standards that corporations can adopt as a framework for sustainability reports was outlined by the United Nations Global Compact (UNGC), the International Organization for Standardization (ISO) and the Global Reporting Initiative (GRI).

International guidelines

The UN Global Compact

The UNGC is a strategic policy initiative for businesses that are committed to the importance of aligning their operations and strategies with the four sustainability objectives. The policies cover a wide range of areas including the Universal Declaration of Human Rights; the International Labour Organization's Declaration of Fundamental Principles and Rights at Work; the Rio de Janeiro Declaration on Environment and Development; and the United Nations Convention against Corruption. In other words, the UNGC formulated guidelines that encouraged or "ask[ed] companies to embrace, support and enact, within their sphere of influence, a set of core values in the areas of human rights, labour standards, the environment and anti-corruption" as part of the UN Global Compact's ten universally accepted principles (UNGC, 2009). "By doing so, businesses, as primary agents driving globalization, can help ensure that markets, commerce, technology, and finance advance in ways that benefit economies and societies everywhere" (UNGC, 2009).

The UNGC has clearly stated that the objectives of the international community and the business world are being aligned around the common goals of building markets, combating corruption, safeguarding the environment and ensuring social inclusion. Over time, these concerns have contributed to increased partnerships and open communication among businesses, government, civil society, labor and the United Nations. Such an understanding among all parties concerned has increased the membership of the UNGC.

> With over 12,000 corporate participants and other stakeholders from over 145 countries, it is the largest voluntary corporate responsibility initiative in the world. Endorsed by chief executive officers, the Global Compact is a practical framework for the development, implementation, and disclosure of sustainability policies and practices, offering participants a wide spectrum of work streams, management tools and resources – all designed to help advance sustainable business models and markets. The UN Global Compact works toward the vision of a sustainable and inclusive global economy which delivers lasting benefits to people, communities, and markets.
>
> (UNGC, 2009)

The UNGC is a public–private initiative that serves as a

> policy framework for the development, implementation, and disclosure of sustainability principles and practices and offering participants a wide spectrum of specialized work streams, management tools and resources, and topical programs and projects – all designed to help advance sustainable business models and markets in order to contribute to the initiative's overarching mission of helping to build a more sustainable and inclusive global economy.
>
> (UNGC, 2009)

Though the initiative is voluntary, it has stressed the importance of corporate accountability and its recognizable benefits to all participants and stakeholders.

The UNGC has outlined the benefits of engagement among its participants as follows:

- adopting an established and globally recognized policy framework for the development, implementation and disclosure of environmental, social and governance policies and practices;
- sharing best and emerging practices to advance practical solutions and strategies to common challenges;
- advancing sustainability solutions in partnership with a range of stakeholders, including UN agencies, governments, civil society, labor, and other non-business interests;
- linking business units and subsidiaries across the value chain with the Global Compact's local networks around the world – many of these in developing and emerging markets;
- accessing the United Nations' extensive knowledge of and experience with sustainability and development issues;
- utilizing UN Global Compact management tools and resources, and the opportunity to engage in specialized work streams in the environmental, social and governance realms.

(UNGC, 2009)

The International Organization for Standardization

The European Union (EU), with its expanding membership, needed to unite its membership corporate standards, as well as the world business organization standards, in a single quality standard to facilitate international commerce and trade. In 1987, the EU devised a set of standards called the International Organization for Standardization. The ISO 9000 outlined a set of procedures, guidelines and standards for world companies to adhere to when conducting business with members of the EU countries. The ISO 9000 incorporated a set of standards governing documentation, work instructions and record keeping that can lead to an ISO certification by qualified external examiners. Once certified, companies are listed in a directory for potential memberships in European and worldwide business organizations. ISO 9000 became one of the first quality standard guidelines recognized around the world. As of 2007, there were over 600,000 certifications awarded to companies in 158 countries around the world (Heizer and Render, 2008).

With the widespread use of ISO 9000 certification throughout the world, there was increasing concern about the world's depletion of natural resources and the environmental risks associated with the globalization of businesses. The International Organization for Standardization responded to this need with the creation of ISO 14000 – environmental management system documentation. It required participating companies to keep track of raw materials usage and the generation, treatment and disposal of their hazardous wastes. Though it did not specify what companies were allowed to emit, it required companies to prepare ongoing improvement plans in their environmental performance (Krajewski and Ritzman, 2005).

According to King (2007), ISO 14001 is used worldwide by large and small organizations in all sectors of the economy. Since its inception, it has become the most well-known and widely implemented set of environmental standards. Though certification is not a requirement, many organizations around the world attained certification because they perceived added value in an independent certification of conformance. By 2005, there were more than 111,000 ISO 14001 certificates in 138 countries. King stated that some of the reasons why firms pursue ISO 14001 certification ranged from a corporate mandate, to regulatory considerations, to environmental benefits. He noted that some of the external benefits realized included the fulfillment of customer requirements, an improved relationship with governmental agencies and stakeholders, positive publicity, competitive advantage, and possibly reduced insurance premiums.

Through the Global Compact's Communication on Progress (COP) policy that promoted transparency and accountability, participating companies were encouraged to provide annual postings. They were required to adhere to policies of transparency and full disclosure; and a failure to abide by these policies was sanctioned by a change of status from participating membership and possibly "delisting" them by excluding their names from the directory. The Global Compact guidelines and policies assisted the private sector in managing and minimizing the potential risks associated with their conduct of business. It encouraged environmental and social governance, and advocated embedding markets and societies with universal humanitarian and societal principles for the benefits of all stakeholders and the community at large.

The Global Reporting Initiative

The GRI was launched in 1997 to develop guidelines for the social and environmental indicators of corporate performance. It followed the guidelines of reporting established in the United States by the Financial Accounting Standards Board (FASB). It developed a standardized voluntary approach to reporting on corporate financial, environmental and social performance to increase the interest and demand for sustainability data and information.

In 2000, the United Nations Environment Programme (UNEP), in cooperation with the Coalition for Environmentally Responsible Economies (CERES) and the TELUS Institute, provided guidance and support for the creation of the GRI. The founders wanted to have general guidelines to compare corporate sustainability performance across industries (Reid, 2013). The goal of the GRI is to provide the international community with a common framework for the reporting of sustainability efforts and initiatives. It is the world leader and largest producer of standards/guidelines for reporting ecological "footprints" in sustainability (UNGC, 2009). The GRI became "a leading organization in the sustainability field. GRI promote[d] the use of sustainability reporting as a way for organizations to become more sustainable and contribute to sustainable development." The GRI policies are integrated with other international organization principles for sustainable development.

> The GRI Guidelines are often used in combination with other international initiatives, frameworks and guidance. GRI has global strategic partnerships with the Organisation for Economic Co-operation and Development (OECD), the United Nations Environment Programme (UNEP) and the United Nations Global Compact (UNGC). Its framework enjoys synergies with the guidance of the International Finance Corporation, the International Organization for Standardization's ISO 26000, the United Nations Conference on Trade and Development, and the Earth Charter Initiative.
>
> (GRI, 2014)

GRI Sustainability Reporting Guidelines was first introduced in 2000 with subsequent amendments in 2002 and 2006. Many European corporations and member U.S. companies follow the GRI when preparing their CSR reports (Jones III and Jonas, 2011). The GRI sustainability guidelines enable corporate organizational sustainability performance to be reported to external and internal stakeholders.

The GRI outlines three forms (i.e., *GRI-G3*) of application disclosure information, which are classified as Organizational Profile, Management Approach and Performance Related Indicators (GRI, 2008, 2010). The *GRI-G3 Organization*

Profile Disclosures include strategic elements (priorities, targets, achievements, failures, challenges, risks and opportunities); profile elements (brands, products, services, operating locations, legal form of ownership, employment levels and assets); and governance structure (officers and independent/non-executive members and linkage to their compensation and performance, guidance processes with regard to the qualifications and expertise of members, codes of conduct, relevant risks, opportunities and adherence/compliance to international standards, codes and principles) (GRI, 2011).

The key areas in the *GRI-G3* guidelines reported under the social category include labor, human rights, society and product responsibility. The main areas of disclosure in the labor category include overall employment, diversity and equal opportunity, occupational health and safety, and labor–management relations among other aspects influencing labor relations (GRI, 2011: 32). Human rights describes an organization's policies and practices on child labor, non-discrimination and indigenous rights (GRI, 2011: 33). The society category provides information on local communities, corruption and compliance (GRI, 2011: 34). Product responsibility represents any information regarding customer health and safety, product labeling and compliance (GRI, 2011: 36). The performance of any type of organization can be measured against these sets of guidelines to determine if specific goals are being met. The GRI includes more specified measures within all the defined categories in order to enhance the information provided by an organization with regards to its socially responsible practices.

The *GRI-G3 Management Approach Disclosures* outline a brief overview of an organizational management approach to aspects defined under each category of performance indicator (GRI, 2009, 2010; see also Etzioni and Ferraro, 2007; Ivan, 2009). The *GRI-G3* performance disclosure indicators are organized into three groups: economic/financial (revenues, operating costs, employee compensation, donations and community investments); environmental (impact upon living/non-living natural systems, emissions, effluents, waste, biodiversity and environmental compliance); and social disclosure (impact upon human rights, labor practices, benefits, training, education, health, safety, diversity, equal opportunity and procurement practices with regard to anti-corruption and anti-trust practices). Of the three types of disclosure that the GRI considers, the most relevant ones for inclusion/discussion in financial and sustainability accounting address economic/financial and environmental disclosures.

The G3 *Sustainability Reporting Guidelines* (SRG) of the GRI stated that new knowledge and innovations in technology, management and public policy are challenging organizations to make new choices in the way in which their operations, products, services and activities affect the Earth, people and economies. It outlined the need for transparency about the economic, environmental and social impacts that are of interest to a diverse range of stakeholders. To ensure that GRI standards provide a consistent general framework to member corporations, the GRI has relied on the collaboration of a large network of experts from all stakeholder groups. These experts provide trusted and credible reporting framework guidelines that have consistent language and metrics, which can be used by organizations of any size, sector or location to prepare a trusted and credible framework for sustainable reporting (GRI, 2011). Hence, the SRG G3 version of the GRI introduced three levels of application declaration ranging from C for beginners to A for advanced reports by corporations who have extensive experience with sustainability reporting. The reporting criteria at each level reflect a measure of the extent of application or coverage of the GRI's SRG. Furthermore, in the self-declaration level, any organization can self-declare a "plus" (+) next to their level, if they have used external assurance, and/or have the external assurance provider (the GRI or other) offer an independent opinion on their self-declaration of meeting sustainability goals (Christofi et al., 2012).

In 2013, the GRI issued G4 *Sustainability Reporting Guidelines*. The GRI stated that:

> The GRI Sustainability Reporting Guidelines are periodically reviewed to provide the best and most up-to-date guidance for effective sustainability reporting. The aim of G4, the fourth such update, is simple: to help reporters prepare sustainability reports that matter, contain valuable information about the organization's most critical sustainability-related issues, and make such sustainability reporting standard practice.
>
> (GRI, 2013a: 3)

The GRI G4 *Sustainability Reporting Guidelines* offer general reporting principles, standard disclosures and an implementation manual for the preparation of sustainability reports by organizations, regardless of their size, sector or location. The guidelines also offer an international reference for all those interested in the disclosure of the governance approach and of the environmental, social and economic performance and impacts of organizations. The guidelines are useful in the preparation of any type of document which requires such disclosure.

To ensure acceptance and adoption, the guidelines are developed through a global multi-stakeholder process involving representatives from business, labor, civil society and financial markets, as well as auditors and experts in various fields; and in close dialogue with regulators and governmental agencies in several countries. They are developed in alignment with internationally recognized reporting-related documents which are referenced throughout the guidelines. The GRI guidelines are developed in consultation with member organizations who are represented by a consortium of public accounting organizations, investment firms and internationally known MNCs (GRI, 2013a).

Reid (2013) summarized the GRI framework as having six main categories for the corporate disclosure of sustainable performance. The "sustainability profiles" included "environmental, human rights, labor practices, society, product responsibility and economic performance – with subcategories to ensure comprehensive reporting" (p29). Similarly, Asif et al. (2013) noted: "The GRI provides an extensive list of 79 sustainability indicators organized along the social, economic and environmental dimensions" (p323).

In addition, the GRI outlines sector-specific indicators that are unique to the industry. While the GRI provides guidelines, there are no specific structured approaches to present the information uniformly. The disclosure guidelines are based on a number of factors related to obtaining legitimacy, transparency, image-building and marketing-related factors. The GRI is based on the notion that "voluntary information dissemination also serves the interests of progressive companies that publicly claim to be socially responsible, transparent and accountable" (Nikolaeva and Bicho, 2011: 138; see also Christofi et al., 2012). It provides public access to information dissemination to the extent to which firms voluntarily comply with the regulatory government environmental and social legislations. The assumption is that competitors will follow and adopt the voluntary approach to comply and report their progress to the public. This approach follows the imitation-followers of the diffusion framework, where sustainability trendsetters are models for others who lag behind to follow the new reporting formats (Lee and Pati, 2012). The trendsetter corporations become a model for the industry, where public interest and marketing efforts shape the voluntary nature of CSR reporting.

The GRI has not only become the underlying framework for CSR strategy and reporting (Wilburn and Wilburn, 2013), it has also evolved into an international and global framework of reference for CSR. Carnevale et al. (2012) denoted the GRI's global framework of reference as facilitating the adoption and diffusion of CSR. In their study of CSR reporting among European banks, they noted that the GRI has provided specific guidelines and frameworks to publish CSR reports that are used by member corporations including European banks. These banks have adopted these "social reporting principles guidelines" (p164). Nikolaeva and Bicho's (2011) findings have corroborated Carnevale et al.'s (2012) findings of the adoption diffusion research that the adoption practices of the GRI among corporations have been shaped by their competitors' adoption of GRI principles (p150). However, they questioned whether universal diffusion of the GRI in the European countries has played a role in their investment decisions, or whether the markets have valued the economic significance of these reports. Nevertheless, banks as financial credit organizations have the leverage to shape and influence the importance of CSR reporting. Their CSR reporting has facilitated the diffusion of GRI practices among the European country-based corporations.

Nikolaeva and Bicho (2011) gave examples of firms in the developing/emerging countries of Brazil and China who are among the early adopters of the GRI to have competitive advantage over their counterparts in the developed countries. Thus the GRI enabled these firms from developing countries to be more transparent, thereby increasing their acceptance and legitimacy as "global stakeholders" in the developed countries (p143). These corporations have used the GRI as a public relations tool to publicize their activities. Their strategy of using the GRI as a public relations medium enabled them to be more responsive to environmental and social issues and stakeholders' interests. They used the GRI as advertising mechanisms to publicize their CSR activities within the GRI framework. Nikolaeva and Bicho suggested that firms with a public relations perspective and who are committed to environmental issues are more likely to adopt the GRI and to manage media and news coverage of their corporate governance by providing CSR disclosures voluntarily to promote their accomplishments (p145). They reported that these corporations effectively used CSR for reputation management, and to enhance and protect their brand names.

As Sisaye and Birnberg (2010b, 2012) noted, the increased rate of the adoption–diffusion of the GRI as corporations responded to competitive pressures as well as corporate support to the GRI can be attributed to the leader–follower (imitators) diffusion approach. This was noticeable among the bigger public corporations that do not want to be left behind, and exhibited a higher adoption of the GRI framework to provide increased CSR disclosure to their stakeholders. Since its inception in 1997, the GRI has received wide acceptance and legitimacy. According to Nikolaeva and Bicho (2011), marketing has played an important role in facilitating the adoption and dissemination of the GRI; managing corporate brand, image, citizenship and reputation; and the legitimacy and institutionalization of CSR for the disclosure of sustainability data and information.

In the marketing literature, the adoption of the GRI has been considered as a "reputation management tool" that enhances the role, visibility and the status of the adopter organization in the international business community (Nikolaeva and Bicho, 2011: 136). That is, the adoption of the GRI has been shaped by competitive institutional and media pressures where the management of public media image and reputation has become a significant determining factor for GRI acceptance and marketing. Nikolaeva and Bicho (2011) suggested that corporations that seek legitimacy and reputation have intensified the need for adopting the GRI as a communication channel to respond to institutional pressures and stakeholders. The adoption of the GRI brought legitimacy and enhanced leadership and organizational reputation and identity for those organizations who responded to current trends in the industry. This ensured that the adoption of the GRI was in accordance to what is considered an appropriate behavior or norm based on industry accounting standards and compliance belonging to the GRI group and community of firms.

As more organizations use the GRI, Nikolaeva and Bicho (2011) noted that there is institutional pressure to adopt the GRI for competitive purposes and the desire to seek legitimacy and become reputable (pp136–140). They emphasized the role of the media in publicizing good corporate practices, and at the same time as a watch dog by exposing unsustainable corporate practices. The media has thus helped to speed up the adoption of the GRI as the GRI received media coverage, publicity and exposure. This is consistent with Sisaye and Birnberg (2010a), who documented the important roles that champions and leaders (early adopters) play as facilitators and trendsetters in the adoption–diffusion innovation processes in organizations.

According to Nikolaeva and Bicho (2011), those corporations who adopted the GRI have used the GRI as a marketing tool to manage the reputation of the company and protect their brand names, logos and identities. They used the GRI to engage in dialogue with stakeholders and manage their relationships and to acquire and maintain their identity and the uniqueness of their goods and services. Moreover, they framed the GRI to gauge as benchmarking for their respective ranking and attain a competitive advantage over others. However, the use and practice of GRI reporting has been influenced by firm and industry characteristics, as well as geographical location (country affiliation).

The GRI guidelines require member organizations that have used the GRI's *Sustainability Reporting Guidelines* (SRG) as the basis for their report to notify the GRI upon the release of the report and provide them with a copy; register their report on the GRI's online database of reports; or request that the GRI checks their self-declared application levels. Although such reporting is voluntary, those organizations that follow these guidelines can benefit from the GRI guidelines to achieve continuous performance improvement over time and communicate their organizational-process performance indicators to their stakeholders.

According to Sobhani et al. (2012), corporations doing business in LDCs, particularly banks, have found the importance of sustainability performance a key policy guideline in their loans and financial services to almost all sectors of the economy (p76). Moreover, Wilburn and Wilburn (2013) argued that the GRI guidelines can be used as reporting devices by corporations to report CSR activities to meet the demands of various constituencies that the corporation depends upon. Sustainability and CSR can provide alliances to these stakeholders in terms of wealth creation, shared values and philanthropic activities that are transparent to benefit both the business and society/community at large. However, Wilburn and Wilburn noted that social disclosure items that are sensitive in the area of human rights and environmental degradations that have adverse impacts upon society are less likely to be reported because of the negative reports and scrutiny over these activities from the press, interest groups and policy-makers. In contrast, Burritt and Schaltegger (2010) viewed the GRI guidelines as an "outside–in approach" to "sustainability accounting and reporting" where the "product is provided by an external institution (the GRI)" (p840). While the GRI guidelines are used to compare sustainability performance, the influence of the GRI on managers of organizations is marginal since CSR disclosure is voluntary and indicators of performance that are selected for reporting are under the discretion of managers.

In spite of these shortcomings, many corporations have adopted the GRI guidelines to prepare environmental reports to the public on the efficient utilization of resources and their policies to reduce emissions and eliminate waste. Creel (2010) provided examples of companies – for example, Apple, Dell, Office Depot and Target, among others – who have complied with these guidelines. Reid (2013) cited companies such as CVS Caremark, who not only use the GRI guidelines to prepare reports, but also use them to provide sustainability information in a separate section in the annual report. There is still a debate about whether or not investors give credence to corporate social responsibility performance in their investment decisions. Some (e.g., Reverte, 2012) have suggested that certification by International Organization for Standardization (ISO) environmental management reporting might also indicate better or improved financial performance.

There has been an increase in the adoption of the GRI guidelines over the years. The 2008 GRI Reporting List included 905 reporting organizations that publish a

GRI report by region, country, sector and adherence level. Most of these organizations represent countries from Western Europe, Australia and the United States (Christofi et al., 2012). Most of these company initiatives and achievements towards sustainability and sustainability reporting are influenced by their local and global regulatory organizations. In 2013, the statistics reveal 6,679 organizations, 20,528 sustainability reports and 16,369 GRI Index reports (GRI, 2013b). Wilburn and Wilburn (2013: 65) claimed that with the increased acceptance of the GRI as an international-based network organization, the number of sustainability experts have reached over 30,000.

Other guidelines

The Dow Jones Sustainability Index

While the GRI is based in Europe, in the United States a comparable institution has advanced the importance of sustainability in its investment portfolio. The Dow Jones Sustainability Index (DJSI) was launched in 1999 by the Sustainable Asset Management (SAM) Group of Zurich and the Dow Jones Indexes of New York. SAM was founded to track the financial performance of the leading sustainability-driven companies worldwide (DJSI, 2010; SAM, 2010). The DJSI screened and listed the leading worldwide companies in terms of environmental, social and economic performance (Reverte, 2012). The objective of the DJSI is to appeal to socially and environmentally conscious investors (Jones III and Jonas, 2011).

The main focus of DJS Indexes is to create performance indicators from investable/traded companies' reports on their financial performance. The DJSI covers the top 10 percent of the biggest 2,500 companies in the Dow Jones Global Index that pursue economic, social and environmental reporting (DJSI, 2009). The selection process is based on the following criteria: tax strategy, social and environmental reporting, human capital development and performance scoring. The assurance of the assessment process is conducted by Deloitte (DJSI, 2014). The DJSI defines corporate sustainability as "a business approach that creates long-term shareholder value by embracing opportunities and managing risks deriving from economic, environmental and social developments" (DJSI, 2009: 2). According to the DJSI, leading sustainability corporations display high levels of management competence in addressing global and industry challenges dealing with economic, environmental and social opportunities and risks that can be quantified and screened for investing purposes.

Similar to the GRI, the DJSI (2009, 2010) used three performance indicators – economic, environmental and social – with associated weights depending on the industry-specific sector to which the corporation belonged. The economic dimensions included codes of business conduct, compliance, corruption and bribery; corporate governance; risk and crisis management; and specific industry criteria. The environmental performance indicators addressed eco-efficiency, environmental reporting and specific industry criteria. The social performance indicators are outlined in corporate citizenship/philanthropy, labor practice indicators, human capital development, social reporting, talent attraction and retention, and specific industry criteria.

The gathering of information for the DJSI is obtained from diverse sources including annual reports, companies' reports, CEO mission statements, press releases, special reports, questionnaires and interviews with managers. The target selection for each eligible DJSI sector is 10 percent of the companies in the industry (Christofi et al., 2007). Although the information obtained is not uniform and comparable across organizations, there is a consensus that the GRI has provided a general standardized framework for sustainability reporting that can assist in comparing performance among organizations in comparable industries, which the DJSI followed in their selection of corporations for inclusion in their list of sustainable leader business organizations.

The DJSI member corporations prepare corporate social reports to highlight their activities to the public. However, there are no assurance reporting standards that are followed. The reports are not uniform and consistent, and may not fully disclose corporate social performance. Nikolaeva and Bicho (2011) pointed out that DJSI members are more likely to use GRI reporting guidelines for disclosure, although they are not required to use that format. Even in the absence of CSR guidelines, the adoption rate of the GRI among the DJSI members has increased, particularly among the most visible corporations with recognizable brand names.

On the other hand, among European organizations, Lopez et al. (2007) found that they follow the GRI guidelines to prepare their sustainability reports to inform stakeholders regarding their practices. The GRI, CSR and DJSI indicators focus on social, environmental and economic performances. "The DJSI introduces a number of indicators that allow us to see what the firm is doing, such as the evaluation of intangible assets, development of human capital, organizational issues, strategic plans, corporate governance and investor relations" (p289). Moreover, Clark and Allen (2012) suggested that firms that have sustainability leadership, where they used a firm listed in the DJSI as a proxy for sustainability leadership, have better financial performances (see also Christofi et al., 2007, 2012). These firms were able to increase shareholders' value based on accounting indicators of their quality earnings and financial performance.

Both the GRI and DJSI collect information on the sustainability performance of companies. However, there are differences in their report disclosure and membership requirements. GRI members are primarily Western European-based corporations, while the members of the DJSI are from both North America and Western Europe. The GRI G3 reports are required by all member organizations, while the DJSI reports are voluntarily disclosed (Christofi et al., 2007).

An overview of GRI and DJSI reports suggests that sustainability reporting provides indicators of performance related to economic, environmental and social goals. Most corporations' external financial accounting reports provide coverage of sustainability activities. There is an increasing trend for sustainability reporting. In 2013 the number reached 20,528 sustainability reports (GRI, 2013b). This may be attributable to the desire of investors, both institutional and individual, to value sustainability as a long-term rather than a short-term measure of economic, social and environmental performance and profitability. While these guidelines enable shareholders and investors to compare business performance across industries, Reid (2013) suggested the goal for the GRI should be for an integrated reporting framework that includes both financial and sustainability (environmental and social) variables in a single report, comparable to the information disclosed in external annual reports. While the DJSI groups were created to track the performance of sustainability-driven companies, there have been other similar indexes that track the performance of leading local and global organizations.

The Sustainability Asset Management group-index research

The SAM Group (SAM, 2010) has developed a SAM Questionnaire specific to each of the DJSI sectors and distributed these to the CEOs and public relations officers of companies who invest in DJSI listed stocks. SAM compiles company documentation from reports on sustainability, the environment, health and safety, as well as social reports, annual financial reports and related special reports (e.g., by gathering information on intellectual capital management, corporate governance, research and development (R&D), as well as employee relations). It also refers to all other sources of company information including internal documentation, brochures and websites.

In addition, it refers to media and stakeholder reports, including other publicly available information (SAM, 2010), and reviews stocks and industry-sector analysts, media and press releases, articles and stakeholder comments available on the internet and from other public sources.

Moreover, they use personal contact with companies to gather information. Each analyst personally contacts individual companies to clarify questions and/or inconsistencies arising from the analysis of questionnaires and information obtained from internal company documents.

The Morgan Stanley Capital International Index

The Morgan Stanley Capital International Index (MSCI) publishes an international and U.S. equity, fixed income and hedge fund index for institutional investors. It has provided global equity indices for over 30 years and has become the most widely used international equity benchmark by institutional investors (Morgan Stanley, 2010). In general, the MSCI is intended to fulfill the investment needs of a wide variety of global institutional market and mutual fund firm participants. Approximately 2,000 organizations worldwide currently use MSCI benchmarks to invest in these funds. When compared to the performance of the DJSI, MSCI listed company performances yielded comparable results, although it was often used as a common benchmark for the "world" or "global" stock market (Sisaye, 2012b). In 2013, Morgan Stanley launched the "Institute for Sustainable Investing to mobilize private sector capital to address major economic, social and environmental challenges" (Morgan Stanley, 2013: 7). The institute sets "a five year goal of $10 billion in total clients' assets invested through the Investing with Impact Platform, which enables clients to choose investments that seek to deliver market-rate returns and positive environmental or social impact" (p7).

The financial accounting triple bottom line (TBL) reporting format follows the DJSI and GRI in three main sectors/groups: economic, environmental and social performance data regarding business organizations (DJSI, 2009; GRI, 2008, 2009). TBL reports have three main parts: economic, social and environmental performance reports. They report both profitability and shareholder value creation as well as social, human and environmental management. The environmental and social indicators of sustainable reporting have become sources of accountability information for indicating levels of commitment to sustainability (Adams, 2010; Aras and Crowther, 2008; Hubbard, 2008; Lamberton, 2005a, 2005b; Pava, 2007). The next section discusses the development of TBL reports within the context of the ecology of the sustainability of businesses.

The evolution of triple bottom line reports: an introduction

In accounting, the disclosure of economic, social and environmental reports is broadly classified as TBL reports that are included in external annual accounting reports. In general, the TBL approach to financial accounting reporting serves as mechanisms to "guide management in balancing economic growth against social and environmental needs" (Saravanamuthu, 2004: 296). It is widely accepted that when accounting reports contain data on the sustainability of social and environmental performance, these indicators can help to advance an organization's social responsibility goals as well as financial and economic management practices.

In accounting, sustainability has formed the basic core assumptions of triple bottom line reporting (Aras and Crowther, 2008; Etzioni and Ferraro, 2007). TBL has incorporated sustainability by incorporating the GRI's three guidelines – economic, environmental and social – to assess the impact of business performance among all sectors/groups of the economy, including profitability and shareholder value creation and associated factors related to social, human and environmental resources management (GRI, 2008, 2009, 2010). Accordingly, TBL reports economic, environmental and social data to indicate levels of sustainability commitment along these three performance measures. Although TBL reports are not mandatory, they are prepared to meet external reporting requirements related to sustainability performances.

The disclosure of TBL reports containing sustainability information on social and environmental issues is currently considered voluntary information. Nevertheless, the accounting profession has emphasized the importance of including standardized sustainability information in annual reports. It has become part of business practice to report social and environmental information when necessary at the discretion of the organization either in footnotes, appendices or supplements to the annual reports. In some instances, sustainability information is also included in the introduction (i.e., text portion) of the annual report as part of the overall report provided by the president or chief executive officer (CEO), included in a separate publication prepared for external constituencies, or posted as a sustainability report on the corporation's website.

Accordingly, business organizations have prepared and issued reports of environmental audits and performance indicators such as the consumption and management of water, energy, toxic materials and assets (see Füssel and Georg, 2000: 41–58). The amount of space they allocate to environmental issues in annual and/or other accounting reports is usually expected to indicate the level of commitment they have on environmental management systems. Corporate management and employees' commitment and participation in the design and implementation of environmental programs has institutionalized environmental concerns and issues on a continuous basis as part of management's continuous improvement programs. Environmental concerns are of interest and attract public attention and desires. It is, therefore, critical that top management recognizes the importance of ecological management programs by issuing TBL reports as mechanisms in resolving contending environmental issues among interest groups. The ecology of environmental management can thus become part of any organization's best management practices to approach sustainable development and business performance.

The Brundtland Report: a resource-based approach to CSR

The GRI and DJSI guidelines for CSR are based on the sustainable development guidelines contained in the Brundtland Report (WCED, 1987). The report highlighted the importance of sustainable development and business performance to manage natural and environmental resources. The report emphasized that national governments and international development organizations play important roles in advancing sustainable development. It embraced sustainability as a self-help mechanism that has to be implemented at the national, regional, local and community levels. Grassroots participation and the recognition and respect of a plurality of cultures, customs and religions are key indicators of success for sustainability. It can be inferred from the Brundtland Report (WCED, 1987) that sustainability is an ecological-systems approach for the preservation, sustenance use and exploitation of natural and environmental resources. At the same time, the report recognizes that both internal and external environmental contexts do influence business organizational objectives and strategies to manage sustainability.

Following the Brundtland Report and the endorsement of international bilateral and multilateral organizations in their sustainability policies, corporations have incorporated sustainable development objectives into their business strategies. According to the ecological framework, firms' commitment and adherence to sustainable development policies are influenced primarily due to the resource-based approach or institutional factors that influence firms' ability to gain acceptance and legitimacy. For example, Bansal (2005) argued that corporate sustainable development is based on balancing and integrating the three pillars of sustainable development: environmental integrity, social equity and economic prosperity (p199). The first pillar involves the management of environmental integrity through the environmental policies of pollution control, pollution prevention and product life-cycle management (p199). The second pillar, social equity, is based on corporate social responsibility concerns to meet the social, ethical and environmental concerns of all stakeholders. Corporations employ stakeholders' management strategies to address the social, economic and environmental issues of their immediate stakeholders, including shareholders, customers, employees and regulatory agencies, as well as local, national and international competitive business organizations (pp199–200). The third pillar, economic prosperity, is achieved by the creation of wealth for shareholders through the development of products that provide value to customers, using resources at a lower cost, the competitive pricing of products, and better pay to workers for improved quality of life and working conditions (p200).

Munck and Borim-de-Souza (2012) concurred with Bansal (2005) that sustainability is centered around "three pillars: economic, environmental and social" (p397). These three pillars have constituted and formed the basis for sustainability reporting outlined in the GRI and DJSI, as well as TBL reporting. Organizational competencies are centered on their endowment of resources to manage these three sustainability objectives. When sustainability is viewed within the context of the ecology of organizational resources, it assumes that resource endowments are key enablers of firms' capacities and competencies to manage and adapt to environmental changes and uncertainties. Organizational competencies to select and manage available resources are essential for the successful management of corporate sustainability performance.

According to Holton et al. (2010), corporate sustainability is also used to manage financial risks, reduce operating costs and make fundamental changes in organizational systems, structures and operating activities (p152). Sustainability can thus enhance competencies by promoting continuous improvement in organizational performance systems, and changing existing cultures and awareness to manage environmental uncertainties. Corporations that have sustainability policies develop fundamental changes in their organizational systems and structures to manage the risks associated with environmental uncertainties. Springett (2003) argued that business organizations need to develop benchmarking to compare their environmental performance with their competitors. The benchmark will have a yardstick to assess economic efficiency to evaluate environmental performance. Springett suggested that organizations with benchmarks have well-developed sustainable strategic plans with established environmental management systems that can meet ISO 14001 accreditation standards for environmental management systems (EMS) certification.

Corporate organizations that are sustainably driven have long-term strategic plans for improving their business performance, attract better employees, attain a positive public image, obtain favorable customer relations and have better compliance and reporting systems to inform the public about their products, services and sustainability performance. While these sustainability reports are voluntary, Hespenheide et al. (2010) indicated that, in Europe, the U.K. government requires business organizations to report "nonfinancial climate-related" performance (p54). Sustainability thus increases environmental business organizations' compliance to social and environmental objectives (Schaltegger and Csutora, 2012). Hespenheide et al. noted that customers and stakeholders, including the shareholders of environmental firms, seek sustainability reports related to "energy-emissions and access to natural resources" (p54). These emissions concern carbon emissions and how they are managed and allocated/exchanged to safeguard environmental assets.

Lee and Pati (2012) have noted that long-term success depends on a TBL approach when a company is devoted to sustainability by committing resources for such purposes. While implementation of sustainability is beneficial to a company, they suggested that sustainability concerns vary by industry, depending upon where they operated and their relationships or interactions with their environments (pp80–81).

In general, the business management and accounting literature suggest that sustainability and corporate social responsibility are associated with improved economic performance (Clark and Allen, 2012; Lee and Pati, 2012). Moreover, sustainability reduces costs associated with government regulation compliance and possible litigation costs to cover liability expenses for environmental degradation and remediation. Sustainability performance contributes to positive media coverage and public image. Corporations following sustainability practices that are endowed with sufficient resources achieve visibility with a positive public image when they deliver reputable products to customers, foster high employee morale and maintain positive stakeholder relations.

The resources-based view to sustainability reporting

A resources-based sustainable development business paradigm is based on the assumption that there are three interrelated ecological systems of development. They are social, environmental and economic. The ecology of sustainability recognizes that while economic growth is a precondition for development, it has to be managed in conjunction with environmental preservation and protection and social and community development. This implies that the production and marketing of goods and services are linked to the ecology of sustainability. In marketing and supply chain management, product development and product life cycles are examined within the context of ecological sustainability.

Environmental resources are scarce, and the resource-based view of the firm suggests that environmental factors do shape corporate strategies and policies addressing environmental concerns. Corporate environmentalism, according to Banerjee (2002), encompasses "the recognition and integration of environmental concerns into a firm's decision-making process" (p177). Managerial perceptions and understanding of their environmental surroundings affect their policies, particularly towards the environmental management of the biophysical environment. Accordingly, firms make strategic alliances with other business organizations, governmental agencies and environmental organizations/groups to better understand and develop collaborative efforts to address environmental issues. Banerjee suggested that corporations that have incorporated corporate environmentalism into their strategic plans and policies addressing pollution control, waste reduction and the efficient utilization of resources do have a competitive advantage in managing environmental resources and constraints in the production and marketing of goods and services.

For example, the American Institute of Certified Public Accountants (AICPA) has noted that going green provides an organization with a competitive advantage. These organizations are "becoming more eco-conscious and searching for environmentally-friendly products and services. By using green practices such as eliminating waste, increasing efficiencies and reducing carbon dioxide emissions, businesses can simultaneously satisfy the green-minded consumers of today" (AICPA, 2010a: 1). The report articulates how a business organization can establish competitive advantage with efficiency of production and promoting green resources to create "new demand for green products and services" that will in the long term create profitability (AICPA, 2010a: 2).

Hanss and Böhm (2012) examined the relationship between the marketing of sustainability products and consumption decisions. They examined five factors associated with the marketing of sustainability products. The first factor is related to environmental factors associated with the preservation of natural resources, recycling, improved production techniques and less energy use; the second, social indicators, is associated with better wages and quality of life; the third addresses economic factors related to access to economic growth prosperity; the fourth is temporal dimensions, which is related to the needs of current and future generations; and the fifth factor, developmental dimensions, addresses technological innovations that support local products, green labeling and changes in product lifestyles. They argued that sustainable products when consumed will "reduce the ecological and social problems associated with production and consumption" (p679). They found that three dimensions – the environmental dimension followed by social and developmental dimensions – were associated with consumers' decisions concerning sustainability consumption (p683). They noted that the temporal and economic dimensions played peripheral roles in consumers' purchasing decisions. They attributed the importance given to the environmental dimensions to the Brundtland Report (WCED, 1987), media coverage, climate change and global financial and market volatility.

In their study of the green marketing of products among European countries, Blengini and Shields (2010) pointed out that green or eco-labeling is part of business organizations' "environmental management system (EMS)" to "minimize their environmental foot print" (p478). They denoted the production of goods and services that are eco-labeled as indicators of sustainability performance. They suggested that proper supply chain management practices for eco-oriented products are essential to manage risks, develop information systems that can report environmental uncertainties, manage sustainable products, and create value to the organization. Accordingly, corporate reporting becomes transparent by sharing information on sustainability issues to all concerned parties. "Sustainable development indicators (SDIs)" include among others "a detailed reporting of financial, environmental and social performance information, in this case with respect to the manufacture of a product and the inputs necessary for its production" (p482). In the long term, sustainability reporting that contains SDI information provides better disclosure that benefits stakeholders and the society/community at large.

The ecology of sustainability in business organizations: recent developments

As discussed earlier, the business approach to sustainability has been largely shaped by the sustainability programs and policies of international bilateral and multilateral organizations as well as the U.S. federal governmental agencies that have regulatory control over business activities. The influence of government regulatory organizations, particularly the U.S. Environmental Protection Agency (EPA) (EPA, 2010), has been notable in business activities in the United States. Moreover, legislators and public accounting firms have shaped environmental regulations and legislations that required business organizations to meet governmental standards of pollution and institute programs that conserve the exploitation and use of natural resources.

The U.S. Environmental Protection Agency guidelines

The EPA has issued guidelines on the accounting and reporting of environmental liabilities that outlines their definitions and the categories of those liabilities. This has been followed by Generally Accepted Accounting Principles (GAAP): the statements on Accounting for Environmental Liabilities, Contingent Liabilities and Asset Retirement Obligations. This act required business organizations to recognize and report corporations' environmental liabilities associated with business innovations and growth, including accounting for loss contingencies and asset retirements. Moreover, the EPA has issued guidelines on the Carbon Disclosure Project USA (2009) Index, greenhouse gas reporting and registers (see Pew Center, 2011; SEC, 2010).

Following the EPA guidelines, environmental preservation and resource conservation has now become the main development effort of business organizations, particularly those organizations whose business is in oil, gas and other types of natural resource utilization, including coal and petroleum, as well as for manufacturing organizations in the automobile, steel and mineral extracting industries. As a result, there has emerged an overlap of concerns among many business organizations on issues of sustainable growth, ethics and corporate social responsibility and conservation issues.

Conservation of wildlife, particularly endangered species, has received the attention of both public and business policy-makers. The effort has intensified due to the growth of private lands where endangered species have been given care and protection. There is recognition of a need for a community-based conservation (CBC) approach in the management of endangered species on private lands. Preservation of private lands for conservation has become a sustainable development issue that has been the topic of public policy debates and private groups' interests. It has attracted publicity since the publication of the Brundtland Report in 1987.

Peterson et al. (2004) have discussed how the community-based conservation approach has been shaped by the Brundtland Report as nations considered the need for the preservation of endangered species. An example of this is the passage of the Endangered Species Act of 1973 (ESA) in the United States (p743). They reported that the CBC approach has encouraged participation among diverse interest groups, contributing to "higher compliance," "lower reinforcement costs" as well as "higher community satisfaction" (p744). They perceived the CBC approach of allowing experimentation and a selective approach to managing endangered species and environmental protection to be beneficial. They noted that while there was conflict between those who advocated preservation and others who advocated for individual rights associated with development (e.g., agriculture, housing, logging), as well as landlords who wanted to sell their land at fair market value (FMV), the CBC approach has allowed local government officials, planners, business groups, advocates of preservation and other interest groups to work together through consensus to select land for preservation, and enforcing government regulation to manage conservation.

Hilborn et al. (1995) used an ecological analogy to approach the sustainable exploitation of natural resources for fishery, wildlife and forestry management. They suggested that sustainable exploitation is an issue in fishery management in the conservation of salmon, marine fishes and the availability of fish stock or surplus for future use. It requires "a reproductive surplus, which is determined by the balance between births, deaths, and somatic growth." The availability of "reproductive surplus differs spatially and temporally as environmental conditions vary" (p45). They noted that the concern for the "sustainable use of natural resources" has been put into prominence by the Brundtland Report (WCED, 1987: 46). They implied that in order to successfully manage sustainable exploitation, advances in the science on sustainability harvesting and "implementation of better institutional arrangements for controlling exploiters and creating incentives for them to behave more wisely" is needed for private owners as well as those public institutions at the local state and national levels of forestry resources (p62).

The Peterson et al. (2004) study of endangered species and the Hilborn et al. (1995) findings of fishery, wildlife and forestry preservation and management are based on the assumption that sustainable development is an ecological approach for the management of conservation and preservation of natural and environmental resources. The concept encompasses "ecological health and social welfare" and "ecology and equity" in the exploitation and conservation of environmental resources (Clark, 1995: 226). However, the public attitude towards environmental conservation is influenced by perceived uncertainty of the future, current levels of consumption and economic growth where favorable economic growth increases the consumption and exploitation of environmental resources. Kama and Schubert (2004) implied that, when there is uncertainty, it leads to concerns for the conservation of natural resources. In developed societies, there is the realization that ecological resources cannot sustain the current level of consumption. There is a joint effort by both business and government policy-makers to align economic growth and the consumption of goods and services consistent with the sustainable exploitation of natural resources. In the United States, the EPA is the federal government agency empowered to enforce regulatory policies and legislations to ensure that business industrial development and growth are consistent with the nation's sustainable development policies with regard to the conservation and preservation of natural and environmental resources.

Similarly, Morrison-Saunders and Retief (2012) found that preservation-related sustainability policies have been incorporated into legislation by many countries after the publication of the Brundtland Report, which encouraged the development of environmental impact assessment (EIA) measures. The U.S. Department of Commerce uses a modified version of EIA in the management of fisheries and other policies related to wildlife. They suggested that

> the worldwide spread of EIA was helped along no doubt by Principle 17 of the *Rio Declaration on Environment and Development* at the 1992 Earth Summit, which provides that signatory nations must employ EIA for proposed activities that are likely to have a significant adverse impact on the environment and are subject to a decision of a competent national authority. (p34)

Since then, international or global sustainability assessment principles and criteria have been framed specifically in relation to the environmental impact assessment. Some of these factors are embedded in "socio-ecological system integrity," which included the sufficiency of livelihood – food and standard of living, equity, resource availability and usage, and adaptation to manage and sustain resource usage for current and future generations. They suggested a systems-based approach to sustainable development to integrate social, environmental and economic dimensions. In general, the ecological framework utilized in this book broadly provides a systems-based approach to sustainable development and reporting.

According to the ecological framework, business organizations' endowment, or the availability or abundance of resources, influences their ability to incur expenditures required to meet environmental and social performance. Resource endowments are usually associated with size, where larger organizations have more surplus resources and management is willing to give priority to environmental performance. Florida et al. (2001) studied the relationships between organizational resources and performance monitoring system influences on the process of environmentally conscious manufacturing (ECM) practices. They defined ECM practices as including "source reduction, recycling, pollution prevention and green product design" (p209). They suggested that ECM practices do improve business and environmental performances when regulatory agencies provide incentives for firms to comply with environmental regulations (p210). In general, they found that when organizational capabilities include specialized environmental resources, these firms have the capacity to analyze and implement environmental performance including innovative programs, such as team work, just-in-time technology (JIT) practices, lean production systems, manufacturing of green products, recycling and pollution control. They are able to monitor and assess the environmental credits and gains obtained from the ECM adoption practices.

The performance monitoring system involves the ability to quantify EMS, conduct environmental monitoring systems and perform supplier audits to address/evaluate and/or to monitor/appraise EMS practices and environmental outcomes. Florida et al. (2001) noted that, in these organizations, ECM practices are part of the overall corporate strategic plan to improve business outcome and meet regulatory requirements. There is also market pressure, competition and stakeholders' interests that influence an organization to meet the environmental performance goals of lowering "environment risks resulting from production operation" (p212).

Environmental assessment techniques have different labels (e.g., EMS) according to Florida et al. (2001). Saeed (2004) referred to such techniques as environmental impact assessment, which has been commonly adopted by many industrialized countries, including the United States, to manage environmental damage caused by industrial development projects. Saeed discussed a comparable approach to EIA, called environmental mitigation banking (EMB), as an institutional innovation approach to conserve and restore valuable natural resources on both public and private lands. The EMB approach allows banks to earn mitigation credits in exchange for land restoration. The bank then sells these credits to developers. The price and the credit that banks charge to developers depend on the type of ecosystem costs for restoration. These ecosystem costs, according to Saeed, depend on the stock of restoration costs to be done to restore the environmental damage and "decay and natural regeneration processes" (p918). According to Saeed, "mitigation banking is concerned with planning and carrying out environmental restorations based on its cash resources and expectations of profit" (p918). Normally, banks follow regulatory policy and comply with these policies when they restore public land.

When banks sell credits to developers, the credits allow the developers to incur the necessary added costs to develop the land. The costs for development are offset by the credits so that the projects are economically viable. The developers are expected to develop the land by following the restoration guidelines where the impact upon the environment remains insignificant or minimal. Mitigation banking thus allows developers to add a production-oriented component to the economy while minimizing the impact of industrial growth. In the long term, mitigation banking can reduce the cost of restoration through tax rebates and credits, improves the returns of mitigation cost, and restores the functionality and ecology of the environment. Many states in the United States (e.g., Minnesota, Michigan, Florida and California) use mitigation banking for the preservation of forests and wetlands (Wildlands Inc.) (Saeed, 2004: 913).

These examples of the preservation of endangered species, forests and environmental resources by EMB demonstrate the evolution and transformation of the EPA from that of a regulatory function of environmental regulations to that with a broader mandate to administer and oversee the federal government sustainability programs, as Grossarth and Hecht (2007) discovered. It should be noted that mitigation banking that is a byproduct of U.S. environmental legislations has granted the EPA the regulatory power to oversee and promote private–public joint efforts for sustainable development in environmental and natural resource conservation policies.

U.S. government legislation: the Sarbanes-Oxley Act of 2002, and the role of public accounting firms in framing sustainability reports

More recently, the passage of the Sarbanes-Oxley Act of 2002 (Environmental and Sustainability Reporting) by Congress broadened the scope of accounting reports to include sustainability programs, and has now been integrated by many organizations into part of their strategic planning processes (Fisher et al., 2007). As a result, many business organizations prepare sustainability reports that account for their social and environmental performances (Accounting for Sustainability Group, 2006). Public accounting firms have started providing consulting services to assist organizations in the design and implementation of sustainability reporting systems, which include sustainability awareness training to employees, performing limited-scope audits requested by top management, conducting supply chain audits, organizing compliance audits, advising on the appointment of outside assessors, and coordinating audit activities by external assessors (KPMG, 2008, 2010; PricewaterhouseCoopers, 2010). Deloitte (2014) issued a report entitled *Sustainability Reporting Services: Sharing the Sustainability Journey with Your Stakeholders* that outlines the consulting services that the firm provides to organizations on the benefits associated with external sustainability reporting.

Most public accounting firms have issued guidelines on sustainability reporting in an attempt to promote consistency and comparability among business organizations' sustainability reports (Wallace, 2000). For example, Ernst & Young (2010) has issued a summary of seven major guidelines that CEOs and board members should consider when planning to adopt and issue sustainability or TBL reporting for the first time. These guidelines address the types of information included; importance, need and the challenges and risks involved in the preparation and disclosure of sustainability reports; the governance, systems, structures and processes that are needed to report on sustainability; and transparency and the need for auditing sustainability reports. The Ernst & Young report concludes with two checklists of "Next Steps" – one for organizations who are not yet reporting, and another for those who are already reporting but may want to think more deeply on subjects related to materiality and stakeholder engagement, as well as assurance services (Ernst & Young, 2010).

For example, the AICPA has issued broad guidelines that define responsible and good corporate governance and sustainability fundamentals for improved business performance (AICPA, 2010b). The declaration initiative has focused on integrated social and environmental performances with financial reporting rather than issuing separate reports addressing social, environmental and economic issues. It has also advocated for an integrated oversight to review these reports, not necessarily mandatory requirements. The goal is to provide assurance on integrated reports (i.e., external opinion validation), which is comparable to the auditing of financial reports by public accounting firms. An example of these oversight and assurance report guidelines has been issued by Ernst & Young (2010). If these attestation guidelines are accepted by many organizations, the trend will be to prepare uniform sustainable reports that can provide comparative data for industries, sectors and competitive organizations.

These guidelines have affected business's approach to sustainability. The ecology of sustainable development in business has focused on ethics and corporate social responsibilities. A synergy developed between environmental ethics and strategic sustainability management which focuses on how corporations can integrate sustainability into their strategies with examples of best practice from business corporations (Bansal, 2005; Dilling, 2009; Epstein, 2008; Sahlin-Anderson, 2006).

Indices and ratings/rankings and examples of best business practices of sustainable companies

As discussed above, the GRI, DJSI and Morgan Stanley Sustainability Index, among others, have been used as sources to develop indicators and rankings for the best sustainable business organizations in the United States and abroad. These rankings are published in magazines and newspapers, as well as in other mass media publications and on the internet. These reports provide details about companies that have sustainable accounting practices. The factors and indicators used to rank these companies are largely based on their sustainability reports.

Such sustainable narrative ratings of companies are available from several sources: Global 100 Most Admired Companies; Bloomberg SRI Index; Fortune's Most Admired Companies; Newsweek Green Ratings; Dow Jones Sustainability Indices; and press releases from sustainable corporations. In general, these published reports are readily available on the internet and/or in libraries that have business reference books and periodical collections. These reports provide information on corporate best sustainability practices.

Corporations' best business practices are designed to promote the value of sharing and ownership of sustainability among all stakeholders. In other words, there is joint ownership or a claim to corporate resources by all stakeholders, not only by shareholders. Moreover, employees are involved in assisting in the formulation of strategic plans for sustained advantage (long-term thinking); promoting green innovation and diffusion strategies; performance issues; linking sustainability with corporate strategy; and rethinking the ownership of corporation resources including both assets and liabilities (Sisaye, 2011).

These corporations assume ownership of local community development programs where they sponsor public cultural and recreational events, supporting museums, art centers, libraries and public parks. The Hershey Candy and Coca Cola Companies are cited as examples of corporations whose business interests have been linked and integrated with local and regional sustainable development. The Hershey Candy Company has long exhibited the value of sustainability by linking business wealth creation to community and societal development where the corporation has been housed and located. The Hershey Candy Company is central to the Hershey community. The company runs schools, parks, recreation centers, hospitals and other facilities that promote sustainable development (Esty and Winston, 2006). Similarly, the Coca Cola Company supports museums, play houses, libraries and recreation facilities throughout Atlanta as part of its sustainable programs and integration within the community.

When corporations join to support community development programs, their names and logos/trademarks are associated with towns, designated streets, parks or recreation centers. When the community becomes dependent on the location of the company's headquarters, any move by the company to relocate is resisted. For example, when the Hershey board of directors voted to sell and relocate Hershey, management, employees and concerned citizens organized to object to the sale. They shared the philosophy that Hershey does not belong to the highest bidder, but to the community where it was founded (Esty and Winston, 2006). This approach is comparable to sustainable credit policies in emerging economies that have well-established community-based practices for micro-small business lending programs and community-owned projects such as dams and irrigation projects. Private business interest is combined with public good to advance the philosophy of sustainability by embedding in it environmental and social responsibility, community benefits and enhancing the well-being of its citizens (Mog, 2004). These examples show that sustainability is rooted in the staged theory of economic growth and the trickle bottom-down effects of industrial development.

The "trickle down" theory of the economics of sustainability analysis in growth and development assumes that there is a synergy between private profit and public welfare, and the link between these assumptions is exhibited in corporations who exemplify best business practices. There are many examples of corporations who regularly contribute (both financially and materially) to support local/community schools, parks, recreational centers, libraries and sponsorship of public events that advance school sports and entertainment groups. Big corporations such as Target, Apple, Microsoft, Wal-Mart and others with chains of stores and merchandise companies regularly raise funds to support public community projects based on percentage of total sales or from sales of special products designated for specific projects in the community where the business segment is located. For them, stakeholders' analysis becomes a strategic initiative to define and identify the value chain between internal and external stakeholders. The yardstick for such analysis focuses on the principle of sustainable accounting if these corporations' best social and environmental practices can simultaneously optimize the wealth created for shareholders in line with the benefits to the external stakeholders – namely, the society and community at large, as well as governmental agencies.

The ecology of sustainability accounting

The ecological approach examines the development of sustainable management reporting as evolutionary that follows a staged process growth in the preparation and disclosure of social and environmental information in financial (external) accounting reports. The subject of sustainability accounting and reporting has benefited from the organizational sociological and ecological anthropological disciplines. Good examples are Social Soundness Analysis (SSA) and Social Impact Assessment (SIA) analysis that are based on anthropological and sociological disciplines (Hoben, 1982; Kottack, 1999; Stone, 2003). SSA and SIA incorporated accounting income and performance indicators in the design and implementation of economic and social programs in developing countries. Most corporations used USAID's SSA and the World Bank's SIA models in their approaches towards business interventions in developing countries.

Although sustainability was initiated in emerging economies by international bilateral and multilateral development organizations to promote social and economic development for community growth, sustainability has also become central to business development in industrially developed countries, particularly in North America and in Western Europe. These organizations have laid the foundation for sustainability reporting that includes both economic and financial performance, as well as social and environmental accomplishments. Accordingly, business organizations began to voluntarily report sustainability information in annual reports, company publications and public media outlets, such as newspapers, magazines and radio and television.

Application of the ecological approach to sustainability reporting

During the late 1990s and early 2000s, economists started advocating for a national accounting information system that keeps inventories of the nation's natural and environmental resources. For example, Nordhaus and Kokkelenberg (1999, 2000) have developed guidelines for accounting information systems that incorporate the costs and effects on financial performance of environmental information associated with the natural and environmental resources of renewable resources related to agriculture, forestry, recreation, land, timber and fisheries as well as livestock and grain; and the non-renewable resources of oil and natural resources. They recommended that organizations prepare environmental reports that focus on pollution, global warming and sustainable resources to determine their costs, if any, and their effect on financial performance. Environmental reports provide information on natural resources management such as air, oceans, water, lakes and fisheries of interest to the general public and regulatory agencies such as the EPA, as well as state, local and municipal governments (see Howes, 1999: 32–33).

The National Research Council report (NRC, 2000) recommended that nature's (environmental) numbers should be included in the national accounting system. That is, the NRC calls for a systematic development of green accounting that will include assets and production activities associated with natural resources and the environment. In other words, national income and product accounts (NIPA) would be extended to include non-market accounts (e.g., air and water quality) beyond consumer products with market accounts. By developing parallel indicators for non-market accounts similar to near-market accounts, the NRC puts forward the importance of protecting the environment – for example, air and water quality contributes to the growth of gross domestic product (GDP). These indicators will increase voluntary environmental disclosures and reporting on environmental policies, expenditures and audits. GDP indicators and processes can include benefits from environmental products and related details on sustainable and renewable resources as well as the limitations that companies in the chemical, forestry, paper, utilities and related sectors face in managing environmental resources. These guidelines provided the general framework for sustainability accounting.

In this context, sustainability accounting and reporting can be viewed as part of either internal and/or external accounting reports prepared by corporations. Accounting reports are broadly classified into two major types: managerial and financial accounting. Managerial accounting reports are prepared for internal use by managers for the planning and control of the operating activities of an organization. On the other hand, financial accounting reports contain economic (financial) information that is mandatory and is prepared periodically. They have a multipurpose function. They are prepared for the general public and/or for government regulatory agencies. They serve various external stakeholders including investors (individual and institutional), financial analysts and creditors. The reports are of interest to government regulatory agencies, which have oversight responsibilities for the activities of business organizations. Accordingly, sustainability reporting has been closely associated with external reporting systems (Sisaye, 2011).

Traditional (conventional) financial accounting rules have focused on measuring the financial resources (assets), debts (liabilities) and owners' (stockholders') equity, as well as the sources of revenues and expenses reported in the income statement. Financial accounting reports contain information on the economic profitability of organizations in relation to the use, control, custody and management of productive assets and resources. Environmental and ecological reports are included in the annual report or prepared as supplementary reports.

Financial accounting reports, in general, present a static/technical view of business, which is consistent with functional assumptions that organizations support incremental changes to maintain the stability of systems to manage and control environmental and social responsibility goals. Nevertheless, these incremental environmental reporting changes have enabled organizations to satisfy their ethical and social responsibility goals as well as meeting investors' concerns and governmental regulatory agencies' external reporting requirements (Herzog, 2010; Hubbard, 2008; Isenmann et al., 2007). Although the trend has been towards increased environmental reports, there is a lack of reporting consistency among organizations in the same industries or markets for comparing performances.

In contrast, sustainability reporting prepared for internal use by management may include (among others): sustainability costs and benefits for decision-making; treatment of sustainability as a capital rather than as a revenue expenditure; when and how to treat sustainability as a long-term cost (deferral) asset rather than as an expense to be reported in a statement of income; to identify and separate the various costs associated in life-cycle costs (i.e., product life-cycle cost assessment); approaching sustainability in terms of a transaction cost approach within a resources-based view of the firm; the application of activity-based costing (ABC) to develop sustainability cost drivers; and use of sustainability in capital budgeting decisions. In a balanced score card (BSC) framework, some of the topics that can be expanded within the context of sustainability accounting include process improvements, market focus, organizational growth and development, cost performance measures and increasing the role and involvement of management/cost accountants in sustainable development (planning and control issues) (Sisaye, 2012a). Within the context of management accounting for internal use, sustainability, which sometimes has been labeled as green accounting, provides a systematic recording and reporting of assets and production activities associated with natural resources and the environment (A. G. Hopwood et al., 2010; B. Hopwood et al., 2005; Lamberton, 2005a, 2005b; Schaltegger and Burritt, 2006).

Sustainability accounting and economic performance

There is a substantial literature to support the link between sustainability and economic/financial performance. These studies have associated sustainability with improved financial and accounting performance. Eccles et al. (2011) classified U.S. companies into high and low sustainability companies based on their sustainability reporting practices, particularly on their disclosure of non-financial information, stakeholders' engagement and social and environmental organizational performance. They reported that high sustainability companies outperformed traditional/low sustainability companies based on accounting rates of return. They suggested that sustainability enhances business economics and financial performance.

In contrast, Koellner et al. (2005) used the balanced score card approach to develop an investment funds rating portfolio as an indicator for sustainability performance. They broadly classified sustainability funds into those funds that take into account social, cultural and ethical aspects in their investments and are included in small, medium and large-scale companies covering a broad range of technologies, including solar energy, and in bond funds as well. They noted that while financial performance indicators are available, social and environmental performances are not readily available for comparison or to provide information to investors and stakeholders. Nevertheless, the BSC-based investment funds rating account indicated that future-projected as well as past performance depended on factors including diversification, market volatility, the quality of service provided and services charged (pp55–57). While the results are mixed, there was a general consensus among researchers that corporate social reporting (CSR) is associated with increased quality of earnings and financial performance.

A study by Hussey et al. (2001) applied quantitative methodologies to compare the environmental reports of ten European-based global companies in energy, oil, consumer goods and healthcare products. They reviewed 23 separate environmental reports covering a wide range of programs including those used by oil refinery companies in "reducing green gas emissions, pushing energy conservation, and exploring renewable energy" (p11). They reported that consumer product companies (e.g., in the automobile and beverage industries) show an appreciation for recycling and environmental health. The automobile industry has responded favorably by gradually meeting specified government emission requirements as well as manufacturing requirements relating to product safety and conservation of resources such as energy, water and waste. Although the trend has been towards increased environmental reports, they noted that there is a lack of reporting consistency for comparative purposes among companies in the same industries or markets.

In general, ecologically responsible companies have provided descriptive and in some instances detailed social and environmental disclosures in their annual reports to document their sustainable management strategies (Wiedmann and Lenzen, 2006). They have disclosed their sustainable use of environmental resources, including energy conservation, development of alternative sources of energy and management of nonrenewable energy sources such as oil, petroleum products, natural gas and coal, as well as renewable energy sources such as trees (Dilling, 2009). Many institutional investors have supported the sustainability programs of corporations because they anticipate positive economic returns in their investments. They have shown a preference to invest in corporations that are listed in the Dow Jones Sustainability Index (see DJSI, 2008, 2009, 2010; Morgan Stanley, 2010; SAM Sustainability Index, 2010). They perceive that the benefits obtained from socially responsible investment policies outweigh the costs associated with these investments.

Business stakeholders, including customers, have shown a preference for corporate social and environmental programs. More recently, socially conscious and affluent customers have expressed preferences to invest in companies whose investment portfolios include sustainable development and ecological conservation policies (Koellner et al., 2005). Accordingly, customers have responded positively and are willing to pay a premium for products and services delivered by companies with reputable environmental sustainability programs (SAM, 2010; SAM Sustainability Index, 2010). For example, paper and bottle recycling companies are advancing social and environmental causes by working with not-for-profit organizations (NFPs). They are placing garbage collection facilities in parks and recreational areas. They also provide sanitation training to public and NFP employees. They work closely with service-sector organizations (e.g., hotels and restaurants) to promote water conservation and the marketing of green-based products (Nelson, 2004).

These reform efforts have also been supported by governmental policies and international organizations in their resource allocation decisions intended to advance the development of environmentally sound technological innovations. When marketing strategies that focus on cultural and humanistic values are used to promote product sales, increase market share and coordinate synergy of production, marketing and distribution linkages, they contribute to the advancement of both environmental management and improved business competitiveness and financial performance (Dilling, 2009).

Accounting guidelines provide the defining methodologies, procedures and key performance indicators for wealth creation, welfare management and corrective action measures to reduce economic and income imbalances within the community (Savitz with Weber, 2006; Schaltegger and Burritt, 2006). To support business development growth and expansion, accounting investment (project) risk analysis strategies centered on cost–benefit analysis for investment in environmental programs that generate high return on projected investment, balance sheet disclosures of integrated reporting on costs and benefits, developing sustainability metrics as cost drivers (assets that have future economic benefits) and lean accounting for perfecting business processes (Koelln et al., 2005; SAM Sustainability Index, 2010; Savitz with Weber, 2006) have been used by many corporations.

Accordingly, sustainability accounting analysis is being incorporated within corporate strategic planning to address environmental factors that mitigate financial risk management associated with investment decisions. These issues are central to financial accounting issues because they address the planning and control issues that top management committees can formulate to manage financial and associated risks. Sustainability analysis in risk assessment focuses on risk-sharing strategies, insurance coverage, divestment and/or acquisition strategies, loans coverage, debt financing, strategies for lean productive operations, survival and sustainable growth strategies (Bowden et al., 2010). If it is strategically used, it can assist managers to develop alternative plans that include the conversion of environmental crises into opportunities for new products and/or services for increasing or maintaining market share. In competitive analysis, sustainability accounting is used to identify and analyze environmental risks, manage political risks through lobbying strategies, mitigate the impact of market volatility on corporate economic performance, link the objectives of greening with the supply chain management process, and enable corporations to take ownership or stewardship of environmental programs (Esty and Winston, 2006; Savitz with Weber, 2006).

For example, Epstein and Young (1999) have suggested that economic value added (EVA) measures can be used to develop profitable investment decisions in line with responsible environmental management policies. In other words, there is a positive relationship between a balanced pro-growth environmentally responsible management program, improved organizational performance and accounting indicators of profitability. In the process, these types of business investment provide simultaneous support for economic community development programs to sustain social, environmental and economic performance and growth among business organizations indefinitely.

As these studies suggest, sustainable development analysis is an evolutionary process for ecosystem advantage: opportunities for business to invest in environmentally sensitive and resource conservation-unaware societies. It is imperative that environmental issues shape market (new and emerging) strategies to focus on a long-term sustainability vision and mission for many organizations. The role of leadership in moving the business organization forward and encouraging employees to embrace sustainability and sustain eco-culture (more value creation with fewer products) has emerged as eco-tracking. It has become the strategy of environmental imprinting. This evolutionary process created a new ecological imprint for some companies who made the transition from product companies (e.g., autos: Volkswagen (VW) and Toyota) that sell cars into service transportation companies that handle financing, leasing, insurance, maintenance, roadside assistance and related services, and operating as a global, mobile integrated sustainable business organization (Esty and Winston, 2006).

The importance of sustainability and corporate social responsibility will continue to grow in the coming years. Investors and other stakeholder groups are increasingly pressuring corporations for transparency and disclosure of information. Stakeholders want to know the details before investing in any organization. "It appears that these companies believe that issuing the report is an essential method of communication with stakeholders" (Idowu and Papasolomou, 2007: 141). It can be argued that corporations have a social contractual obligation to provide sustainability reports as a platform to display their public image. They use sustainability reports as forums to show all of the positive influences the organizations have on the community as well as the environment.

This strategy will create additional customers which support community involvement and initiatives in which the organization operates (Turcsanyi and Sisaye, 2013). Environmental concerns have attracted public interests and desires. It is, therefore, critical that top management recognizes the importance of ecological management programs as mechanisms in resolving contending environmental issues among several interest groups, including governmental organizations. Environmental management can thus become part of any organization's best management practices. The principles of sustainability have become sources of legitimization that are embedded in corporate citizenship and responsibility and accountability. Accordingly, sustainability has served as a source of operating guidelines to increase the frequency of corporate environmental and social disclosures to their stakeholders (i.e., institutional investors).

The importance of legitimization and institutionalization has been reflected in many organizations' sustainability reports. Many business organizations have incorporated into their corporate social reports the interests of the various stakeholders, such as employees and/or regulatory agencies, as well as investors/owners. Once social and environmental criteria are established, corporate activities are then evaluated with reference to the relationship they have with the interests of different stakeholders (i.e., the general public, employees, customers, suppliers and competition). This formed the basis for sustainability to become integral to CSR in response to the information needs of the various stakeholders of business organizations.

Corporate social reporting

CSR provides disclosure on the environmental, economic and social aspects that both directly and indirectly influence business activities. These topics can include, among others, issues related to pollution, charitable work or indirect economic impacts. However, there is no "globally accepted definition" or framework that is mandatory (Dilling, 2009: 20). Companies are free to disclose any and all environmental and social activities that they have implemented. Corporations are motivated to engage in social responsibility for a number of reasons: to follow government regulations, to improve public image, to provide transparency to investors, and to improve economic performance. All of these reasons and others can help to improve the overall financial portfolio of a company.

CSR "suggests that businesses are motivated by more than just self-interest and it actually promotes the collective self-interest of society" (Idowu and Papasolomou, 2007: 139). CSR directly affects not only the corporations or organizations that implement these practices but also stakeholder groups (e.g., investors, employees, regulators, activists and communities). Socially conscious investors are using socially responsible investing techniques that incorporate financial, ethical, social and environmental requirements to determine whether or not these companies meet socially desirable investment guidelines (Turcsanyi and Sisaye, 2013). CSR can aid companies in attracting socially responsible investors who would be interested in investing in the company.

Blowfield (2007: 692) reported that "there are roughly 200 social funds in the USA and 800 in Europe, and there has been growth in ethical mutual funds, especially in the UK, which accounts for two-thirds of the European market." If these ethical mutual funds are found to compete or possibly outperform other mutual funds, then this could encourage more companies to publicize their ethical business practices in order to be included in these mutual funds. Investors may choose to continue to invest in socially responsible companies to benefit themselves financially but also to support the sustainable practices employed by these organizations.

Employees can benefit from corporate social responsibility if the organization promotes initiatives that improve the work environment and work–life balance. Regulators are able to measure reported progress in a CSR report issued by a company against specific government standards to determine if regulations are being satisfied. CSR can keep activists informed of a company's commitment and progress towards more sustainable business activities. Communities benefit from CSR since corporations can influence a community's living space positively or negatively through active involvement in social and environmental programs such as pollution control, housing and road constructions, resource sustenance policies in recycling, land, forestry and natural resources management, as well as supporting cultural and civic activities.

Since businesses are deeply intertwined with communities, it is important that businesses can function as part of society by working closely with their stakeholders to positively manage external environmental and competitive influences. "As a result, CSR is not something with its own discrete outcomes, but an approach that helps business manage its relationship with society" (Blowfield, 2007: 693). With so many interest groups to satisfy, organizations are challenged to find ways to communicate social and sustainability information to all of these concerned groups. CSR provides the mechanism for the reporting and dissemination of this information.

An organization that is acting in a socially responsible manner needs to establish guidelines on how best to publicize its positive impact upon society. There are a variety of methods that organizations can choose to disseminate their sustainability practices. While there is no mandatory or regulated method for reporting CSR or sustainability, most companies choose to include the information in their published annual reports, while others announce information through a separate sustainability report or sustainability website (Christofi et al., 2012). To this effect, Arrow et al. (2003) argued that sustainable development needs to be measured to figure out whether or not "an economy's production possibility set is, in a loose sense, growing" (p653). Their analysis is based on an interpretation of sustainability that is based on the maintenance of social welfare, rather than on the maintenance of the economy's productive base.

Sustainability has its basis in the principles of the life-cycle approach that links environmental criteria with productivity and economic growth. According to Rennings and Ziegler (2003: 38), the life-cycle approach focuses on evaluating those "corporate activities aiming at a reduction of environmental impacts … along the entire value chain (pre-production, production, and during use of products and services)." Sustainability in business incorporates the interests of the various stakeholders, such as investors/owners, employees, the general public, customers, suppliers, competitors and/or regulatory agencies. Once social and environmental criteria are established, corporate activities are then evaluated, considering the relationship they have with the different stakeholders. This has formed the basis for the life-cycle assessment (LCA) argument for sustainability to be integral in corporate reports in order to respond to the information needs of the various stakeholders of business organizations.

Implementation of the GRI guidelines: the CSR evidence

The GRI is mandatory for member business organizations. When compared to the GRI, members of the DJSI are not required to disclose sustainability information. In contrast to the European countries of the GRI, U.S. external reporting issues related to sustainability are voluntary, even though the subject of sustainability has become important for business and governmental organizations. Nevertheless, there are public information reports of current sustainability trends among U.S. companies. It is still in the evolutionary process of development, reflecting the voluntary – that is, first – stage of information reporting.

Despite the consistency and uniformity constraints of reports, Thomson and Bebbington (2005) appraised U.K. social and environmental reporting (SER) as presenting "an objective view of the reality of an organization's social and environmental interactions ... with its broader ecological and social environments" (p15). However, these reports present a static/technical view, which is consistent with the functional assumptions that organizations maintain stability of systems to manage and control environmental and social responsibility goals. Despite these limitations, they affirmed that UK companies' environmental reporting formats could serve as model guidelines for many European countries.

A comparative study by Boons et al. (2000) advocated the need for environmental management systems (EMS) as an important component of the strategic planning processes of the highly industrialized European countries. They provided examples from Western Europe and Scandinavian countries where socially responsible firms have integrated ecological and environmental concerns within their strategic plans and policies. For example, in Sweden, some organizations have environmental managers who are responsible for managing issues related to the environment. These managers prepare and report the organization's activity on environmental and ecological matters on the principle that environmental reporting advances a fairer and more responsible society. These firms have developed strategies where the developments of new products and services are firmly grounded on the principles of EMS (see also Füssel and Georg, 2000: 50). EMS has been employed as an effective management strategy to minimize the negative impact of the unintended consequences of production activities on ecological systems and human welfare.

Solomon and Darby (2005) advanced the view that social, ethical and environmental (SEE) disclosure/reporting builds a mutual understanding between companies and investors (individual and/or institution). These disclosures can promote dialogue, problem-solving and education processes that are essential for socially responsible investment guidelines (p27). Thomson and Bebbington (2005) affirmed that SEE disclosures provide educational and pedagogical processes to understand the environmental and ecological dimensions and objectives of sustainable reporting (p2). As an educational process, companies can selectively prepare reports where they have significant impact in social and environmental programs such as pollution control, resource conservation and control of environmental degradation. According to Solomon and Darby (2005), SEE reporting has become "increasingly important for companies and shareholders" because of "the growing awareness that SEE risks are linked closely to company reputation and consequently to financial performance" (p28). Although SEE reporting was relatively new, it has showed a relatively slow growth over time as more social issues are raised and discussed in private and public forum engagement. These studies corroborate the fact that corporations that value sustainability have increased the amount of space devoted to account for their environmental and social impacts in their annual reports as well as in the publication of standalone (separate) environmental reports.

The GRI has shaped the external financial reporting of many European countries. Hedberg and von Malmborg's (2003) study reveals that, because of the GRI, the environmental reports of Swedish-based companies showed comparable formats to those practiced by U.K. companies. In other words, the guidelines of the GRI established for the development of CSR reports, both internal and external, are comparable, but not necessarily uniform, among European countries.

Hedberg and von Malmborg (2003) indicated that Swedish-based corporations prepare both internal and external financial reports. The internal reports are used to assist management in the planning and controlling of their operating activities. The financial (external) reports contain sustainability data to address stakeholders' interest in corporate social responsibility. They are separate voluntary reports prepared to satisfy CSR guidelines. Managers use these reports to seek "organizational legitimacy" for visibility and control (p153). CSR reports have dual purposes. First, they can serve as a public relations medium to educate stakeholders of their social and environmental programs. Second, they can assist as guidelines to motivate employees to become socially responsible actors. Accordingly, these CSR guidelines have integrated "accounting on environmental, social and economic issues" into "so-called 'triple bottom line' (TBL) accounting" (Hedberg and von Malmborg, 2003: 154). The guidelines are not uniform across industries. These variations amongst companies reflect differences in their environmental and social programs. Accordingly, the relative absence of authoritative environmental reporting standards has contributed to the generation of reports that are not uniform across organizations (Wallace, 2000). This has affected the comparability and verifiability of environmental reports among organizations.

Since the GRI guidelines for reporting have established a general framework for reporting that member corporations have to adhere to in order to disclose sustainability information, it has reinforced the importance of voluntary (self-reported) conformance to these requirements through the issuance of CSR reports. In contrast, in the United States, sustainability reports are voluntary and provided at the discretion of management; nevertheless, managers do recognize the value that their stakeholders attach to sustainability reports. A study by White (2005) affirmed that 81 percent of senior executives at large U.S.-based businesses contended that sustainability practices are very important to their company's strategic mission. Management indicated that social and environmental responsibilities have influenced their financial performance. White suggested that the continuous scrutiny of corporate practices by consumers, employees, investors and local communities, and government's oversight of pollution and wastes from the mismanagement of resources, have increased corporations' compliance with improved environmental resource management (pp36–43). Although the number of U.S. companies that reported sustainability practices was limited in the early 1990s, it increased by the mid-2000s and accounted for over two-thirds of the Fortune 500 companies (White, 2005). By late 2000, according to Dilling (2009: 22), "about 70% of the studies reviewed showed a positive and statistically relevant relationship between CSR and financial performance."

As the number of corporations who voluntarily disclose social and environmental reports increases, the need for better disclosure on the effective utilization and management of environmental resources has become important in corporate sustainability reports (Sisaye et al., 2004). These reports most often contain economic, environmental and social performance data. They provide information on management's commitment to responsibly manage environmental resources and future social and environmental strategies.

Organizations can use CSR to document their adherence by publicizing the report on the declining or decreasing amounts of fines paid out to implement or continue their sustainable practices. Compliance and the reporting of CSR are expected to improve the financial performance of a company in the long term. There is empirical evidence to support the theory that there are positive relationships between business sustainability practices and improved organizational (financial) performances. For example, Rennings and Ziegler (2003) suggested that there are two measures for sustainability performance:

> The first measure evaluates the environmental and/or social risks of the industry to which a company belongs (i.e. compared with other industries). The second measure evaluates the environmental and/or social activities of a corporation relative to the industry average.
>
> (p36)

These social activities become sources of social awareness to minimize the negative environmental consequences that include emissions or other harmful substances that would result in lawsuits or regulatory penalties due to noncompliance. They found that companies with a "higher environmental sector performance" (i.e., a lower degree of environmental risks) had a significant positive effect on the average monthly stock return between 1996 and 2001 (p40). According to their results, the investment in the stock market rewards corporations with clean environmental sectors or policies (with otherwise similar economic characteristics measured by financial variables) with a "premium" when compared to companies with high social performance (Rennings and Ziegler, 2003: 40). Their study suggests that environmental and/or social factors play important roles in reducing costs and thereby increasing economic performance. Organizations follow environmental policies to restructure their investment portfolios towards industries that simultaneously reduce sector-specific environmental and/or social risks and increase economic performance.

Gray (2006), for example, suggested that ecologically responsible companies are likely to have better financial performance reports to establish whether or not they are "socially and environmentally sustainable" (p805). He suggested that those companies with sound financial economic performance disclosed the benefits and costs (risks) associated with the management of social and environmental programs in their annual reports. These corporations provided descriptive and in some instances detailed social and environmental disclosures in their annual reports to document their sustainable management strategies. Most investors perceive a positive link between social, ethical and environmental reporting and financial performance. Accordingly, companies over the years have increased the amount of space devoted to environmental reports and accounts of social impacts in their annual reports as well as in the publication of standalone environmental reports.

CSR has the potential to decrease regulatory costs or fines that come from following regulations. If an organization must highlight its wrongdoings, it is more likely to fix the problem than incur the costs associated with legal fees and adverse corporate publicity. CSR also requires companies to treat employees better; this, in turn, can help to improve the productivity and then profitability of the organization. "With employees, CSR activities may lead to the ability to hire and retain high quality staff as well as to improve worker health and morale" (Lankoski, 2008: 540). If corporations are more transparent with stakeholders, this could help to improve customer loyalty and satisfaction, improve the firm's public image and attract additional customers who might not have known about products and services without the issuance of a sustainability report (see also Turcsanyi and Sisaye, 2013).

When marketing strategies that focus on cultural and humanistic values are designed to promote product sales, maintain customer loyalty, increase market share and facilitate synergy of production, marketing and distribution linkages, they advance both environmental management and improved business competitiveness and financial performance. In other words, when corporations combine effective environmental management strategies with culturally and socially oriented marketing programs, they will be able to gain relative competitive advantage over those organizations without environmental strategies and policies (Christmann, 2000). Dilling (2009) stated that there is a relationship between "long-term growth in sales revenue" and "the publication of a G3 report" (p21). It should be noted that there are incremental costs associated with sustainability reporting; however, it is assumed that the benefits for corporations adopting these practices into their business strategies outweigh the costs incurred in the voluntary disclosure of CSR reports.

The adoption of CSR is usually associated with increased costs if it required the hiring of additional employees or securing the services of consulting professionals or experts who are able to advise, plan and implement sustainable practices in an organization. Lankoski (2008) noted that CSR is part of overall corporate reports (CRs). These "CR activities may increase production costs because they may require management time, capital investments, and operating costs" (Lankoski, 2008: 540). Moreover, the implementation of a sustainable practice requires a long-term timeframe, and due to management or strategic changes it may be discontinued without realizing the added value to the business. Because of these associated costs, organizations have become reluctant to adopt sustainability practices due to uncertainty of the future business environment that may affect the potential to realize improved financial performance in the long run.

The current literature on the subject of CSR and sustainability suggests that the benefits from sustainability reports may outweigh the costs incurred to prepare these reports. Organizations are motivated to report and engage in socially acceptable practices (Sisaye, 2012b). Many organizations who issue sustainability reports to their stakeholders have employed sustainability as the underlying framework to legitimize profitability goals through sustained social–environmental programs and economic performance objectives (Parker, 2005: 845–846). There is no question that social and environmental accounting has a broader impact nowadays across business and governmental organizations. It has received significant public policy attention and political profile. The issues are not only rich and complex, but also have long-term impacts in society and the world community at large (Parker, 2005: 856–857). The culmination of ecological issues in public and policy debates and their subsequent impact at local, regional, national and global/international levels have generated interest in accounting research and practice, notably in CSR.

In general, CSR has enabled organizations to satisfy their ethical, environmental and social responsibilities as well as meeting investors' concerns and government regulatory agencies' external reporting requirements. Responsible environmental strategies are considered as enabling organizations to protect the environment and reduce the transaction costs associated with regulation, litigation and liabilities and clean-up costs to maintain and preserve natural resources. Organizations have benefited from cost advantages associated with responsible production processes, better product design through improved manufacturing processes and disposal of wastes, and access to manufacturing and distribution facilities.

The growing emphasis on environmental and natural resource conservation management and their voluntary disclosure in accounting reports supports the convergence of ecological and institutional research. Singh and Lundsen (1990) indicated that if a convergence between them occurred, it can be examined in terms of how institutional environment variables have influenced the ecological dynamics of organizational populations and the role of legitimacy and institutionalization in population dynamics. Institutional variables such as customers, competitors, suppliers and government regulatory agencies have profound effects on vital organizational rates: founding, disbanding, mortality/death or performance change rates. On the other hand, legitimacy or external institutional support reduces selection pressures on organizations. In general, legitimacy in the institutional environment "provides access to resources, which reduces mortality rates" (Singh and Lundsen, 1990: 184). While young organizations lack legitimacy and institutional support due to liability of newness assumptions, those organizations that do have them have relatively easier access to resources, which reduces their mortality rates. Over time, these organizations develop rules and regulations to maintain their legitimacy. As the number of rules increase, organizations become inert. Chapter 6 presents the effects of legitimacy and institutionalization on the bureaucratization of rules and their impact upon accounting rule-making (i.e., rule birth and the proliferation of rules and procedures).

References

Accounting for Sustainability Group (2006). *Accounting for Sustainability: Introduction and Executive Summary*, Report from Accounting for Sustainability Group convened by HRH The Prince of Wales, December 5, 2006, Mimeo.

Adams, R. (2010). "Accounting report," Association of Chartered Accountants, www.accaglobal.com (accessed January/February 2015).

AICPA (American Institute of Certified Public Accountants) (2010a). *The Fundamentals of Going Concern, Part II: The Competitive Edge Sustainability Can Provide to a Business*, www.globalreporting.org/resourcelibrary/g3.1-guidelines-incl-technical-protocol.pdf (accessed February 6, 2015).

AICPA (2010b). "Good governance and sustainability: Fundamental for improved business reporting," *Accountants Today*, July.

Aras, G. and Crowther, D. (2008). "Developing sustainable reporting standards," *Journal of Applied Accounting Research*, Vol. 9, No. 1, pp4–16.

Arrow, K. J., Dasgupta, P. and Maler, K. G. (2003). "Evaluating projects and assessing sustainable development in imperfect economies," *Environmental and Resource Economics*, Vol. 26, No. 4, pp647–685.

Asif, M., Searcy, C., dos Santos, P. and Kensah, D. (2013). "A review of Dutch corporate sustainable development reports," *Corporate Social Responsibility and Environmental Management*, Vol. 20, No. 6, pp321–339.

Banerjee, S. B. (2002). "Corporate environmentalism: The construct and its measurement," *Journal of Business Research*, Vol. 55, No. 3, pp177–192.

Bansal, P. (2005). "Evolving sustainability: A longitudinal study of corporate sustainable development," *Strategic Management Journal*, Vol. 26, No. 3, pp197–218.

Blengini, G. A. and Shields, D. J. (2010). "Green labels and sustainability reporting: Overview of the building products supply chain in Italy," *Management of Environmental Quality: An International Journal*, Vol. 21, No. 4, pp477–493.

Blowfield, M. (2007). "Reasons to be cheerful? What we know about CSR's impact," *Third World Quarterly*, Vol. 28, No. 4, pp683–695.

Boons, F., Baas, L., Bouma, J. J., Groene, A. D. and Blansch, K. L. (2000). "Trajectories of greening: The diffusion of green organizational routines in the Netherlands, 1986–1995," *International Studies of Management and Organization*, Vol. 30, No. 3, pp18–40.

Bowden, A. R., Lane, M. R. and Martin, J. H. (2010). *Triple Bottom Line Risk Management: Enhancing Profit, Environmental Performance, and Community Benefit*. John Wiley, New York.

Burritt, R. L. and Schaltegger, S. (2010). "Sustainability accounting and reporting: Fad or trend?," *Accounting, Auditing & Accountability Journal*, Vol. 23, No. 7, pp829–846.

Carbon Disclosure Project USA (2009). "Carbon Disclosure Project Leadership Indexes," New York, Mimeo.

Carnevale, C., Mazzuca, M. and Venturini, S. (2012). "Corporate social reporting in European banks: The effects on a firm's market value," *Corporate Social Responsibility & Environmental Management*, Vol. 19, No. 3, pp159–177.

Christmann, P. (2000). "Effects of 'best practices' of environmental management on cost advantage: The role of complementary assets," *Academy of Management Journal*, Vol. 43, pp663–680.

Christofi, A., Christofi, P. and Sisaye, S. (2012). "Corporate sustainability: Historical development and reporting practices," *Management Research Review*, Vol. 35, No. 2, pp157–172.

Christofi, P., Sisaye, S. and Bodnar, G. (2007). "The integration of total quality management into sustainability: The case of the Dow Jones Sustainability Index," *Internal Auditing*, Vol. 23, No. 1, pp33–39.

Clark, J. G. (1995). "Economic development vs. sustainable societies: Reflections on the players in a crucial contest," *Annual Review of Ecology and Systematics*, Vol. 26, pp225–248.

Clark, T. S. and Allen, D. S. (2012). "Shareholder value from sustainability leadership: Comparing valuation ratios within industry groups," *International Research Journal of Finance & Economics*, Issue 89, April, pp108–117.

Creel, T. S. (2010). "Environmental reporting practices of the largest U.S. companies," *Management Accounting Quarterly*, Vol. 12, No. 1, pp13–19.

Deloitte (2014). *Sustainability Reporting*, http://www2.deloitte.com/content/dam/Deloitte/au/Documents/audit/deloitte-au-audit-sustainability-reporting-services-0814.pdf (accessed February 3, 2015).

Dilling, P. F. A. (2009). "Sustainability reporting in a global context: What are the characteristics of corporations that provide high quality sustainable reports – an empirical study," *International Business & Economics Research Journal*, Vol. 9, No. 1, pp19–30.

DJSI (Dow Jones Sustainability Index) (2008). *Dow Jones Sustainability Indexes: Annual Review, September 24, 2008*, www.sustainability-indices.com/images/review-presentation-2008.pdf (accessed January/February 2015).

DJSI (2009). *Corporate Sustainability*, www.sustainability-Index.com/07_htmle/sustainability/corpsustainability.html (accessed January/February 2015).

DJSI (2010). *Dow Jones Sustainability Indexes in Collaboration with SAM*, www.sustainability-index.com (accessed January/February 2015).

DJSI (2014). *DJSI 2014 Review Results*, www.sustainability-indices.com/images/DJSI_Review_Presentation_09_2014_final.pdf (accessed January/February 2015).

Eccles, R., Ioannou, I. and Serafeim, G. (2011). "The impact of corporate sustainability on organizational processes and performance," *Harvard Business School Working Paper*, November 25, pp1–46.

EPA (U.S. Government, Environmental Protection Agency) (2010). "Sustainable development," Washington, DC, www.epa.gov/ebtpages/pollsustainabledevelopment (accessed January/February 2015).

Epstein, M. J. (2008). *Making Sustainability Work: Best Practices in Managing and Measuring Corporate Social, Environmental and Economic Impacts*. Greenleaf Publishing and Berrett-Koehler Publishers, San Francisco, CA.

Epstein, M. J. and Young, S. D. (1999). "'Greening' with EVA," *Management Accounting*, Vol. 80, No. 1, pp45–49.

Ernst & Young (2010). "Sustainability reporting: Seven questions CEOs and boards should ask about triple bottom line reporting," www.ernst-young.de/Publication/vwLUAssets/Seven_things_CEOs_boards_should_ask_about_climate_reporting/$FILE/

Seven_things_CEOs_boards_should_ask_about_climate_reporting.pdf (accessed February 2, 2015).

Esty, D. C. and Winston, A. S. (2006). *Green to Gold*. Yale University Press, New Haven, CT.

Etzioni, D. and Ferraro, F. (2007). "Accounting for sustainability: Analogical work and the Global Reporting Initiative," IESE Business School, Barcelona, Spain, June 27.

Fisher, D. G., Swanson, D. L. and Schmidt, J. J. (2007). "Accounting education lags CPE ethics requirements: Implications for the profession and a call to action," *Accounting Education*, Vol. 16, No. 4, pp345–363.

Florida, R., Atlas, M. and Cline, M. (2001). "What makes companies green? Organizational and geographical factors in the adoption of environmental practices," *Economic Geography*, Vol. 77, No. 3, pp209–224.

Füssel, L. and Georg, S. (2000). "The institutionalization of environmental concerns: Making the environment perform," *International Studies of Management and Organization*, Vol. 30, No. 3, pp41–58.

Gray, R. (2006). "Social, environmental and sustainability reporting and organizational value creation? Whose Value? Whose creation?," *Accounting, Auditing & Accountability Journal*, Vol. 19, No. 6, pp793–819.

GRI (Global Reporting Initiative) (2008). *Sustainability Reporting Guidelines*, www.globalreporting.org/resourcelibrary/G3-English-Financial-Services-Sector-Supplement.pdf (accessed January/February 2015).

GRI (2009). *About GR*, www.globalreporting.org/information/about-gri/what-is-GRI/Pages/default.aspx (accessed January/February 2015).

GRI (2010). *G3 Guidelines, G3.1 Developments and Organizational Stakeholders*, www.globalreporting.org/resourcelibrary/G3-Guidelines-Incl-Technical-Protocol.pdf and www.globalreporting.org/resourcelibrary/G3.1-Sustainability-Reporting-Guidelines.pdf (accessed January/February 2015).

GRI (2011). *GRI – G3.1 Reporting Guidelines*, www.globalreporting.org/resourcelibrary/g3.1-guidelines-incl-technical-protocol.pdf (accessed January/February 2015).

GRI (2013a). *G4 Sustainability Guidelines*, www.globalreporting.org/resourcelibrary/GRIG4-Part1-Reporting-Principles-and-Standard-Disclosures.pdf (accessed February 3, 2015).

GRI (2013b). *Sustainability Disclosure Data Base*, http://database.globalreporting.org (accessed October 21, 2014).

GRI (2014). *GRI and Sustainability Reporting*, www.globalreporting.org/information/about-gri/Pages/default.aspx (accessed January/February 2015).

Grossarth, S. K. and Hecht, A. D. (2007). "Sustainability at the U.S. Environmental Protection Agency: 1970-2-20," *Ecological Engineering*, Vol. 30, No. 1, pp1–8.

Hanss, D. and Böhm, G. (2012). "Sustainability seen from the perspective of consumers," *International Journal of Consumer Studies*, Vol. 36, No. 6, pp678–687.

Hedberg, C.-J. and von Malmborg, F. (2003). "The Global Reporting Initiative and corporate sustainability reporting in Swedish companies," *Corporate Social-Responsibility and Environmental Management*, Vol. 10, No. 3, pp153–164.

Heizer, J. and Render, B. (2008). *Operations Management*, 9th edition. Pearson Prentice-Hall, Upper Saddle River, NJ.

Herzog, C. (2010). "Internet-supported sustainability reporting: Empirical findings from the German DAX 30," Centre for Sustainability Management, Leuphana University of Luneburg, Germany.

Hespenheide, E., Pavlovsky, K. and McElroy, M. (2010). "Accounting for sustainability performance," *Financial Executive*, Vol. 26, No. 2, pp52–58.

Hilborn, R., Walters, C. J. and Ludwig, D. (1995). "Sustainable exploitation of renewable resources," *Annual Review of Ecology and Systematics*, Vol. 26, pp45–67.

Hoben, A. (1982). "Anthropologists and development," *Annual Review of Anthropology*, Vol. 11, pp349–375.

Holton, I., Glass, J. and Price, A. D. F. (2010). "Managing for sustainability: Findings from four company case studies in the UK precast concrete industry," *Journal of Cleaner Production*, Vol. 18, No. 2, pp152–160.

Hopwood, A. G., Unerman, J. and Fries, J. (eds) (2010). *Accounting for Sustainability*. Earthscan, London.

Hopwood, B., Mellor, M. and O'Brien, G. (2005). "Sustainable development: Mapping different approaches," *Sustainable Development*, Vol. 13, No. 1, pp38–52.

Howes, R. (1999). "Accounting for environmentally sustainable profits," *Management Accounting*, Vol. 77, No. 11, pp32–33.

Hubbard, G. (2008). "Beyond accounting: Assessing the impact of sustainability reporting on tomorrow's business," University of Adelaide Business School, Australia, Mimeo.

Hussey, D. M., Kirsop, P. L. and Meissen, R. E. (2001). "Global reporting initiative guidelines: An evaluation of sustainable development metrics for industry," *Environmental Quality Management*, Vol. 11, No. 1, pp1–20.

Idowu, S. and Papasolomou, I. (2007). "Are the corporate social responsibility matters based on good intentions or false pretenses? An empirical study of the motivations behind the issuing of CSR reports by UK companies," *Corporate Governance: The International Journal of Business in Society*, Vol. 7, No. 2, pp136–147.

Isenmann, R., Bey, C. and Welter, M. (2007). "Online reporting for sustainability issues," *Business Strategy and the Environment*, Vol. 16, No. 3, pp487–501.

Ivan, O. R. (2009). "Sustainability in accounting-basis: A conceptual framework," *Annales Universitatis Apulensis Series Oeconomica*, Vol. 11, No. 1, pp106–116.

Jones III, A. and Jonas, G. A. (2011). "Corporate social responsibility reporting: The growing need for input from the accounting profession," *The CPA Journal*, Vol. 81, No. 2, pp65–71.

Kama, A. A. L. and Schubert, K. (2004). "Growth, environment and uncertain future preferences," *Environmental and Resource Economics*, Vol. 28, No. 1, pp31–53.

King, Jr., R. (2007). "Strategic sustainability: The state of the art in corporate environmental management systems," pp9–11 in Sroufe, R. and Sarkis, J. (eds) *The State of the Art in Corporate Environmental Management Systems*. Greenleaf Publishing Ltd, San Francisco, CA.

Koellner, T., Weber, O., Frenchel, M. and Scholz, R. (2005). "Principles for sustainability rating of investment forms," *Business, Strategy and the Environment*, Vol. 14, No. 1, pp54–70.

Kottack, C. P. (1999). "The new ecological anthropology," *American Anthropologist*, Vol. 101, No. 1, pp23–35.

KPMG (2008). "Introduction to the Revised AA 1000 Assurance Standard and the AA 1000 Accountability Principles Standard 2008," *Accountability*, October 24, 2008, www.kpmg.com/us/en/Pages/default.aspx (accessed January/February 2015).

KPMG (2010). "Reporting: Sustainability briefing paper," in partnership with *Accountability Journal*.

Krajewski, L. J. and Ritzman, L. P. (2005). *Operations Management: Processes and Value Chains*, 7th edition. Pearson Prentice-Hall, Upper Saddle River, NJ.

Lamberton, G. (2005a). "Sustainable sufficiency – An internally consistent version of sustainability," *Sustainable Development*, Vol. 13, No. 1, pp53–68.

Lamberton, G. (2005b). "Sustainability accounting – A brief history and conceptual framework," *Accounting Forum*, Vol. 29, pp7–26.

Lankoski, L. (2008). "Corporate responsibility activities and economic performance: A theory of why and how they are connected," *Business Strategy and the Environment*, Vol. 17, No. 8, pp536–547.

Lee, J. and Pati, N. (2012). "New insights on the operational links between corporate sustainability and firm performance in service industries," *International Journal of Business Insights & Transformation*, Vol. 4, No. 3, pp80–93.

Lopez, M. V., Garcia, A. and Rodriguez, L. (2007). "Sustainable development and corporate performance: A study based on the Dow Jones Sustainability Index," *Journal of Business Ethics*, Vol. 75, No. 3, pp285–300.

Mog, J. M. (2004). "Struggling with sustainability – A comparative framework for evaluating sustainable development programs," *World Development*, Vol. 32, No. 12, pp2139–2160.

Moir, L. (2001). "What do we mean by corporate social responsibility?," *Corporate Governance*, Vol. 1, No. 2, pp16–22.

Morgan Stanley (2010). *Sustainability*, www.morganstanley.com/globalcitizen/sustainability.html (accessed January/February 2015).

Morgan Stanley (2013). *2013 Sustainability Report*, www.morganstanley.com/globalcitizen/pdf/2013_MS_Sustainability_REPORT.pdf (accessed February 10, 2015).

Morrison-Saunders, A. and Retief, F. (2012). "Walking the sustainability assessment talk – Progressing the practice of environmental impact assessment (EIA)," *Environmental Impact Assessment Review*, Vol. 36, No. 1, pp34–41.

Munck, L. and Borim-de-Souza, R. (2012). "Sustainability and competencies in organizational contexts: A proposal of a model of interaction," *International Journal of Environment & Sustainable Development*, Vol. 11, No. 4, pp394–411.

Nelson, K. (2004). "How small firms innovate sustainability," *In Business*, Vol. 26, No. 6, pp24–26.

Nikolaeva, R. and Bicho, M. (2011). "The role of institutional and reputation factors in the voluntary adoption of corporate social responsibility reporting standards," *Academy of Marketing Science Journal*, Vol. 39, No. 1, pp135–157.

Nordhaus, W. D. and Kokkelenberg, E. C. (1999). "Overall appraisal of environmental accounting in the United States," *Survey of Current Business*, Vol. 79, November, pp50–65.

Nordhaus, W. D. and Kokkelenberg, E. C. (2000). "Accounting for renewable and environmental resources," *Survey of Current Business*, Vol. 80, March, pp26–51.

NRC (National Research Council) (2000). "Nature's numbers: Expanding the national economic accounts to include the environment," National Academy Press, Washington, DC, Mimeo.

Parker, L. D. (2005). "Social and environmental accountability research: A view from the commentary box," *Accounting, Auditing & Accountability Journal*, Vol. 18, No. 6, pp842–860.

Pava, M. (2007). "A response to 'getting to the bottom of triple bottom line,'" *Business Ethics Quarterly*, Vol. 17, No. 1, pp105–110.

Peterson, M. N., Allison, S. A., Peterson, M. J., Peterson, T. R. and Lopez, R. R. (2004). "A tale of two species: Habitat conservation plans as bounded conflict," *Journal of Wildlife Management*, Vol. 68, No. 4, pp743–761.

Pew Center (2011). *Pew Center on Climate Change Greenhouse Gas Reporting and Registries*, Pew Center on Climate Change, Arlington, VA, Mimeo, February 10.

PricewaterhouseCoopers (2010). *A Framework for Greenhouse Reporting*, PricewaterhouseCoopers, New York, Mimeo, September 20.

Reid, R. (2013). "Integrated and GRI reporting," *NACD Directorship* (National Associations of Corporate Directors), March/April, pp28–30.

Rennings, M. S. and Ziegler, A. (2003). "The economic performance of European stock corporations: Does sustainability matter?," *Greener Management International*, Vol. 44, Winter, pp33–43.

Reverte, C. (2012). "The impact of better corporate social responsibility disclosure on the cost of equity capital," *Corporate Social Responsibility and Environmental Management*, Vol. 19, No. 5, pp253–272.

Saeed, K. (2004). "Designing an environmental mitigation banking institution for linking the size of economic activity for environmental capacity," *Journal of Economic Issues*, Vol. 38, No. 4, pp909–937.

Sahlin-Anderson, K. (2006). "Corporate social responsibility: A trend and a movement, but of what and for what?," *Corporate Governance*, Vol. 6, No. 5, pp595–608.

SAM (Sustainable Asset Management) (2010). *About SAM: Company and Responsibility: SRI & ESG Policies of sustainable investing*, www.sustainable.com.sg/company/about-sustainable-asset-management (accessed January/February 2015).

SAM Sustainability Index (2010). *Dow Jones Sustainability Indices: Sustainability Assessment*, www.sustainability-indices.com (accessed January/February 2015).

Saravanamuthu, K. (2004). "What is measured counts: Harmonized corporate reporting and sustainable economic development," *Critical Perspectives on Accounting*, Vol. 15, No. 3, pp295–302.

Savitz, W. with Weber, K. (2006). *The Triple Bottom Line*. Jossey-Bass, San Francisco, CA.

Schaltegger, S. and Burritt, R. L. (2006). "Corporate sustainability accounting: A nightmare or a dream coming true?," *Business Strategy and the Environment*, Vol. 15, No. 5, pp293–295.

Schaltegger, S. and Csutora, M. (2012). "Carbon accounting for sustainability and management: Status quo and challenges," *Journal of Cleaner Production*, 36, November, pp1–16.

SEC (Securities and Exchange Commission) (2010). *SEC Issues Interpretive Guidance on Disclosure Related to Business or Legal Developments Regarding Climate Change*, U.S. Securities and Exchange Commission, Washington, DC, Press Release, January 27.

Singh, J. V. and Lundsen, C. J. (1990). "Theory and research in organizational ecology," *Annual Review of Sociology*, Vol. 16, pp161–195.

Sisaye, S. (2011). "Ecological systems approaches to sustainability and organizational development: Emerging trends in environmental and social accounting reporting systems," *The Leadership & Organization Development Journal*, Vol. 32, No. 4, pp379–396.

Sisaye, S. (2012a). "An ecological approach for the integration of sustainability into the accounting education and professional practice," *Advances in Management Accounting*, Vol. 20, pp47–73.

Sisaye, S. (2012b). "An ecological analysis of four competing approaches to sustainability development: Integration of industrial ecology and ecological anthropology literature," *World Journal of Entrepreneurship, Management and Sustainable Development*, Vol. 8, No. 1, pp18–35.

Sisaye, S. and Birnberg, J. G. (2010a). "Organizational development and transformational learning approaches in process innovations: A review of the implications to the management accounting literature," *Review of Accounting and Finance*, Vol. 9, No. 4, pp337–362.

Sisaye, S. and Birnberg, J. G. (2010b). "Extent and scope dimensions of diffusion and adoption of process innovations in management accounting systems," *International Journal of Accounting and Information Management*, Vol. 18, No. 2, pp118–139.

Sisaye, S. and Birnberg, J. G. (2012). *An Organizational Learning Approach to Process Innovations: The Extent and Scope Dimensions of Adoption and Diffusion in Management Accounting Systems*, Studies in Managerial and Financial Accounting Series, Vol. 24, Emerald Publications, UK.

Sisaye, S., Birnberg, J. G., Bodnar, G. H. and Christofi, P. (2004). "Total quality management and sustainability reporting: Lessons from Social Soundness Analysis," *Internal Auditing*, Vol. 19, No. 5, pp32–39.

Sobhani, F. A., Amran, A. and Zainuddin, Y. (2012). "Sustainability disclosure in annual reports and websites: A study of the banking industry in Bangladesh," *Journal of Cleaner Productions*, Vol. 23, No. 1, pp75–85.

Solomon, J. F. and Darby, L. (2005). "Is private social, ethical and environmental reporting mythicizing or demythologizing reality?," *Accounting Forum*, Vol. 29, No. 1, pp27–47.

Springett, D. (2003). "An 'incitement to discourse': Benchmarking as a springboard to sustainable development," *Business Strategy and the Environment*, Vol. 12, No. 1, pp1–11.

Stone, M. (2003). "Is sustainability for development anthropologists?," *Human Organization*, Vol. 62, No. 2, pp93–99.

Thomson, I. and Bebbington, J. (2005). "Social and environmental reporting in the UK: A pedagogic evaluation," *Critical Perspectives on Accounting*, Vol. 16, No. 5, pp507–533.

Turcsanyi, J. and Sisaye, S. (2013). "Corporate social responsibility and its link to financial performance: Application to Johnson and Johnson, a pharmaceutical company," *World Journal of Science, Technology, and Sustainable Development*, Vol. 10, No. 1, pp4–18.

UNGC (United Nations Global Compact) (2009). *Overview of the UN Global Compact*, www.unglobalcompact.org/AboutTheGC/index.html (accessed October 20, 2014).

USAID (U.S. Government, Department of State, Agency for International Development) (2002). *Social Soundness Analysis*, Washington, DC, Mimeo.

USAID (2010). *What We Do*, www.usaid.gov (accessed January/February 2015).

Vondal, P. J. (1988). "Social and institutional analysis in agriculture and natural resources management project assistance: Suggestions for improvement from Africa Bureau experience," USAID, Bureau of Africa: Social/Institutional Analysis Working Paper No. 2, Office of Development Planning, March.

Wallace, P. (2000). "Assurance on sustainability reporting: An auditor's view," *Auditing: A Journal of Practice and Theory*, Vol. 19, Supplement, pp53–65.

WCED (World Commission on Environment and Development) (1987). *Our Common Future*, The Brundtland Report. World Commission on Environment and Development (WCED) and Oxford University Press, New York.

White, G. B. (2005). "How to report a company's sustainability activities," *Management Accounting Quarterly*, Vol. 7, No. 1, pp36–43.

Wiedmann, T. and Lenzen, M. (2006). "Triple-bottom-line-accounting of social, economic and environment indicators: A new life-cycle software tool for UK businesses," Third Annual International Sustainable Development Conference, Sustainability – Creating the Culture. Perth, Scotland, November 15–16.

Wilburn, K. and Wilburn, R. (2013). "Using Global Reporting Initiative indicators for CSR programs," *Journal of Global Responsibility*, Vol. 4, No. 1, pp62–75.

World Bank Group (2003). *Social Analysis Sourcebook*, www.worldbank.org/socialanalysis (accessed January/February 2015).

6 Ecology of sustainability accounting

Environmental and social influences on corporate reporting systems

The ecological systems approach focuses on populations of organizations in order to examine the effect that the environment, market forces, technology, natural resources and geographical locations have on sustainable development and accounting processes. Ecology views organizations as communities having interdependency relationships among multiple and diverse populations (Astley, 1985). Similarly, accounting systems, including sustainability accounting reporting, are viewed as populations or groups instead of as units or individuals.

Accordingly, the evolutionary process in organizational ecology suggests that the number of trials for organizational forms to find a better fit is a continuous process until a point is reached where organizational learning contributes to an increase in population density in the environment without selection (Aldrich, 1979; Amburgey and Rao, 1996; Carroll, 1984). At the same time, the evolutionary process may create conditions for inertia, thereby allowing organizations to compete in order to secure the scarce resources needed for sustained survival and growth. Consequently, only the "fittest" performing organizations survive (Freeman, 1982; Pfeffer, 1985).

The ecological implications for sustainability accounting are that, for accounting rule changes to materialize, there have to be corresponding increases in variations of sustainability assumptions that would allow for the replacement of existing assumptions. In other words, the selection process allows for the substitution of existing assumptions by newer approaches, in this case sustainability accounting principles, which contribute to the death of old assumptions that are no longer amenable to change. At the same time, inertia within accounting enables changes in existing assumptions to accommodate the new emerging philosophies of sustainability accounting and reporting. Thus, accounting rule-making has followed the adaptation process strategy, which accommodates and revises existing accounting rules and regulations without the substitution of newer principles. The current developments in sustainability accounting and reporting guidelines are byproducts of organizational ecological systems and structures.

An overview of organizational ecology system approaches to sustainability

Organizational ecology is a sociological deterministic approach for the study and analysis of the evolutionary process of growth, change, survival and death in organizations. It assumes that those organizations that are not able to learn, adapt and survive will be eliminated by a natural selection process. When organizations are inert, they are unable to reorganize their goals, strategy, authority, technology, markets, systems and structures in a relatively short time. This inertia results in the replacement of one form of organization with another, or eventual death over time (Amburgey and Rao, 1996). Yet, even if inertia is minimal, there still exists the potential for evolutionary organizational change and development through adaptation and learning.

This evolutionary adaptation process may involve both gradual and organizational transformation changes (Lant and Mezias, 1992: 52). The change process requires organizations to go through a series of incremental/gradual innovation changes which may involve cost reduction (accounting) strategies and growth and development stages (life cycles) to maintain stability and continuity. Accordingly, strategy, competition and cultural adaptations – both organizational and anthropological ecological practices – are intertwined to form the basic foundation for sustainable development and reporting. These assumptions are rooted in the sociological functional approaches of organizational change and development (Sisaye and Birnberg, 2010a).

The structural functional theoretical framework

The structural functional (SF) approach takes a more focused view of the functional and institutional importance of structures in societal change. It studies the most important components of the social system and the characteristics of the organization as a whole. Because the SF approach considers each organization to be unique, the approach advocates a contingency view of organizations (i.e., the appropriate course of action for a specific organization is dependent on the characteristics of the organization's internal and/or external environmental factors) (Sisaye and Birnberg, 2012, 2014).

When there are volatile changes in the external environment, the SF approach puts emphasis on the organization's choice of leadership to direct the organizational growth and development strategies. In other words, leadership is fundamental and critical to sustained change. If these turbulent changes cause an organization's level of performance to fall below some internally acceptable target or benchmark (e.g., the industry average), it can create a crisis within the organization. This can lead to the perception of the need for change. Often this takes the form of new leadership and/or the subsequent formation of work teams to solve the organization's crisis through organizational learning and process innovations.

The SF institutional approaches in sociology emphasize the key role of the leader in the early stages, evolution and the gradual adaptation of organizations to environment changes. Moreover, managing the crisis stage also depends on the ability of the leadership to institute adaptive organizational system change through a gradual, orderly and consensual process. While environmental changes generate discontinuity and "dysfunction" in social systems, the institutional approach justifies the ability/necessity of leaders to facilitate an orderly adaptation process (Perrow, 1986). The resulting change may be an incremental innovation in existing systems as they adapt to the new environmental changes, while others may require that the accounting systems must be totally changed to adapt to the new environment (Giddens, 1987). The internal characteristics of mechanistic systems may create structural conditions that can alter or modify the existing accounting systems and prevent the effective adoption of alternative approaches that will replace existing rules with newer rules, which will form the foundation for sustainability accounting systems.

The contingency approach accounts for those particular social relationships that define a given system (i.e., organization, sub-unit or group of sub-units), where changes occur within the system, and what types of change characterize the system. To set the social context of a given organization, the SF contingency approach defines the test of significance in terms of its functional relevance for the maintenance of the organization's social systems that are being studied.

SF assumptions of organizational structures and systems

The SF functional assumption argues that social structures, in turn, affect actors' (e.g., individuals and groups) behaviors and social relationships. The structures provide networks where actors can interact in meaningful exchange relationships (Whitmeyer, 1994: 153–156). When exiting structures modify or change, it is legitimate to expect actors to change/modify their behaviors in search of fit with organizational changes.

According to the SF framework, when organizations search for legitimacy, they adopt structures and procedures that are acceptable in their political and social environment. These structures are diffused across organizations that operate in the same cultural environment (Ribeiro and Scapens, 2006: 96). Organizations that successfully operate in similar environments can be expected to exhibit similar structures. According to Ambrose and Schminke (2003), these structures consist of those charters, power relationships, rules and regulations that determine work behaviors, power relationships and decision-making processes in the organization.

The SF approach argues that the organization consists of two major goal-directed systems or functions. These are task and social systems. Ambrose and Schminke (2003) labeled these two systems as "mechanistic" and "organic" (pp295–296), respectively, following the Burns and Stalker (1961) typology. SF researchers who view organizations as *task* systems focus on the technical and productive orientation of the organization. Under the production view, the concern is on *task* accomplishment, and the primary consideration is economic efficiency and effectiveness of process innovation programs and initiatives (Kabanoff, 1991: 419). Researchers such as Morgan (1986) who follow the mechanistic view assume that organizations function like machines. Such organizations can be made to operate efficiently and in predictable ways. They are controlled by management through budgets and standards, and accounting performance indicators play important roles in measuring individual/organizational performance.

The second systems view focuses on the organic view of the organization, which is concerned with relational issues that affect the maintenance of the system components of the organization. According to Kabanoff (1991), the social-system view stresses those factors that are related to employee orientation and consideration, social environment and personal work relationships. In the organic view, the objective is the maintenance and preservation of the arrangement of roles or relationships created by the production subsystems. The fundamental dynamic here is the maintenance of the organization's social environment (i.e., cohesiveness, solidarity or a sense of common fate among system members) (Kabanoff, 1991: 419).

Accordingly, the organic view is more flexible than the mechanistic view and is focused on system maintenance to promote broader organizational issues such as stability, adaptability and survival. The goal of management is to ensure that the organization is orderly and integrated so that input–output relationships and labor productivity are maximized. In this environment, accounting systems and practices have technical roles to play in the appraisal, evaluation and rewarding of employees.

In general, the SF system focuses on modifications and/or experimentations to improve existing systems, technologies, products and services on a continuous basis (Lant and Mezias, 1992; Mezias and Glynn, 1993). Given the SF emphasis on operating efficiency and effectiveness, it is logical that organizations characteristically follow a reactive/adaptive strategy to change that focuses on incremental, quick-fix solutions rather than on a long-term solution. SF utilizes a step-by-step incremental strategy to institute modifications and small-scale improvements to correct problems without major organizational commitment in technical, financial and human resources (Mezias and Glynn, 1993). Accordingly, the SF approach is incremental where the outcome process supports the stability and maintenance of the existing social systems.

The mechanistic-organic organizational structure assumptions of SF address those organizational factors related to structural arrangements, contextual factors, job-task work activities, and human resources management policies. In the SF approach, structures manifest themselves in centralized (mechanistic) and/or decentralized (organic) form. These structures can be loose in the organic approach or tightly controlled in the mechanistic approach; they can involve independent or interdependent tasks. These conditions have a direct impact upon the operation of management information and accounting control systems that will, in turn, affect organizational performance.

As noted earlier, Burns and Stalker's (1961) description of the two types of organizational structure, organic and mechanistic, affects the size, work structure, task complexity and structural arrangements of an organization, which affects the accounting systems. Ozsomer et al. (1997) have noted that organizations that exhibit organic systems have "flexible structures [that] facilitate the development and implementation of new ideas" (p401). As compared to centralized rigid structures, organizations with decentralized-flexible structures support innovations because their structures facilitate open communication and less formal decision-making processes that help to accelerate innovations. It also permits managers in individual units to undertake changes that later may be adopted by other units in the organization. These structures can affect the flow of information in accounting and reporting systems. Accordingly, if we view sustainability accounting as a process innovation, its adoption–diffusion strategy can be affected whether or not the organization has a mechanistic and/or organic structure and system.

Organizational structure and the control of information flow

The form of the organizational structure (i.e., whether tightly or loosely controlled), the form of the control system and the flow and accuracy of information have an effect on the innovation strategies (i.e., mechanistic or organic) adopted by the organization. When the organization is highly structured and mechanistic, it gives rise to what Ezzamel and Willmott (1998) described as group-based power control or what Etzioni (1961) referred to as a coercive control system. Under this type of control system, a dominant actor or coalition would centralize the accounting information system and the coordination and flow of information.

The centralization of control systems has been accelerated by recent advances in information technology, which has contributed to increased management demand for accounting information for strategic planning purposes. The tendency is to centralize mechanistic structures with command/coercive control mechanisms because of the desire to control the utilization of the outputs of the information system. Administrative innovations, as significant as sustainability accounting, can best be addressed in mechanistic structures that require the support and championship of top management for their adoption and diffusion throughout the organization.

It is worth noting that, with advances in information technology, the use of accounting information has expanded beyond the traditional mechanistic management control function. Thus, in these contexts, the SF approach has focused on supporting the functional maintenance of the social system (i.e., the power of the dominant individual or group). In order to enhance their legitimacy and maintain their power, the dominant individual or group adopts an incremental innovation process. These innovations tend to be autonomous or standalone innovations (Sisaye and Birnberg, 2010b). This is because innovations of this type lead to a minimum amount of change and disruption of the organization's functions, thereby minimizing the likelihood of an opportunity for a change in the power structure.

Functionalism and differentiation

Specialization and differentiation increase the size and complexity of organizations. In addition, organizations tend to grow over time, and as a result they tend to become more complex. This complexity creates a need for the organization to divide into more independent sub-units or departments (Boeker, 1989). This suggests that there will be a significant need for the formation of cross-functional work teams.

Population growth and technological changes that improve productivity, advance specialization and promote functional differentiation contribute to an increase in social stratification. When technological advances increase functional differentiation, they create administrative and distributive needs. Society develops subsystems to meet those needs. Improvement in information and transportation technology allows interaction and communication, thereby reducing the effect of geographical distance on spatial and social differentiation (Mark, 1998). While many studies have suggested that these approaches have significant relevance to the study of organizational change (Aldrich, 1979; Hannan and Freeman, 1984), it can also be extended to study sustainability accounting systems within the context of changes in management control systems.

Technological developments in organizations have contributed to specialization of organizations' structures, and eventually has changed the unitary (U-form) functional organization into multiple (M-form) divisional structures. The internal structures of divisionalized organizations are highly differentiated, bureaucratized and formalized, and less democratic. Managers seek to solidify their power by controlling the decision-making process for resource allocation decisions. They develop several levels of hierarchy to solidify their control over employees, consumers and suppliers (Sisaye and Birnberg, 2014). It is these types of organizational structure that can adopt and implement sustainability accounting methods and practices.

Teece (1996) noted the drawbacks associated with the bureaucratic features of functional organizations which exhibit several levels of management hierarchy. Accordingly, "decision-making processes in hierarchical organizations almost always involve bureaucratic structures" (p200). There are formal procedures for budget preparations and approval, committee structures, reporting systems and budget appropriations. Politics becomes important as committees "tend toward balancing and compromise in their decisions. These structures may inhibit innovations as each group attempts to appeal to its constituents. Funding decisions are biased to these constituents than to the merits of the programs under review" (p201).

It is apparent that, as organizations grow in size, internal structures become highly differentiated and bureaucratized, more formalized and less democratic. The decision-making process is politicized and tends to be dominated by a few groups who exercise hierarchical control over resources, employees, consumers and suppliers. As Vogel (1987) argued, organizations that exercise political power do not follow the democratic principles of power. When there is a coalition of interest groups, decisions are reached through compromise and negotiated agreements (pp63–68).

The question of politics and organizational performance is of importance to management researchers. Eisenhardt and Bourgeois III (1988) argued that politics leads to poor performance because "it is time-consuming to engage in politics" (p761). Politics takes time away from management and diverts their attention from work and responsibilities. Eisenhardt and Bourgeois III suggest that management teams of high-performance firms avoid politics while those of low-performance firms use politics in strategic decision-making (pp760–761). They found that "where power was relatively decentralized … the [management] team maintained a collaborative viewpoint. In effect, [they] found cooperative behavior focusing on group, rather than individual, goals" (p753). The best-performing firms are those that are decentralized, less subject to political power, and share information amongst themselves (p764). Divisionalized structures that allow autonomy in decision-making tend to be prevalent in high-performing firms.

While divisionalized structures are arranged to counter the coordination problem created by organizational size and to manage businesses in order to maximize profits, the corporate bureaucracy, according to Galbraith (1967), has been transformed into "techno-structures." Corporate management became technocratic rather than bureaucratic by relying on accounting information systems to evaluate performance and to control behavior. Management control systems have reinforced goal congruence through reward incentive systems, including coercion.

Characteristics of mechanistic accounting systems

Mechanistic accounting systems follow bureaucratic-behavior control systems where budget targets and standards are used to evaluate divisional performance. Mechanistic structures support the institutionalization of management control systems featuring increased bureaucratization and the tightening of control of resource-sharing and allocation mechanisms through operational procedural manuals that require documentations and adherence to operating procedures (Kober et al., 2007: 446–447). Although these management control structures change to fit management's strategies, the changes are not likely to be extensive. Rather, they will encompass incremental and procedural changes. Jamali (2005) has attributed this gradual change process to the traditional management model of functional centralized structural systems being driven primarily by rules, prescriptions, efficiency, cost reduction, hierarchical structures and division of labor to improve production. It is derived from scientific management principles of division of labor, the functional management of centrality, stability, planning, organizing and controlling organizational operations, and the bureaucratic management of subordination and hierarchical authority. This view critically assumes that organizations operate in a stable environment where any changes in markets and competitive environments are predictable (Jamali, 2005: 105).

When accounting control systems are mechanistic and tight, and follow detailed bureaucratic-behavior evaluation rules and procedures in performance evaluations, they are referred to as restrictive control exchange systems. When mechanistic structures prevail, management planning and control systems become more formal and institutionalized. Formal rules specify procedures and employee roles. Accounting numbers in effect control employee behavior as well as the operating activities of the organization. Accounting and audit tasks are centralized to handle operation and production activities that are routine, repetitive and programmable (Dirsmith and McAllister, 1982). Management reliance on accounting control systems to monitor employee performance restricts the use of personal feedback and interpersonal relationships in management control systems. The predominance of a superordinate–subordinate relationship in performance evaluation and reward systems reduces coordination among departments and divisions. In these settings management typically has institutionalized several accounting systems, including budget targets, profit goals and performance evaluation systems, in order to evaluate divisional performance, control management behavior and develop a commonly shared corporate culture among employees and team members. As a result, management accounting systems have become critical to securing employee and team compliance with organizational rules, procedures and goals.

However, over the long term, bureaucratic rules and formal control systems may be dysfunctional if there are continual turbulent changes and discontinuity in the organizational environment. These structures may not be responsive to sustainability accounting and reporting systems that are current and require changes/modifications in response to environmental and regulatory requirements. Thus, institutionalization becomes an effective process through which a planned change program, such as sustainability accounting, can be incorporated within the organizational culture and control systems. However, over the longer term, after the new control systems have been implemented and integrated into the organization's systems, it is apparent that bureaucratic rules and formal control systems may again become institutionalized. This can be dysfunctional for any organization where there are continual turbulent changes and discontinuities in the organization's environment. This calls for innovations that are incremental and can respond to sudden changes in the competitive environment.

Mechanistic accounting systems that are based on SF assumptions are not well suited for dealing with environmental changes that management view as "crises." However, those economic changes that the organization may view as "crises" may have resulted over the years in changes in the organization's formal control systems. In such a turbulent environment, standardized mechanistic accounting control systems will not contribute to improved divisional and corporate performance. If control systems are institutionalized as highly mechanistic and orderly systems, they create an organizational climate that promotes compliance and cooptation. These systems also discourage managers from taking risks that innovative changes require. The cost of an unsuccessful deviation from organizational norms is likely to be perceived as much higher than the gains that accrue to the manager of any successful innovation.

Thus, while management control systems are necessary for motivation, coordination and performance evaluation purposes, they can have serious dysfunctional consequences if they are implemented, so as to create a restrictive and tightly controlled environment in the organization that discourages needed changes. On the other hand, a loosely structured control system may also not facilitate innovative behavior in the absence of an organizational structure and norms that promote autonomy, independence and coordination of activities, team work and accountability of individual performance. In general, the design and implementation of control systems that facilitate sustainability accounting and reporting systems will be shaped by structural contingency variables such as organizational size, technology and business competitive environment, as well as by internal political processes of management coalition groups and external stakeholders. Sustainability accounting is a byproduct of the mechanistic functional SF system. Under the functional system, the environment is assumed to be predictable, which leads to the bureaucratization of accounting rules that are restrictive and less conducive to adaptive learning to environmental changes. This is accompanied by growth in the population of accounting rule-making, where the birth of sustainability accounting rules and procedures can be classified as a byproduct of the proliferation of accounting rule-making.

The evolution and birth of sustainability accounting rules and reporting

Organizational growth, development and transformation require accounting innovations and learning. As organizations evolve over time, they create accounting mechanisms that among other purposes serve to maintain organizational stability and the status quo. Mechanistic accounting systems are revised and changed to accommodate changes in structures and systems brought about by organizational growth and development. In some instances, when changes in the organization's structures are significant, it may require a complete change and overhaul of the existing accounting rules and regulations.

Accordingly, organizations develop new accounting rules *only* when they are necessary to address "new problems that do not seem to be covered by existing rules and when these problems are fairly recurrent, consequential or salient" (Schulz, 1998: 845). This enables the organization to retain what has been learned from past experiences in the form of "codified" rules and regulations. Thus, bureaucratization takes place (Schulz, 1998).

Sustainability accounting and reporting as a current phenomenon has received prominence among accountants, particularly accounting firms and policy-makers in the United States and abroad. Its development can be viewed as requiring or involving a codification of new accounting rules. In the United States, there are guidelines that the accounting firms and researchers have suggested to advance sustainability accounting. These guidelines are voluntary and not mandatory, and have not yet been formalized to be classified as bureaucratic accounting rules. These rules are not codified because they have not been institutionalized as legitimate by accounting rule standard organizations. Moreover, sustainability issues are broader in orientation and they pose difficulties in following prescribed, defined and well-specified rules for reporting. For example, Gary et al. (2011) have noted that sustainability goes well beyond "environmental (ecological) and social reporting," and that sustainability accounting should "be much broader to include such activities as risk assessment and providing assurance including auditing" (p99). In general, sustainability includes the whole business enterprise systems. They encompass the organization's strategic, legal and personnel issues as well as sales, production, supply chain management, marketing and finance functional areas.

One of the most important developments in the sustainability accounting rule-making process was the birth of the Sustainability Accounting Standards Board (SASB). The SASB was developed and incorporated in July 2011 as an independent not-for-profit (NFP) organization in the United States. In 2010, researchers at Harvard University's Initiative for Responsible Investment (IRI) conducted the applicability of non-financial indicators of performance associated with specific industry sectors. Their studies, which were widely received, resulted in the birth of the SASB.

The SASB is not affiliated with the FASB, or any other accounting standards boards, including public accounting organizations. It is an incorporated NFP organization that is in the business of assisting business and governmental organizations in developing sustainability accounting standards. Its services encompass several industries operating in the health and environmental and other related sectors. Its mission is "to develop and disseminate sustainability accounting standards that help public corporations disclose material, decision-useful information to investors." These disclosures are intended to provide public information on those sustainability outcomes that determine the performance of business organizations. The board provides consulting, advising and educational services to inform investors, financial analysts, management and leaders of public organizations on the importance of sustainability accounting standards to supplement financial accounting standards when having a complete appraisal of organizational performance (SASB, 2015).

It is evident from the SASB website that sustainability approaches to business become broader when they address economic and sustainability performance issues. Sustainability performance can thus encompass business as an enterprise as a whole or can address specific areas when related to a functional area: for example, marketing or production management. In this context, while sustainability is broader and covers the entire business enterprise system, sustainability accounting rules can be contextual and specific, covering particular areas, whether they are environmental or social. The prescription of these rules tends to follow the current accounting rules and modes of operations. Any deviations for current rules that are not coded are expected to be dysfunctional and do not conform to operating procedures consonant with the management of organizational performance.

While sustainability involves managing future risks to make business more competitive through a better understanding of social and environmental risks using several strategies, including "carbon trading and compliance" (Hespenheide et al., 2010: 58), there is consensus that current accounting techniques are functional and can provide cost–benefit analysis for internal decisions on how sustainability can become beneficial in cost savings associated with product costing, manufacturing efficiency, product life analysis and supply chain management. In product management, life-cycle assessment (LCA) is used to trace the product through its life cycles and the resulting impact upon the environment and the community at large (Hespenheide et al., 2010: 57). This approach is incremental, where innovations in accounting such as sustainability are adopted if they meet the cost–benefit threshold, not in terms of future risks, but that may affect the overall sustenance of the business enterprise.

When sustainability is used for managing future potential risks, it involves the examination of both internal and external environmental factors that affect the organization's current and expected future performances. In accounting, internal and external environmental factors are viewed within the context of the internal and external reporting functions of accounting systems. In this regard, Joshi and Krishnan (2010) appraised the relationship of the internal and external reporting formats of accounting systems with sustainability functions. They viewed the internal use of sustainability as having a strategic planning framework to manage financial risk associated with environmental issues and regulatory compliance for air and water quality, as well as environmental protection. Externally, sustainability reporting discloses the organization's social and environmental performance to the various stakeholders (Joshi and Krishnan, 2010: 21–25).

Similarly, Asif et al. (2013) reported that the World Business Council for Sustainable Development (WBCSD, 2000) has considered sustainable development reports as part of the internal and external reports of a company to provide stakeholders with information on social, environmental and economic activities and performance. These reports may contain qualitative and quantitative data of a company's strategy, and long-term as well as short-term sustainability objectives (p322). It can be argued that both the Joshi and Krishnan (2010) and Asif et al. (2013) studies extended the SF assumptions in sustainability accounting to meet the internal and external reporting objectives of the organization. Accordingly, it can be inferred that sustainability values and principles have functional roles to shape organizations' strategic plans, missions and policy guidelines. Since sustainability is functional, there is an evolutionary development of sustainability principles, which can eventually result in the proliferation of accounting rules.

The SF assumptions in accounting have been embedded in materiality principles. In other words, for a rule to be functional, it has to be based on the principles of materiality. The materiality assumption has been extended to provide theoretical foundations to sustainability accounting. For example, Ivan (2009) pointed out two interrelated factors – materiality (from accounting theory) and sustainable development – as contributing to the general guidelines for integrated sustainability accounting and reporting systems. The first factor is related to the "materiality of sustainability and its relationship to firm performance," derived from the GRI and DJSI, which provided reporting guidelines for sustainability performance. The second factor is related to the extent to which business organizations "respond to issues of sustainable development" as defined by the Brundtland Report (WCED, 1987: 107). Similarly, Gary et al. (2011) extended the accounting materiality argument to advance the importance of sustainability accounting. They implied that sustainability in business is based on the group concern principle in accounting because a business entity that is sustainable meets the concept of a going concern; otherwise, if it is not sustainable, "it implies a lack of going concerns" (p101).

The second factor, sustainable development, mentioned by Ivan (2009), has been advanced by the Brundtland Report (WCED, 1987), which made sustainability a global issue. The report highlighted that the availability of resources for current and future generations depended on resource conservation and environmental protection management practices. International development organizations, government regulatory agencies, society and policy-makers' awareness of climatic change, and business policies to meet regulatory requirements and legislations to avoid unexpected costs and consequences have led to the incorporation of sustainability indicators into financial accounting reporting systems. Sustainability accounting rule-making has evolved, and eventually there will be a proliferation of accounting rules to establish the foundation for an integrated reporting system for sustainability and economic performance.

An integrated accounting reporting system is based on the SF approach, that when reports cover the three interrelated areas of the financial, environmental and social performances of the organization, the organization is assumed to be functional, enduring and a living entity (i.e., going concern). For example, Gary et al. (2011) saw integrated reporting as being more systemic and holistic to include the interconnection of several factors that affect a business enterprise, including financial, environmental, social and others, including cultural and corporate control and management, and stakeholders' governance issues (p105). Burritt and Schaltegger (2010) have listed four qualitative indicators to make sustainability environmental performance reporting a part of the integrated business enterprise system. They comprise environmental management activities where reporting, first, can facilitate environmental compliance; second, aids the implementation of policies and regulations; third, assists in the management of continuous improvement programs and generates data for decision-making; and, fourth, produces external reports (p842). They referred to the first three as having internal orientation, and the fourth (last) one as having external focus. They referred to this approach as being integrative to address the business interests and stakeholder relations of organizations. In other words, sustainability accounting is functional, and can help to develop performance indicators, assist compliance, set specific targeted goals and link the business and environmental goals of organizations and society at large. They suggest that these approaches entail developing a sustainability score card of performance indicators (Burritt and Schaltegger, 2010: 842–843). In other words, they argue that a sustainability score card can be adapted to the indicators developed in the balanced score card (BSC) formats. This approach calls for an incremental change consistent with the SF assumptions of organizational change and innovations.

The triple bottom line (TBL) approach, which encompasses sustainability, has been referred to as an extension of BSC, which integrates accounting indicators into the marketing, production and human resources functions of the organization. In the accounting literature, sustainable development has been interpreted as encompassing the concept of TBL: economic, environmental and social performances. It has expanded the financial/economic perspective to incorporate environmental and social attributes that enhance overall business performance. Creel (2010) discussed the three aspects of TBL where social indicators include the company's (business) relationships to the community, employees and other stakeholders. Financial and economic performance is related to profitability and return on investment. The environment is related to the management of resources such as energy, water, pollution control, reduction of products and services. Waste product management through recycling, composting and careful disposal has become part of environmental sustainability functional goals.

Mitchell et al. suggested that, if TBL is used in conjunction with BSC, sustainability accounting contributes to learning through dialogue, engagement and transparency. Noting that water is an example of a scarce natural resource, Mitchell et al. (2012) suggested that sustainability can enhance the ability of the organization to work together with the community on how best to distribute scarce water resources from irrigation to the community. Since the organization uses BSC to formulate corporate objectives, involves the staff in the decision-making process, and obtains support and feedback from the community on ways of conserving and improving current water practices, the BSC approach enables the use of sustainability score cards in TBL reporting that are disclosed to the public (pp1058–1064). Mitchell et al.'s study shows that current accounting principles, such as BSC, have been used to incrementally modify and adapt sustainability accounting principles.

While the TBL and BSC formats have improved sustainability accounting and reporting, it should be mentioned that the approach, since it is incremental, has drawbacks and limitations. The debate has centered on whether sustainability narrowly focuses on the organization rather than the ecosystem at large and the socio-political system that regulates business and environmental regulations and the management of resources. Burritt and Schaltegger (2010) questioned whether or not sustainability as a corporate strategic management tool can assist decision-making to assess business performance through the development of sustainability score card and management control systems that condense sustainability into performance-related indicators and information processing for external reporting (p833). They saw sustainability environmental accounting as highlighting only the economic importance/significance of the environmental business aspects of business (p835). Although there are limitations, the TBL and BSC approach to sustainability accounting has incrementally contributed to the development of an integrated reporting system that encompasses the economic/financial, environmental and social performance disclosures of business organizations.

For example, da Rosa et al. (2012) highlighted that environmental disclosure management can be viewed "as a set of methods used by businesses to disclose their environmental responsibilities to their stakeholders" (p1117). In general, environmental sustainability disclosures address ecosystems, natural resources such as air and water, and other non-renewable resources. Corporations report environmental compliance when they have accomplished sustainable performance. Corporations disclose their compliance to local, state and federal regulations in adhering to those environmental policies, rules and regulations (Sobhani et al., 2012: 79). While business organizations voluntarily disclose environmental information including emission control, it is apparent that, for those corporations who operate in environmentally sensitive areas, sustainability reporting has enabled them to gain public approval in the conduct of their businesses. Therefore, when corporations incrementally improve their sustainability accounting reporting formats, they receive public acceptance and favorable media coverage, and reduction in compliance and externality costs associated with government regulatory organizations.

Sustainability accounting and reporting is in the development stage, and requires time to significantly change from the current functional reporting formats. While there are constraints and limitations in the development of sustainability accounting and reporting, the examples cited above demonstrate a progress and evolutionary change for the development of an integrated sustainability reporting guideline that incorporates both the TBL and BSC formats.

Sustainability accounting: the case of carbon reporting

Carbon dioxide is the main form of greenhouse emissions from industrial activities in areas such as manufacturing of consumer goods, durable household products, transportation, mining, oil exploration and drilling, and food processing in the agricultural sector. These carbon emissions have been noted to be big sources of pollutants to the environment, contributing to environmental degradation and jeopardizing the health and integrity of natural resources, plants and endangered species.

As the concern for greenhouse emissions and the potential threats to climate change and the environment have increased, sustainable investment in managing natural resource stocks has become attractive to major investment firms (e.g., Morgan Stanley). Morgan Stanley's Sustainable and Responsible Equity Research Team's report (Morgan Stanley, 2015a) outlined several sustainable stocks that can offer investors capital growth and at the same time minimize the impact of climate change. These areas include non-renewable resources such as the management of water; agriculture and food technology; reduction in municipal waste disposal; improving health styles by controlling non-communicable diseases, such as cancer, cardiovascular diseases, diabetes and chronic respiratory diseases; improving life styles and the standard of living in developing societies; as well as changing the demographics of ageing in the global population (Morgan Stanley, 2015a).

In addition to sustainably investing in a climate change stocks portfolio, the management of environmental issues and reduction of carbon emissions gained recognition among governmental and national and international development organizations. It called for governmental regulatory organizations to monitor carbon emissions. Business organizations recognized that the costs of meeting government regulations through compliance would be high, as these regulations may require structural changes in the methods of their operating manufacturing activities. They adopted carbon trading as a low-cost, flexible approach for corporate carbon governance (Kolk et al., 2008). Carbon trading provided them with an alternative approach that is market based and voluntarily used by those corporations who choose to participate in the carbon trading market.

According to Hespenheide et al. (2010), for environmental firms, managing carbon emissions is an important goal. Companies formulate "carbon positions" from which they develop plans to reduce overall emissions or identify targeted opportunities for energy efficiency, cost savings and eventually trading of carbon allowances to offset credit. They refer to this type of carbon accounting as "carbon counting," "carbon footprint" and "carbon inventory" (p57).

Carbon trading is a relatively new approach that corporations have adopted to address the issue of carbon emissions. Schaltegger and Csutora (2012) suggest that carbon accounting is an evolving area in sustainability accounting for transparency and decision-making purposes. When there is an environmental management accounting system, carbon accounting can have monetary approaches in decision-making contexts. They noted that "carbon accounting" has become important "in the context of climate change and sustainable development" (p2). They argued that there is a form of institutionalized corporate governance that has developed to establish bureaucratic procedures for setting carbon emission baseline standards, allocation of carbon credits among participating corporations, exchange rates and structural legal mechanisms to govern the carbon trade. Institutionalism and bureaucratization are based on SF assumptions, where recent developments in sustainability accounting (i.e., carbon accounting) can be viewed as being embedded in the functional assumptions of organizational change and innovations.

Many corporations, whether they participate in carbon trading or comply with governmental carbon emission standards, have sought to reduce carbon emissions and issue carbon disclosure projects. A good example is the launching of Morgan Stanley's bloom energy technology to reduce emissions of greenhouse gases at their headquarters in New York (Morgan Stanley, 2014).

As part of Morgan Stanley's sustainable investment management policy, Morgan Stanley's Sustainable and Resource Equity Research Team (Morgan Stanley, 2015b) Morgan Stanley has issued an executive summary report on carbon capture and storage (CCS) as an alternative solution to managing carbon emission. The report highlights that

> CCS works by capturing carbon dioxide emissions pre- or post-combustion, thus preventing CO_2 from entering the atmosphere. Once captured the carbon dioxide is transported through pipelines to geological reserves where it is then stored deep underground, preventing carbon dioxide from entering the atmosphere, which would otherwise contribute towards global warming.
>
> (p1)

While CCS has the potential to limit global warming to a 2-degree scenario (2DS), it will require substantial investment in new technologies, making CCS prohibitively expensive to fully operate globally. Morgan Stanley's SRER Team suggests that, for CCS technology to become a solution, it requires a supportive regulatory environment that provides incentives and subsidies to CCS. The report noted that

> CCS is a significant initial investment whilst ongoing subsidies, or a much higher carbon price, are also essential. In an environment where there is increasing pressure to keep electricity prices low and much uncertainty about the carbon price, these costs remain unattractive. As a result, full commercialisation of CCS is dependent on supportive regulation and commitment to investment in this technology.
>
> (Morgan Stanley, 2015b: 2)

Public accounting firms are in the process of developing guidelines for carbon accounting and disclosures. For example, PricewaterhouseCoopers (2010b) issued a report entitled *Greenhouse Gas Emissions Report*. The PwC report is designed to help U.K.-based business organizations to interpret reporting guidelines from the U.K. Climate Disclosure Standards Board. The reporting format is based on a fictitious U.K.-listed technology company, Typico plc, producing consumer durables and information technology products with operations in Asia, the United Kingdom and the United States. The document has guidelines on how to report the strategy, targets, performance and benchmarking approaches of Typico plc to reduce the impact of climate change. PwC prepared a very detailed *Greenhouse Gas Emissions Report* for the year ended December 31, 2009 for Typico plc. The carbon emissions reporting format prepared by PwC is an illustrative guideline that can serve as a model for business organizations to adopt and report climate change and greenhouse gas emissions activities in their sustainability reports (PricewaterhouseCoopers, 2010b).

A report prepared by Michael Levitsky for the International Bank for Reconstruction and Development (World Bank) for the international development community documented the links between black carbon (BC) and climate change. The report discussed the potential benefits of limiting BC emissions on the environment. It identified alternative considerations for development organizations to manage climatic change, including climate modeling to reduce global sources of BC emissions, and direct current investments and policies supported by development agencies on those programs that have impacts upon the emissions of BC and organic carbon (World Bank, 2011).

A follow-up report in 2014 was prepared by Koko Warner for the World Bank, addressing climate change and global warming. The report noted the potential risks that climate change poses to sustainable development and discussed issues associated with managing that risk. Sustainable development efforts could target greenhouse gas (GHG) emission reductions globally when there is support and broad participation among both the developed and developing countries. The paper argued that economic development models focusing on industrialization and societal transformation should include low-carbon emission policies that complement climate-resilient sustainable development policies to manage the risks associated with climate change. However, the political and economic challenges related to climate change risk management continue to undermine international development policies (World Bank, 2014).

Moreover, PwC has released a *Global Sustainability and Climate Change* report for the years 2009–2015 addressing strategic sustainability, assurance and reporting, and several sustainability and climate change case studies (PricewaterhouseCoopers, 2009–2015).

In 2008, the International Organization for Standardization (ISO) issued a summary report entitled *ISO International Standards: Practical Tools for Addressing Climate Change*. The report highlighted the importance of monitoring climate change, quantifying GHG emissions and communicating on environmental impacts, promoting good practice in environmental management and design, and opening world markets for energy-efficient technologies (ISO, 2008). In terms of quantifying,

> the newly developed standards ISO 14064 and ISO 14065 provide an internationally agreed framework for measuring GHG emissions and verifying claims made about them so that "a tonne of carbon is always a tonne of carbon." They thus support programmes to reduce GHG emissions and also emissions trading programmes. ISO 14064 is emerging as the global benchmark on which to base such programmes.
>
> (ISO, 2008: 4)

In 2004, the World Resources Institute (WRI) and the World Business Council for Sustainable Development (WBCSD) issued the Greenhouse Gas Protocol entitled *A Corporate Accounting and Reporting Standard, Revised Edition*. The Greenhouse Gas Protocol Initiative is a multi-stakeholder partnership of businesses, non-governmental organizations (NGOs), governments and others convened by the WRI, a U.S.-based environmental NGO, and the WBCSD, a Geneva-based coalition of 170 international companies. Launched in 1998, the initiative's mission is to develop internationally accepted GHG accounting and reporting standards for business and to promote their broad adoption. Similar to financial accounting and reporting Generally Accepted Accounting Principles (GAAP), the initiative sought to develop generally accepted GHG accounting principles intended to underpin and guide GHG accounting and reporting to ensure that the reported information represents a faithful, true and fair account of a company's GHG emissions.

Accordingly, the GHG Protocol Initiative comprised two separate but linked standards. In the *GHG Protocol Corporate Accounting and Reporting Standard*, the document outlined "a step-by-step guide for companies to use in quantifying and reporting their GHG emissions." It provided "specific principles, concepts, and methods for quantifying and reporting GHG reductions – i.e., the decreases in GHG emissions, or increases in removals and/or storage – from climate change mitigation projects (GHG projects)." The second standard was a proposal for the *GHG Protocol Project Quantification Standard* to develop "a guide for quantifying reductions from GHG mitigation projects" (WRI and WBCSD, 2004).

Recognizing the importance of climate change, Schaltegger and Csutora (2012) pointed out that the plan for developing a standardized carbon disclosure format was led by the WRI and WBCSD. They perceived the importance of sustainability accounting in assisting companies to develop transparent policies for reporting their current environmental performance in carbon emission reduction policies, forecast future emissions, identify steps to control or reduce future emissions, and develop implementation policies to manage and reduce carbon emissions. It is evident that carbon accounting can document ecological plans and can be used to budget for investment in the cleaner production of products and services of corporations. In consumption decisions, carbon labeling of products helps consumers to make informed choices in their purchase of products and services (Schaltegger and Csutora, 2012: 5–10).

In July 2014, the WRI issued a final draft report for public comment entitled *Mitigation Goals Standard: An Accounting and Reporting Standard for National and Subnational Greenhouse Gas Reduction Goals*. The document outlined the proposed *GHG Protocol Project Quantification Standard* that was initiated in 2004. It formulated accounting methods for tracking the progress of GHG reductions and calculating allowable emissions in the target year(s) in order to understand future emission levels associated with meeting the Mitigation Goals Standard (WRI, 2014).

The Organisation for Economic Co-operation and Development (OECD) has been at the forefront of encouraging member European countries to introduce technologies to reduce carbon emissions. In 2010, it issued a report that summarized the policy frameworks and guidelines for corporate action in support of a low-carbon economy. The report suggested strategies for business organizations in addressing climate change, and building on principles of responsible business conduct, as outlined in the guidelines for multinational corporations, around three broad areas of corporate engagement: accounting for GHG emissions; achieving reduction of GHG emissions; and reaching out to suppliers, consumers and other stakeholders (Kauffmann and Less, 2010).

The Schaltegger and Csutora (2012) study and WRI (2014) and OECD (2010) reports focused on carbon accounting and emission reduction management policies among European countries. In the United States, the Securities and Exchange Commission (SEC) (SEC, 2010) has provided guidelines on carbon accounting and disclosures for U.S. firms (see also CERES, 2014).

Carbon accounting is a good example that documents the functionality of sustainability accounting, which is adopted to reduce carbon emissions of products and services, and their labeling for marketing purposes. Carbon accounting is a byproduct of current accounting practices such as ABC and BSC, where there are no fundamental changes in existing financial and cost accounting techniques for product costing, pricing and market planning. It has brought incremental changes to the methods in which corporations can extend financial accounting rules to manage carbon trading. When carbon accounting is widely accepted, sustainability accounting focusing on environmental protection and reduction of carbon emissions not only reduces government oversight and the need for regulatory compliance, but it also serves as a mechanism to enhance corporate image and citizenship with the community and society at large. In terms of accounting rules, carbon accounting has contributed to the proliferation of rules on how to record, price, exchange and disclose carbon emissions.

Sustainability and the adoption of GRI guidelines in environmental reporting: examples from manufacturing organizations

Sustainability reporting discloses environmental data to the various interest groups to enhance and solidify a positive corporate image. Sustainability, in this regard, provides a public relations medium to disclose corporate environmental activities and performance. There is evidence from various studies examined that there are increasing trends by manufacturing organizations to prepare and disclose information to the public, particularly in the United States, Canada and Western European countries, who have adopted GRI guidelines for their sustainability reporting.

For example, Eugenio et al. (2010), after reviewing the annual reports of several countries in both the developed and emerging economies, reported that there are variations of social and environmental reporting (SER) among countries in Asia and Europe and in Australia. These SER variations differ largely by industry and the size of the company. Among industries, those that have environmental impacts in the automobile, chemical and mining industries provided more disclosure, including the impact of government regulations on their industries. They found the report to vary and lack consistency in disclosure formats.

While there are several reporting formats for disclosing sustainability information, Joshi and Krishnan (2010) found that GRI guidelines have been widely accepted by many business organizations for external reporting purposes. Iyer and Lulseged (2013) reported that in the United States, among Standard & Poor's (S&P's) listed firms that appear in the GRI Sustainability data base, for both family and non-family status ownership and involvement, there was no difference in the extent and level of detail of sustainability disclosures. In other words, both family and non-family-affiliated S&P-listed firms that are included in the GRI followed the same reporting guidelines. That is, GRI guidelines have been adopted by member firms, contributing to uniform and comparable sustainability disclosures.

Bansal (2005) found that corporate sustainable development for forestry, mining and oil gas industries in Canada was being shaped according to media pressure, mimicry and organization size. Larger firms with slack resources adopted earlier, but, over time, media coverage played a role in the adoption of sustainable practices to manage forestry. Treffers et al. (2005) gave examples from the Netherlands where the government, through tax credits and the establishment of centers and research institutes, worked with both international and local institutions to develop new infrastructures and technological development to reduce emissions of greenhouse gases in housing construction, agricultural and rural development projects. Holton et al. (2010) provided case studies from various industries in the United Kingdom, and reported that these companies follow both GRI reporting guidelines and ISO 14011 certified environmental guidelines and the British Standard BS8900: 2006 *Guidance for Managing Sustainable Development*. These organizations used the guidelines to "monitor" through "continuous performance improvement" management and culture systems to achieve both "eco-efficiency" and "socio-efficiency" of sustainability objectives (p136). These examples indicate that, in environmentally sensitive industries, management has introduced gradually planned sustainable development programs to protect the environment, reduce emissions and conserve resources, and to report these activities to the public, government and media.

Birkin (2003) viewed environmental and resources management as part of ecological accounting, and applied this to study the ecological impact of the tourism industry on Ponza Island, Italy, focusing upon resource consumption (water), energy usage and waste management. The study revealed that there was community participation and involvement in shaping the industry within the context of the growth of tourism to the island from European and Asian countries, and tourism sustainability policies of bordering European countries that compete in the tourism industry. The study addressed the impact of the tourism industry on the country's economic development and the well-being of the community as it relates to jobs, standard of living, education, environmental resources, water, landscape, forestry, natural vegetation and the ecosystem at large, focusing on tourist attraction areas, particularly on the Italian islands (pp59–60). The study linked the importance of ecological resources in the preservation of island resources and the long-term sustainable growth of the tourist industry.

Another study by Contrafatto and Burns (2013) noted the importance of ecological resource management within the context of environmental and social accounting. They reported a longitudinal case study of an Italian company, MARIO, which has adopted the GRI's social and environmental accounting principles within the context of broader social, economic and environmental development contexts. They suggested that administrative routines over time can become an ongoing organizational process that can have "normative traits and become institutionalized" (p353). In other words, norms and behaviors can develop into rules when these norms are institutionalized. From the Birkin (2003) and Contrafatto and Burns (2013) studies, it can be inferred that, in European countries where environmental concerns have been incorporated into government policies and GRI reporting requirements, accounting rules for sustainability have been institutionalized. Even in emerging developing countries, multinational corporations (MNCs) that operate worldwide do provide sustainability disclosures. Dutta (2012) reported that, among Indian companies that are GRI listed, they prepare their external financial reporting following GRI guidelines. They issue corporate social reports to be competitive internationally, but Dutta noted that the reports are not as comprehensive when compared to those of European-based corporations (pp654–655).

These studies corroborated Joseph's (2012) argument that the GRI has set up a multi-stakeholder perspective in defining sustainability. Although the GRI reporting guidelines are widely used for sustainability reporting, it is not required except for GRI member corporations. The GRI and DJSI reporting guidelines have both contributed to the development of integrated reporting for the disclosure of sustainability information.

Sustainability reporting: the need for attestation and assurance services

If sustainability disclosures and reporting formats are integrated as part of the annual report, transparency, attestation and verification of the information by an external party ensures the validity of the information contained in the report. While external auditing is mandatory for external annual reports, it is not required for voluntary sustainability reporting. However, there is a general consensus that external party assurance services provide credibility to the information disclosed in sustainability reports.

For example, Evans and Campos (2009) stressed the importance of transparency in all types of corporate activities including sustainability reports. Accordingly, transparency includes all transactions that the business has conducted, and the accounting principles that are used to measure, record and report them. When these reports can be independently examined and verified, an assurance report by an independent organization follows, such as by an accounting firm. Although assurance is not mandatory, Evans and Campos highlighted the importance of having assurance reports to ensure transparency of the information disclosed. Certified public accountants (CPAs) and auditing firms can provide assurance services to assist businesses to develop internally consistent and uniform reports encompassing all areas of accounting and their adherence to accounting theories, principles and practices (Jones III and Jonas, 2011).

Cho et al. (2012) qualified the need for external auditors and advocated for the increased role of CPAs in providing assurance services for CSR performance reports as the number of companies disclosing sustainability activities increases over time. Attestation enhances the transparency and accuracy of sustainability reporting. While not mandatory, independent assurance services enhance the accountability and verifiability of reports. They also provide guidelines for managers to act in the best interests of the corporation and society. If sustainability disclosure is audited, the attestation function for sustainability accounting and reporting establishes the initial procedure for a rule-making bureaucratization process of sustainability information disclosure by accounting rule-making organizations such as the Financial Accounting Standards Board (FASB). Sustainability accounting has evolved from a mandatory practice to that of a rule-based principle where the FASB and the auditing firms coordinate their activities to ensure that corporations' annual reports have complied with sustainability rules.

The EPA and the Sarbanes-Oxley Act of 2002 (SOX) have provided guidelines and regulations for integrated environmental reporting, albeit voluntary.

At the same time, environmental legislation is enforceable by government regulatory agencies such as the EPA. The American Institute of Certified Public Accountants (AICPA) and the big four accounting firms have developed sustainability accounting and corporate social reporting (CSR) guidelines (Lusher, 2012). The accounting firms provide consulting and assurance services to assist corporations in formulating guidelines, and to document and prepare environmental reporting that meets regulatory agencies' requirements and adheres to corporate financial performance. They advocate making environmental management an important component of the financial and operating performance of an organization, and the need to disclose sustainability information/data that is certified and assured by public accounting firms as part of an integrated external reporting system.

It should be noted that accounting guidelines for reporting are based on theoretical assumptions and principles. Transparency is based on the principles of accounting for the full disclosure of information to report to the stakeholders who have an interest in the organization or to those groups where the firm's activities have a direct impact upon their economic well-being. This is a normative approach where principles are based on accounting rules and regulations. Joseph (2012) argued for a normative sustainability approach to transparency rather than rule-based objectivity that adheres to profitability goals. Nevertheless, rule-based sustainability principles in accounting have transparency and full disclosure practices that promote corporate profitability goals in line with sustainability objectives (i.e., the sustenance of scarce environmental and natural resources is profitable in the long run).

The ecology of rule-making and bureaucratization of accounting rules

From an ecological perspective, the drawback in principles and rule-making is that, over time, it increases the number of rules. Proliferation of rules leads to bureaucratization and adherence to the enactment and implementation of the rules. The different formats used to account for environmental and social costs and associated liabilities incurred by businesses in their industrial development activities have contributed to the development of ecological rules and principles for sustainability accounting.

Ecology has a systemic approach in addressing interdependent and interconnected transaction costs that affect humans' interaction with the environment. Accordingly, ecological accounting advances sustainable economic development by broadening accounting to include "the larger, practical limits to our dependencies and provides a means of living according to these dependencies" (Birkin, 2003: 51). In ecological accounting, business activities are linked to regional and community development as well as their impact upon the economy and the ecosystem at large.

However, this bureaucratization is not without its costs. It contributes to incremental learning and innovation. In the case of accounting, this would mean that learning and innovation would lead to the birth and codification of new accounting rules. As organizations over time develop more rules, the potential for greater bureaucratization is increased, which, in turn, may result in inhibiting future learning experiences.

Specifically, Schulz (1998: 872) stated:

> As lessons from past experiences get encoded in rules or other systems of automated (organizational) responses, new experiences become scarce. As a result, learning through further codification of experiences declines. Making rules and routines helps organizations respond to problems in a programmed and efficient way, but, at the same time, rules create a dangerous sense of familiarity with arriving problems that reduce the likelihood that new problems will be seen as opportunities to draw new lessons.

The rule-based approach to managing organizations has been noted by Lawrenson (1992), who described the bureaucratization of organizational decision-making in British Rail systems. Prior to Margaret Thatcher becoming prime minister, British Rail was engineering driven. Its incremental learning created values and mechanisms that reinforced the importance of maintaining superior engineering. Decisions were made with the intent of maintaining an organization that reflected the highest engineering standards. British Rail responded to changes in the competitive environment by searching for engineering innovations. Financial measures played a secondary role in their decisions. As the environment changed and economic issues became more important under the late prime minister, with Thatcher's plan to privatize it, the organization remained insensitive to the changing political environment. It required an explicit intervention by the government to override the existing bureaucratic rules and alter the organization's orientation to learning and innovation (Dent, 1991).

When technical accounting procedures are bureaucratized, accounting tasks become centralized to handle the operation and production activities that are routine, repetitive and programmable (Dirsmith and McAllister, 1982). Formal accounting control systems monitor employee performance, and the existence of quantitative reports leads to them replacing the use of personalized and qualitative feedback and interpersonal relationships in control systems. The predominance of a formal intra-unit orientation, i.e., controllability, in the organization's performance evaluation and reward systems has another important effect. It reduces the interactions among units and discourages/inhibits the diffusion of a potential innovation within the organization. Each unit operates as a distinct and separate unit within the organization's hierarchy. Thus, members minimize their relationship with or connection to any other unit. This inhibits the flow of innovations across units and favors standalone innovations.

The awareness of the need for inter-unit cooperation may increase when organizational problems have "thematic relatedness" (i.e., possess a high degree of similarity, or reflect a joint dependence on the same resources, as is often the case with accounting problems or procurement problems) (Schulz, 1998). Although these changes might lead to acceptance by some and resistance by others, the uncertainties surrounding these changes might require members to accept them or else leave the organization. Under these circumstances, the central management of the organization can develop relatively generic common rule(s) that can be disseminated to and utilized by many or all of the organization's sub-units. This generic rule may involve the adoption of sustainability reporting.

Accounting legitimacy and the functionality of sustainability reporting: the case of corporate social reporting

When organizations incorporate sustainability growth strategies in cost and management accounting systems to remain competitive and profitable, they have adopted incremental changes in their business operations. Over time, when these changes are institutionalized, they provide legitimacy for sustainability accounting and reporting systems. Organizations justify legitimacy to generate prescription of rules, routine procedures and to define supporting functions to guide their daily operating activities. Eventually, when accounting rules become close to the core of the organization's administrative activities, they tend to become mechanistic and shielded from external environmental changes.

Although changes in a business's environment necessitate changes to its accounting systems (e.g., sustainability reporting), the impact of these changes upon accounting regulations has been limited. These rule changes (e.g., sustainability accounting) become bureaucratic when they perpetuate and co-opt into existing administrative procedures. However, incremental changes in accounting reporting systems, including sustainability reporting, prescribe to the functional assumptions of system maintenance. When accounting systems become functional, they exhibit characteristics that are associated with inertia, becoming less flexible and resistant to change. However, inertia in accounting is a relatively short-term phenomenon that is amenable to environmental changes. CSR is an example of a functional sustainable accounting reporting format that has incorporated environmental and social disclosures as part of external reporting systems.

Corporate social reporting has its theoretical foundations in the stakeholder theory of the firm which assumes that CSR objectives are in line with corporate interest groups who seek information on environmental protection, consumer safety and social philanthropic activities. CSR is voluntary and is based on the assumption that business contributes to the betterment of society, thereby enhancing its corporate image within the community and society.

The stakeholder view of business

The stakeholder theory assumes that business organizations have several stakeholders besides stockholders. They "include employees, customers, the local community, government agencies, public interest groups, trade associations and competitors." They are "legitimate partners in a business" that the business organizations have to account for (Banerjee, 2002: 179). Accordingly, business organizations' responsibility to manage these relationships is an aspect of an external corporate environmental orientation. Sustainable development is an external corporate environmental orientation that advocates for environmental protection and natural resources preservation, social responsibility and ethical performance. In the process, business recognizes its responsibility and manages the need of the community for sustained economic growth. Sustainability concerns such as greening influence new product development, investment in research development, location of new industries and managing pollution control.

Kotonen (2009) interpreted the stakeholder point of view as implying a "regulated CSR reporting" both nationally and internationally to increase the importance of CSR reporting as part of companies' official information (p198). However, CSR reports are voluntary, and if reported are prepared to meet government regulation guidelines and accounting disclosure requirements. Since CSR is not regulated, there is a debate as to whether the disclosure of CSR information has relevance for economic and sustainability investment decisions. Nevertheless, business organizations that have a proactive view of CSR show more responsiveness to stakeholders' interests through compliance of government regulatory guidelines – working with customers, civic groups, organized interests and the community as well as shareholders in addressing environmental concerns and aligning their strategies with their competitors and industry requirements.

Buysse and Verbeke (2003) associated a proactive corporate strategy with environmental leadership. In their study of water pollution and solid waste production management in Belgium, they reported that firms with an environmental leadership strategy were responsive to various stakeholders, including customers, shareholders and employees, as well as international competitors, if they operate globally – that is, if they are MNCs. The size of the company and affiliation to MNCs as a subsidiary have resulted in affiliates being more responsive to environmental strategies. These MNC affiliates attach importance to international competition and show responsiveness to overall environmental strategies. The MNC affiliates are bigger in size, have resources and value the importance of environmental leadership to international competition rather than local concerns (pp466–467). Since most of these MNCs follow the GRI guidelines in their CSR, their strategy for meeting international environmental standards exceeds those of local regulatory requirements.

Kotonen (2009) reported that Finnish companies have utilized the stakeholder approach in their CSR disclosure where CSR complied with the GRI guidelines to meet the various stakeholders' interests, including the international community. Moreover, CSR was integrated with annual reports to present the companies' social, environmental and economic performances.

In natural resource management, the stakeholder approach has shaped CSR policies in terms of the sustainable management of renewable resources, which has its basis in the Brundtland Report guidelines (WCED, 1987). Sharma and

Henriques (2005) examined forestry management sustainability practices in Canada. They reported that Canadian firms have managed sustainability through pollution control, reduction of usage and conservation policies that do not require substantial investment in resources. The bigger firms have undergone ISO certification to satisfy stakeholder demands on the sustainable harvesting of lumber products. However, they did not find Canadian firms embracing the advanced stages of sustainability performance such as "eco-design, eco-stewardship, and business redefinition" unless there was significant pressure from consumers through the boycott of products and environmental groups, stockholders and regulatory agencies calling for enforcement of policies (p175). Accordingly, government policies in Canada are ambiguous on jurisdictions and responsibilities. However, there has been consideration among all parties (national, state, local and business) to respond to stakeholders' interests and demands. In general, environmental management enhances the corporate/business image as the organization establishes better public awareness and working relationships with the community.

The functionality of CSR in improving organizational performance

CSR is an organization-wide strategic initiative (Asif et al., 2013). Lopez et al. (2007) summarized CSR strategies as comprehensive and include or integrate policies ranging from "management quality environmental arrangement, brand reputation, customer loyalty, corporate ethics and talent retention," as well as practices that are related to better corporate management, environmental protection, ethics and full disclosure of sustainable development practices. The accounting implications are cost savings, improved internal control and quality decision-making. These policies are expected to create long-term value and performance for the organization (p286).

According to Branco and Delgado (2012), CSR discloses information on "CSR reporting" and is associated mainly with voluntary disclosures of information pertaining to "several economic, social and environmental aspects upon which companies' activities may have an impact: employee-related issues, community involvement, environmental concerns, other ethical issues, and so on" (p357). CSR discloses all business activities, including labor practices, consumer protection, community involvement, human rights and corporate governance, as well as social welfare (Reverte, 2012: 255). It is assumed that corporations are less likely to be involved in ethically questionable activities, such as corruption, which is incompatible with CSR. When reported, CSR disclosures supplement external financial reporting by incorporating social and environmental data into these reports.

CSR has thus become an avenue to reduce risk (risk reduction strategy) in environmental matters; it provides competitive advantage over others; it enables employee retention; and it increases the ability to respond to media and regulators' compliances (Morhardt, 2010). Since CSR is hard to quantify, the focus is on the long-term economic impact upon the community, society and ecosystems.

CSR legitimizes corporate social and environmental activities, leading to acceptance and institutionalized norms and behavior.

Morhardt (2010) found that organizational size and industrial sectors do account for differences of whether or not companies attempt to provide sustainable reporting on their social performance. In terms of size, medium- and large-sized firms respond to social issues in response to their internal and external pressures. In small companies, information cost becomes a factor in not fully adopting CSR. Moreover, industrial-sector characteristics do account for CSR differences. In industries that have "established environmental sensitivity and substantial direct impact in sectors such as manufacturing, resources, utilities, chemicals, pharmaceuticals, motor vehicles and parts" as well as in banks, retailing, food, etc. with direct contact with customers, there is a CSR orientation to inform the public (p408). These sectors show awareness and responsibility by issuing CSR disclosures.

There is a consensus among researchers that CSR is more likely to provide firms with long-term competitive advantage compared to others who exhibit lower CSR concerns/orientations (Lee and Pati, 2012). It is likely that many organizations are more likely to initiate CSR if environmental and social concerns are associated with competitive advantage that improves financial performance.

Clark and Allen (2012) examined the relationship between sustainability leadership (CSR) and accounting performance. They used DJSI listings and memberships as a proxy to account for sustainable leader companies. They reported that sustainable leader companies improved the financial valuation and quality of earnings. Their study indicated that, while sustainability leadership is a qualitative attribute, the market perception was positive, and "that achieving sustainability leadership is a strategy that is consistent with maximizing shareholder value" (p115). Overall, their study indicated that even though sustainability investments are considered as "operating expenses allocated to 'nonmarket' activities" that may affect the accounting bottom-line factors of net income and other profitability indicators, because of these investments "shareholder wealth may still increase if investors assign a higher valuation multiple to lower earnings" (p116). In other words, investments in discretionary areas that may not increase bottom-line performance measures may contribute to "increases in shareholder value," which is associated with sustainability leadership. They valued membership in DJSI as contributing to higher valuations of financial assets and earnings quality when compared to those non-DJSI member firms.

However, the relationship between sustainability/CSR and firm economic performance is mixed. Reverte (2012) questioned whether or not improved CSR increases firm value through reduction of the cost of equity capital. While improved CSR provides more disclosure on a company's sustainability performance by reducing information asymmetry and increasing transparency, Reverte suggested that, if an increase in the contents of CSR is evidenced in an increase in CSR rating, it has the potential to decrease the cost of equity capital. That is, "the cost of equity capital is an important channel through which the market prices CSR disclosure" (Reverte, 2012: 263). However, the results showed that "a negative relationship between CSR disclosure quality and cost of equity capital is more pronounced for those firms operating in environmentally sensitive industries" (p266). They reported that CSR disclosures indicated quality of management and responsible reporting that are value neutral and did not contribute to market valuation of the firm by reducing the cost of equity capital.

CSR reports are mostly non-economic and financial, and contain more information disclosure for manufacturing organizations that operate in environmentally sensitive areas such as the mining, oil, chemical and pharmaceutical industries (Reverte, 2012: 255–258). In general, CSR disclosures are voluntary processes that provide sustainability information and data to supplement mandatory external financial reporting.

Examples of studies of CSR reporting in the developed and developing economies

There are variations in the CSR disclosure formats within developing and developed economies, and within the developed economies, they vary according to the political orientations of the country (e.g., among the Nordic, West European and other industrially developed countries). The Nordic countries have liberal political government and democratic institutions that encourage CSR disclosures that are detailed and comprehensive. Kotonen (2009) described the CSR of Finnish companies as comprehensive, following GRI guidelines by reporting environmental issues, employee welfare and ethical behavior, as well as corporate involvement in community-based projects, natural disaster help, support for education and donations to charities and youth groups, among others. The reports include both qualitative and quantitative information, including "transparency, openness, materiality, and in some cases fairness" (p190). Siew et al. (2013) studied the CSR disclosure practices of Australian construction companies. They found sustainability disclosure related to environmental conservation, climate change and carbon emission control to be limited, but noted an increased trend in CSR activities. These two studies indicate that sustainability reporting among developed countries is not uniform and varies according to political and institutional differences. It is evident that the Nordic countries, with their social democratic political systems, are more likely to require more sustainability disclosures when compared to those countries with pro-business conservative environmental policies, such as Australia.

Moreover, the extent of disclosure of CSR information also varied according to industries, size of the company, and whether or not the corporations are privately or publicly owned and operated nationally or internationally. Reverte (2012) reviewed the contents of CSR for several industrial organizations and reported that industries from oil, mining, chemical and pharmaceutical companies disclose information on environmental and health and safety issues related to their operations and the industry at large. Turcsanyi and Sisaye (2013) reported on the CSR disclosure of a pharmaceutical industry, Johnson & Johnson, and found that the company disclosed sustainability information on the medical health and safety impacts of medication pills on consumers, and safety measures that the company instituted to protect consumers' safety and welfare. These studies indicate that the size of the company, public ownership and international involvement were associated with an increased trend in CSR.

In contrast, in the financial industry, CSR disclosure is limited. Carnevale et al. (2012) appraised the CSR disclosure of banks. They reported that banks do consider CSR disclosures as non-financial variables, and do not attach importance to them since they have no impact upon accounting earnings' performance and profitability. However, they concluded that since banks' economic performance is not affected by CSR disclosure and behavior, CSR does not indicate future performance and profitability and the market does not assign any significant economic importance for banks' commitment to publish CSR (pp172–173). The CSR report only has significance in showing banks' commitment to social and environmental concerns, and their civic relationships to the society and community at large.

Branco and Delgado (2012) studied the relationship between CSR and corruption – that corruption is inconsistent with the objectives of sustainable development, and that OECD member countries have policies to combat against corruption. They argued that the concepts of CSR and sustainable development enhance economic growth, competition and environmental protections, as well as consumer protection and social responsibility. Since corruption increases the costs of doing business, it "constrains economic growth by distorting public investments"; CSR reports can make corruption transparent by disclosing and exposing business organizations' corruption practices (pp360–361).

There are also variations in the CSR disclosures within the developing and emerging economies. An example of a country considered to be an emerging economy is China. A study of CSR reporting in mainland China by Noronha et al. (2012) indicated that the disclosed information was not as comprehensive as in developed economies. CSR disclosure is quite recent since the publication of the 2006 Shezhen Stock Exchange CSR guidelines. These guidelines include environmental and social data related to stakeholders' interests and impact upon society and community. These reports, while voluntary, were suggested to be published as part of annual reports or in separate CSR reports. Although CSR reports are provided by major companies, the information provided is preliminary and not as comprehensive as that of the developed economies. Nevertheless, there is a realization that these reports can improve the public image of Chinese companies, and thereby help them to become competitive in international business. Even among major Chinese companies that have adopted or begun to use the GRI guidelines, Guan and Noronha (2013) reported that the scope of CSR disclosure has been limited. The reports are qualitative and descriptive, and do not include accounting data to empirically support their CSR activities.

There are several studies of CSR disclosures in the developing economies. Sobhani et al. (2012) studied CSR disclosures in Bangladesh by examining the annual reports of banks. They found a lack of a standardized format, no standalone sustainability reports, and the absence of environmental information in these disclosures. They reported that, while environmental disclosure was not available, banks reported in their annual reports social sustainability information related to their employees' rights, product responsibility as well as supporting community development through credits, loans and the financing of small and medium businesses. The banks also sponsored sport and cultural activities in the community, extended grants to address poverty programs by financing low-cost housing projects, provided quality customer service, and offered healthy and safe working environment conditions for their employees (pp79–80).

Ussahawanitchakit (2011) studied the relationship between sustainability accounting and corporate image in Thailand. The study indicated that, since sustainability is associated with transparency, inclusiveness and auditability, it enhanced the corporate image and business ethics of companies that disclosed CSR information, thereby contributing to investors', consumers', the community's and society's increased confidence in business activities. Kaeokla and Jaikengkit (2013) found that in Thailand companies that used the GRI guidelines reported sustainability information that is qualitative and they are only beginning to provide a credible comparison among the cement and public power companies they studied.

In contrast, Aghashahi et al. (2013) studied CSR reporting in the food industry in Malaysia. They noted that CSR in Malaysian food industries is a competitive tool that indicates the capability of the corporations to meet socially and environmentally desirable characteristics. It is not only food safety, but also animal rights, labor issues, pollution, trade, safety and bio-technology issues. Corporations are responding to these issues in their CSR reports. They disclose the impact of their business activities upon the environment, including energy use, pollution and emission control, water cleanliness and product labeling and safety. Labor issues on health, education and working conditions are reported to meet stakeholders' demand for CSR reports.

A related study by Jalaludin et al. (2011) examined the adoption of environmental management accounting (EMA) practices in Indonesia. They argued that EMA adoption provided legitimacy and political support for the manufacturing sector. They suggested that normative pressures from the accounting profession and practices (norms, rules and standards among accountants) have affected and influenced EMA adoption. Government organizations issued awards and certificates to recognize and institutionalize best practices of environmental management accounting in Malaysia, which increased adoption and compliance (pp540–552). These awards followed the Malcolm Baldrige Award in the United States and the Deming Award in Japan to recognize organizations with best business practices in their respective industries.

These studies indicate that CSR has been associated with sustainability disclosure (Kotonen, 2009). The current trend is in increased CSR disclosures among U.S. and European business organizations. These reports do contain the costs incurred in meeting regulatory requirements and the future liabilities associated with these costs. They are, in general, considered incremental reports – in other words, supplementary voluntary reports provided in addition to the mandatory annual report. Accordingly, CSR reports do contain accounting capital and operating budgeting issues and the financial future risk strategic implications of corporate sustainability activities. This trend shows that finance and accounting can provide a multifunctional and multipurpose approach to sustainability accounting by integrating environmental issues, the management of risk, as well as measuring operating performance and strategic plans for the future.

Learning and innovation occur when institutional pressures create the need for organizations to change existing accounting practices (Sisaye and Birnberg, 2014). In accounting, government regulations, stakeholders, competitive forces and market conditions have required changes in CSR, EMA and carbon accounting for pollution control and the management of environmental degradation. These accounting rules constitute a byproduct of current sustainability reporting. The adoption of EMA by manufacturing organizations is to comply with government regulations and avoid penalties, fines, liabilities and financial risks. These practices have been common in both developed and emerging countries.

Moreover, institutional forces, such as legal, governmental and competitive, as well as international factors, have affected organizational structures and systems' ability to imitate and conform by adopting social and environmental accounting standards in organizations' administrative procedures to meet the demands of their diverse constituents. By mimicking and accepting normative industry standards, conformance and compliance provided legitimacy and stability for the adopting organizations.

The ecological system's functional assumptions of sustainability reporting

The functional assumptions in the ecological systems approach presume that there is a growing interest among accountants to integrate sustainability within financial and managerial accounting reports as long as these reports satisfy and meet the reporting requirements of both external and internal users (Sisaye, 2011). In other words, sustainability has advanced the prescription and institutionalization of social and environmental reports to be presented along with external financial (economic) information disclosure. The ecological systems approach goes beyond the functional and incremental rule-making principles for CSR disclosures as part of sustainability accounting.

Ecology involves adaptation and social transformation systems. Walker et al. (2004) indicated that there are three interdependent factors that govern the dynamics of ecological systems. The first is resilience, which is the capacity of the system to deal with disturbances/turbulences and its ability to adjust and reorganize while going through the required changes for sustaining balance and performance. The second factor addresses ecological adaptation as occurring through managing the change and its ability to influence and monitor environmental changes. The third factor addresses transformation when new systems and structures are developed by altering and replacing existing systems. Walker et al. viewed sustainable development as involving social–ecological systems that can be best explained as having these three interrelated and interdependent characteristics. However, the current rule-making process in sustainability accounting is characterized as having resilience and adaptability dimensions. The first two ecological dimensions specified by Walker et al. address a set of interrelated social, economic and political systems that may shape and influence the interaction of businesses with the immediate environment. The sustainability rules that are formulated have not addressed the issues of transformability, as a third dimension of ecology as defined by Walker et al., that organizations adopt in order to alter and change the systems entirely.

In transformation, ecological systems may be configured to have new landscapes, wildlife habitat for tourism purposes, new cattle ranching for rangeland management, forest management and tourism for economic development and international trade purposes. Using the same analogy, in sustainability accounting, ecological transformation requires the development of radically different accounting guidelines and principles. Currently, sustainability accounting has a wide range of accounting rules (e.g., CSR, carbon accounting) that are implemented to revise existing practices that are considered outdated in managing the conservation and preservation of natural resources. Accounting rules have generally prescribed to the ecology of resilience and adaptation. They follow the SF approaches to process innovations and change, and represent incremental changes that are functional to modify accounting rules to meet sustainability reporting requirements.

The ecological transformation approach thus considers both external and internal factors as being critical to the growth and failure rates of organizations. As organizations grow larger, inherent structural problems associated with growth arise. When organizations become established and gain legitimacy, they develop prescribed rules, routine procedures and defined functions to guide daily operating activities. The ecology of resilience and adaptation approach implies that organizations grow accustomed to these rules, making it difficult to change routine procedures. Because internal procedures and structures become rigid over time, resilience manifests in resistance to change, resulting in organizational inertia that constrains the birth of new accounting rules. Accordingly, social and environmental reports operate through existing rules and administrative structures. Ecological adaptation is used as a strategic process to overcome organizational inertia and accounting constraints to meet current environmental changes. Adaptation occurs when organizations adopt innovation strategies in environmental and management accounting systems to remain competitive and profitable in their business operations.

A comparable framework developed by Hailey and Balogun (2002) has related the adaptation and incremental-transformation strategies of growth to evolution and adaptation typologies. The approach assumes that the environment has a significant influence on organizational growth and adaptation strategies. This includes the organization's business boundaries, the community in which the business or industry is located to conduct its business, and its economic and social relationship to this community. In this regard, ecology integrates a community-based approach to business strategies where sustainable development and environmental accounting provides business organizations with competitive advantage. The ecological use of natural ecosystems links organizations to their communities, and the effectiveness of these links is included in organizations' sustainability reports. Accounting reports record, accumulate, measure and disseminate sustainability information to the public. In the process, accounting changes, although incremental, become institutionalized in sustainability reporting.

The institutionalization of sustainability accounting and reporting

It can be inferred that implementation of sustainability reports and environmental concerns and practices in organizations, if accepted and practiced regularly, and repeated over time, can develop into norms of acceptable behavior and serve as a frame of reference to meet the demands of the dominant constituencies/stakeholders: shareholders, customers, employees, regulatory organizations and the community at large. It can also provide organizational visibility and legitimacy.

Sustainability is based on greening and pro-environmental issues; when they are institutionalized, they become legitimate, and could develop into collective sense-making that can provide employees with norms and a shared ideology to guide their actions in day-to-day activities and for turning organizational policies into operational practices. Accordingly, organizations develop new routines to manage emerging environmental and ecological issues to legitimize their actions and ensure stability over time to balance institutional pressures for legitimacy, efficiency and responsible environmental practices which could eventually advance competition and the collective sharing of environmental concerns among organizations (Boons and Strannegård, 2000; Füssel and Georg, 2000).

However, the long-term effect of the institutionalization of environmental reporting rules and regulations over time is that, once these rules are established, they become fixed, uniform and tend to be bureaucratic in nature, making the density effect of rules in accounting significant. Schulz (1998) inferred that low levels of business environmental turbulence (i.e., sustained incremental changes over time) have resulted in a low level of accounting rule production and a very low "birth rate" for accounting rule change. The consequential effect of low birth rates has brought about the proliferation of existing accounting rules, which has been the case in environmental reporting systems and disclosures. As accounting rules receive more scrutiny by parties including external governmental agencies, they develop more rules that use sustainability reporting to accommodate these changes.

The movement towards proliferation of accounting rules was intensified by international competition and the development of new accounting techniques such as ABC in the 1990s and BSC in the late 1990s and early 2000s. These developments transformed accounting systems from a more functional-restrictive role to that of an organic-relaxed structure that is able to develop new routines, rules and codifications in response to environmental and regulatory changes. These changes in accounting systems were particularly significant during the 1990s. The 1990s was a period of time in which international competition, global business changes and environmental uncertainties brought significant developments in organization management. Moreover, in the 1990s and 2000s, public interest in environmental and natural resources conservation and management contributed to a gradual/incremental increase in the birth and growth of rules governing environmental disclosures and requirements in accounting reporting systems and their institutionalization across public and business organizations.

However, changes in accounting reporting practices have occurred gradually over time. Incremental changes in accounting reporting systems have prescribed to the SF assumptions that, although accounting systems are inert, less flexible and resistant to change, inertia in accounting is a relatively short-term phenomenon. Rather, changes in accounting systems evolve in increments over the years to changes in business requirements and environmental conditions.

The ecological approach suggests that there are long-term effects of the institutionalization of environmental reporting rules and regulations. During the course of the organizational growth and development stages, accounting rules are formulated and established to administer organizational activities. Over time, once these rules are established, they become fixed and uniform and tend to be bureaucratic in nature, making the density (population) effect of accounting rules in organizations significant. These rules become mechanistic when they perpetuate and co-opt into existing administrative procedures. Although business environmental changes necessitate changes to accounting systems, the impact of these changes in accounting regulations has been limited.

It needs to be noted that environmental movements in the 1990s and 2000s did result in the acceptance and institutionalization of sustainability reports across many public and business organizations. This has been evidenced in the highly industrialized nations of Europe. The corporations of Western European and Scandinavian countries represent exemplary organizations for taking the lead in sustainability reporting in response to national and international standards on social and environmental reporting. For example, the GRI disclosures format has established guidelines that follow the ISO 9001 and ISO 14001 certifications that specify business operating procedures and guidelines on social, ecological and natural resources management, as well as environmental systems documentation on the disposal of hazardous wastes associated with utilization of natural resources.

The 2008 GRI report has specified three types of disclosure information related to organization profile, management approach and performance-related indicators. Of these three disclosures, the performance-related indicators specify TBL reporting. The first type relates to performance indicators and deals with the economic/financial-related measures associated with revenues, operating costs, employee compensation, donations and community investments. The second type of disclosure addresses the environmental management impact upon living/ non-living natural systems, emissions, effluents, waste, biodiversity and environmental compliance. The third, related to performance measures, is concerned with social disclosure assessment and impact upon human rights, labor practices, benefits, training, education, health, safety, diversity, equal opportunity and procurement practices related to anti-corruption and anti-trust practices. GRI member European companies have adopted the GRI guidelines in the preparation of their financial reports.

These developments have shaped financial accounting and reporting systems, particularly the methods that accountants use to gather, measure, interpret and report social and environmental data. The adoption of ISO 9000 and ISO 14001, and GRI disclosures, have shaped TBL reports. However, the trend for U.S. corporations to adopt the GRI guidelines has been mixed since very few are members of the GRI and those who are not members voluntarily provide information on social and environmental programs. This may change in the near future. Both the Securities and Exchange Commission (SEC) and the Financial Accounting Standards Board (FASB) have shown interest in the inclusion of sustainability information in external financial reports. The FASB is considering the adoption of the International Financial Reporting Standards (IFRS) so that U.S. corporations can be comparable with their European-based counterparts. When adopted, this will make TBL reporting mandatory. It will allow comparisons of social and environmental performance reports among corporations that are within the same industry and/or compete for increased market share for their products and services. When the IFRS is adopted in the United States and accepted nationally and internationally as the generally accepted financial accounting reporting guidelines, the standardization is expected to have significant impact upon the overall format and presentation of TBL reports.

An overview of sustainability reporting: emerging trends

In addition to growth and development, sustainability also involves conservation which entails reduction in resources for economic purpose – consumption and an attempt to redirect economic gains to social concerns for disadvantaged members of society. These elements of sustainability include social justice, eco-efficiency and eco-effectiveness, among others.

There is recognition that, in general, accounting has a social responsibility construction dimension. Saravanamuthu (2004) argued that accounting standards can promote sustainable management practices – what are measured counts to enable the financial accounting framework to "guide management in balancing economic growth against social and environmental needs" (p296). However, accounting rules have been largely geared towards measuring financial resources, assets, liabilities, equity, expenses and revenue. The emphasis of accounting on efficacy and efficiency has left concerns of social justice, education, ethics, morality and sustainability to social processes of democracy and reliance on a corporate voluntary effort to promote them (Saravanamuthu, 2004: 296–298). Social responsibility of the control, custody and management of a company's resources, as well as environmental and ecological issues, have been left to corporations to voluntarily report them.

Most of the sustainability accounting issues are related to voluntary environmental reporting. Some accountants argue that qualitative research in accounting is appropriately suited to address issues related to the environment, ethics and social justice. For example, Lee and Humphrey (2006) noted that accounting is not a neutral technique, but viewed as being constituted within the social and economic relations it operates – the social significance of accounting and its legitimization of rules. They suggest that "qualitative research methods are particularly well suited to studies that seek to understand the origins and role of accounting into specific historical, social and organizational context" (p183). These concerns are related to the historical emergence of management accounting, the relationship between accounting and other dimensions of organizations, and whether or not management accounting practices are resistant to change, and if not how accounting research has contributed to organizational change including sustainable development.

In terms of sustainability, accounting standards have promoted sustainable management practices to balance economic growth against social and environmental needs. Gray (2006) suggested that socially responsible companies focus on the issuance of ecological and environmental management reports to the public. This is because ecologically based reports are important in order to establish whether or not organizations are socially and environmentally sustainable (Colbert and Kurucz, 2007). There is an increasing trend in social and environmental reporting, as evidenced in the annual reports of socially responsible companies.

Sustainability accounting and external financial reporting guidelines: the journey towards standardization

Social and environmental accounting has a broader impact nowadays across business and governmental organizations. These reports are valued by the company's stakeholders and the market (Hedberg and von Malmborg, 2003; Hussey et al., 2001; Parker, 2005). Corporations have realized that when sustainability is incorporated within the business strategies of social and environmental performance, it complements economic profitability objectives. In other words, sustainability promotes transparency, adherence and disclosure that incorporates and promotes social equity, environmental restoration/renewal and financial performance.

In the long run, business organizations will pursue economic growth and profitability performance consistent with social, natural and environmental resource conservation, and align future technological developments with sustainability programs. When TBL reporting is standardized and adopted, corporations will voluntarily prepare and disclose uniform and comparable social and environmental reports along with economic performance trends in their annual external financial reports.

Although sustainability reporting is a voluntary disclosure, there is a movement towards the standardization of sustainability data reported by organizations for auditing and comparison purposes. In this regard, it is necessary to note that the most important source of information on sustainability is incorporated under external reporting requirements. These include Generally Accepted Accounting Principles (GAAP) and the Sarbanes-Oxley Act of 2002.

Generally Accepted Accounting Principles

The FASB issued SFAS No. 5, Accounting for Environmental Liabilities, Contingent Liabilities and Asset Retirement Obligations, to recognize and report corporate environmental liabilities associated with business innovations and growth. In addition, the Environmental Protection Agency (EPA) has established guidelines on environmental liabilities by providing specific definitions and categories, topics that are relevant for intermediate accounting courses (EPA, 2010). Most financial accounting text books include materials that address accounting loss contingencies and accounting for asset retirement. The Securities and Exchange Commission (SEC, 2010) has disclosures of climate change risks and opportunities that are considered material (e.g., the BP *Deep Horizon* spill).

Other topics of interest related to environmental issues include reports on climate change from meteorological and geographical reports (weather and maps). The 2011 *Pew Center on Climate Change Report* issues greenhouse gas reporting. Another source is the Carbon Disclosure Project USA (2009) Index. Moreover, PricewaterhouseCoopers (2010a) has issued guidelines entitled *Report on a Framework for Greenhouse Gas Reporting*. These reports provide guidelines for inclusion of environmental and social data in sustainability reports.

Sarbanes-Oxley Act of 2002 (environmental and sustainability reporting)

The Sarbanes-Oxley Act of 2002, also known as the Public Company Accounting Oversight Board (PCAOB), has oversight functions to oversee the quality control of the auditing performance of public corporations. The Act has broadened the scope of accounting reports to include sustainability programs, which have now been integrated by many organizations into some of their strategic planning processes.

The PCAOB is "empowered to regulate the auditors of public companies, investigate rules violations, and sanction accordingly. Overseen by the SEC, PCAOB replace[d] the old system of accounting firm self-regulation administered by the AICPA" (Fisher et al., 2007: 53). The board also oversees the quality of auditing tasks and reviews auditor practices and procedures. It reviews the compensation, professional competency and compliance of auditors and partners, as well as policies governing retention of auditors by client firms. It also appraises the overall human resources management policies of auditing firms (Cheng et al., 2009).

The Sarbanes-Oxley Act increased oversight and intervention by governmental organizations at the national and state levels in order to monitor the performance of corporations, accounting firms and professional organizations, including the AICPA. The Act required the audit committee of the boards of directors of corporations to select an independent firm to audit financial statements by limiting the role of accounting firms providing non-auditing (e.g., consulting) services (Fisher et al., 2007).

The implications of the Sarbanes-Oxley Act for the auditing profession are substantial. The Act has reinforced the requirement of auditor independence, commitment for quality service and independence from outside interference in conducting their auditing functions. It established continued professional education, particularly on accounting ethics and corporate governance, as basic to maintaining professional certification. In addition, it provided guidelines for the separation of auditing and consulting services (Misiewicz, 2007; Sisaye, 2011). Thus, SOX provides a strong basis for the recognition of some form of uniform data related to sustainability accounting.

Auditing: attestation of sustainability disclosure and management

The general guidelines for sustainability and assurance reports are outlined by the GRI, WBCSD and the International Auditing and Assurance Standards Board (IAASB). The four big accounting firms and the AICPA have issued auditing guidelines for sustainability reporting. According to O'Dwyer et al. (2011), the four big CPA firms support an integrated sustainability reporting system, which includes third-party assurance statements from CPA firms. Moreover, both international and national standard setting boards have included guidelines for the development and conduct of sustainability assurance reports. These assurance audit services are co-evolving to secure legitimacy with clients, stakeholders, external regulatory agencies and users of these reports and within the "auditing/assurance" firms who provide these services (pp38–39). The objective is to seek consensus on the structure of the sustainability reports among the assurance service providers and to achieve general legitimacy on the importance, value and instrumentality of these reports.

O'Dwyer et al. (2011) noted that legitimacy of the reports cannot be attained or sustained for the long term unless there is demand from stakeholders. They reported that most of the firms they studied used the assurance services certification to secure pragmatic legitimacy through the exchange and reproduction of assurance reports (p42). It is apparent that internal legitimacy cannot be maintained unless it is enforced and audited through oversight and external regulatory enforcements.

Management accounting: internal reporting and decision-making

While the focus of sustainability reporting has primarily been on financial (external) reporting and the auditing of the information, the managerial (internal) accounting and decision-making aspects have not received much research attention. Nevertheless, sustainability is a management issue which requires the formulation of strategic planning and the implementation of operational guidelines. It shapes and influences the internal decision and operating functions of organizations. Within this context, it is apparent that sustainability's integration into managerial accounting and control is critical in improving corporate economic, social and environmental performances.

Within the context of management accounting, sustainability has become a strategic planning initiative (e.g., in the BSC framework for managing product and manufacturing cost analysis, new product development and organizational transaction cost management, as well as personnel training and development). Along with economic performance, environmental and sustainability dimensions can be integrated within the BSC as important determining factors in organizational resource allocation decisions. Internal sustainability reporting provides information to management that can be used in managing the operational activities of the organization (Hopwood et al., 2010). Sustainability reporting prepared for internal use by management may include the identification of the various costs associated with organizational life cycle (OLC) costs (i.e., product life cycles' cost assessment); approaching sustainability in terms of a transaction cost approach within a resources-based view of the firm; the application of ABC to develop sustainability cost drivers; and the use of sustainability in capital budgeting decisions.

In sustainability accounting, ABC can be used as a cost control program to manage both costs and organizational change processes. Similarly, in BSC, sustainability accounting can be used to manage process improvements, market focus, organizational growth and development and cost performance measures, as well as increasing the role and involvement of management/cost accountants in sustainable development (planning and control decisions). In other words, sustainability integration in managerial accounting, particularly ABC and BSC, involves planning, budgeting, internal control and reporting systems that shape sustainability disclosure and decision-making processes.

More recently, the management of climate change has been recognized as a sustainability goal that is addressed as a strategic risk management process as developed economies have faced environmental uncertainties associated with natural disaster and loss of biodiversity among freshwater and ocean species (Adams and Frost, 2008; Larsen et al., 2013). Strategic planning for environmental assessment has focused on managing carbon emissions and reduction policies and conserving energy and non-renewable oil resources to align carbon management policies with population growth and increased human industrial development activities (Amekudzi, 2011). Accounting techniques and measurements have been integrated to improve eco-efficiency and effectiveness in managing climate changes, implementing carbon management tools, public procurement policies and aligning carbon trading with sustainability objectives. The use of ABC and BSC for assessing sustainability performance can assist strategic management decisions in improving the quality of voluntary social and environmental disclosures.

In general, the ecological approach has examined the development of sustainable financial and management accounting reporting as evolutionary in that it follows a staged growth process in the preparation and disclosure of social and environmental information in financial (external) accounting reports. While sustainability reporting is a recent development in the accounting literature, the subject has benefited from governmental and public accounting organization guidelines on how to voluntarily prepare and report sustainability information on corporate social and environmental performance to stakeholders. These developments from the public, business and accounting practice (professional) organizations have increased the demand for the integration of sustainability education within the accounting curriculum, and the need for accounting professionals who have the expertise and educational background to prepare sustainability reports.

The question of integrating sustainability within the overall accounting curriculum is a subject of paramount interest from business schools and accounting firms, as well as government regulatory organizations. The integration of sustainability into accounting education and the role that the accounting practice profession has played in promoting sustainability reporting reflect how environmental and ecological issues are important for the long-term management of the natural resources of nations to advance the social and environmental well-being of individuals, business organizations and societies at large. Chapter 7 addresses the integration of sustainability into accounting education and practice from the perspectives of both organizational sociological and ecological anthropological social sciences.

References

Adams, C.A. and Frost, G.R. (2008). "Integrating sustainability reporting into management practices," *Accounting Forum*, Vol. 32, No. 4, pp288–302.

Aghashahi, B., Rasid, S. Z. A., Sarli, M. and Mand, A. A. (2013). "Corporate social responsibility reporting of food industry major players," *Interdisciplinary Journal of Contemporary Research in Business*, Vol. 5, No. 2, pp751–761.

Aldrich, H. E. (1979). *Organizations and Environments*. Prentice-Hall, Englewood Cliffs, NJ.

Ambrose, M. L. and Schminke, M. (2003). "Organization structure as a moderator of the relationship between procedural justice, interactional justice, perceived organizational support, and supervisory trust," *Journal of Applied Psychology*, Vol. 88, No. 2, pp295–305.

Amburgey, T. L. and Rao, H. (1996). "Organizational ecology: Past, present, and future directions," *Academy of Management Journal*, Vol. 39, No. 5, pp1265–1286.

Amekudzi, A. (2011). "Planning carbon reduction in the context of sustainable development priorities: A global perspective," *Carbon Management*, Vol. 2, No. 4, pp413–423.

Asif, M., Seacy, C., de Santos, P. and Kensah, D. (2013). "A review of Dutch corporate sustainable development reports," *Corporate Social Responsibility and Environmental Management*, Vol. 20, No. 6, pp321–339.

Astley, W. G. (1985). "The two ecologies: Population and community perspectives on organizational evolution," *Administrative Science Quarterly*, Vol. 30, No. 2, pp224–241.

Banerjee, S. B. (2002). "Corporate environmentalism: The construct and its measurement," *Journal of Business Research*, Vol. 55, No. 3, pp177–192.

Bansal, P. (2005). "Evolving sustainability: A longitudinal study of corporate sustainable development," *Strategic Management Journal*, Vol. 26, No. 3, pp197–218.

Birkin, F. (2003). "Ecological accounting: New tools for sustainable culture," *International Journal of Sustainable Development and World Ecology*, Vol. 10, No. 1, pp49–61.

Boeker, W. (1989). "The development and institutionalization of subunit power in organizations," *Administrative Science Quarterly*, Vol. 34, No. 3, pp388–410.

Boons, F. and Strannegård, L. (2000). "Organizations coping with their natural environment: A laboratory for institutionalization," *International Studies of Management and Organization*, Vol. 30, No. 3, pp7–17.

Branco, M. C. and Delgado, C. (2012). "Business, social responsibility, and corruption," *Journal of Public Affairs*, Vol. 12, No. 4, pp357–365.

Burns, T. and Stalker, G. M. (1961). *The Management of Innovation*. Tavistock, London.

Burritt, R. L. and Schaltegger, S. (2010). "Sustainability accounting and reporting: Fad or trend?," *Accounting, Auditing & Accountability Journal*, Vol. 23, No. 7, pp829–846.

Buysse, K. and Verbeke, A. (2003). "Proactive environmental strategies: A stakeholder management perspective," *Strategic Management Journal*, Vol. 24, No. 5, pp453–470.

Carbon Disclosure Project USA (2009). *Carbon Disclosure Project Leadership Indexes*, New York, Mimeo.

Carnevale, C., Mazzuca, M. and Venturini, S. (2012). "Corporate social reporting in European banks: The effects on a firm's market value," *Corporate Social Responsibility & Environmental Management*, Vol. 19, No. 3, pp159–177.

Carroll, G. R. (1984). "Organizational ecology," *Annual Review of Sociology*, Vol. 10, pp71–93.

CERES (Coalition for Environmentally Responsible Economies) (2014). "SEC climate guidance & S&P 500 reporting: 2010 to 2013," www.ceres.org/resources/reports/cool-response-the-sec-corporate-climate-change-reporting (accessed February 13, 2015).

Cheng, Y.-S., Liu, Y.-P. and Chien, C.-Y. (2009). "The association between auditor quality and human capital," *Managerial Auditing Journal*, Vol. 24, No. 6, pp523–541.

Cho, S., Lee, C. and Park, C. K. (2012). "Measuring corporate social responsibility," *The CPA Journal*, Vol. 82, No. 6, pp54–60.

Clark, T. S. and Allen, D. S. (2012). "Shareholder value from sustainability leadership: Comparing valuation ratios within industry groups," *International Research Journal of Finance & Economics*, Issue 89, April, pp108–117.

Colbert, B. A. and Kurucz, E. C. (2007). "Three conceptions of triple bottom line business sustainability and the role for HRM," *Human Resources Planning*, Vol. 30, No. 1, pp21–29.

Contrafatto, M. and Burns, J. (2013). "Social and environmental accounting, organizational change and management accounting: A processual view," *Management Accounting Research*, Vol. 24, No. 4, pp349–365.

Creel, T. S. (2010). "Environmental reporting practices of the largest U.S. companies," *Management Accounting Quarterly*, Vol. 12, No. 1, pp13–19.

da Rosa, F. S., Ensslin, S. R., Ensslin, L. and Lunkes, R. J. (2012). "Environmental disclosure management: A constructionist case," *Management Decision*, Vol. 50, No. 6, pp1117–1136.

Dent, J. (1991). "Accounting and organizational cultures: A field study of the emergence of a new organizational reality," *Accounting, Organizations and Society*, Vol. 16, No. 8, pp705–732.

Dirsmith, W. M. and McAllister, J. P. (1982). "The organic vs. mechanistic audit," *Journal of Accounting, Auditing and Finance*, Vol. 5, No. 3, pp214–228.

Dutta, S. (2012). "Triple bottom line reporting: An Indian perspective," *International Journal of Contemporary Research in Business*, Vol. 3, No. 12, pp652–659.

Eisenhardt, K. M. and Bourgeois III, L. J. (1988). "Politics of strategic decision making in high-velocity environments: Toward a midrange theory," *Academy of Management Journal*, Vol. 31, No. 4, pp737–770.

EPA (Environmental Protection Agency) (2010). *Sustainable Development*, Washington, DC, www.epa.gov/ebtpages/pollsustainabledevelopment.html (accessed January/February, 2015).

Etzioni, A. (1961). *A Comparative Analysis of Complex Organizations: In Power, Involvement, and Their Correlates*. The Free Press, New York.

Eugenio, T., Lourenco, I. C. and Morais, A. I. (2010). "Recent developments in social and environmental accounting research," *Social Responsibility Journal*, Vol. 6, No. 2, pp286–305.

Evans, A. M. and Campos, A. (2009). "Open government initiatives: Realizing principles of citizen participation," Lyndon Baines Johnson School of Public Affairs.

Ezzamel, M. and Willmott, H. (1998). "Accounting for teamwork: A critical study of group-based systems of organizational control," *Administrative Science Quarterly*, Vol. 43, No. 2, pp358–396.

Fisher, D. G., Swanson, D. L. and Schmidt, J. J. (2007). "Accounting education lags CPE ethics requirements: Implications for the profession and a call to action," *Accounting Education*, Vol. 16, No. 4, pp345–363.

Freeman, J. (1982). "Organizational life cycles and natural selection processes," *Research in Organizational Behavior*, Vol. 4, pp1–32.

Füssel, L. and Georg, S. (2000). "The institutionalization of environmental concerns: Making the environment perform," *International Studies of Management and Organization*, Vol. 30, No. 3, pp41–58.

Galbraith, J. K. (1967). *The New Industrial State*. Houghton-Mifflin, Boston, MA.

Gary, C. M., Fagerström, A. and Hassel, L. G. (2011). "Accounting for sustainability: What next? A research agenda," *Annals of the University of Oradea, Economic Science Series*, Supplement, pp97–111.

Giddens, A. (1987). *Social Theory and Modern Sociology*. Polity Press, Cambridge, MA.

Gray, R. (2006). "Social, environmental and sustainability reporting and organizational value creation? Whose value? Whose creation?," *Accounting, Auditing & Accountability Journal*, Vol. 19 No. 6, pp793–819.

GRI (Global Reporting Initiative) (2008). *Sustainability Reporting Guidelines*, www.globalreporting.org/resourcelibrary/GRI-Sustainability-Report-2008-2009.pdf (accessed January/February, 2015).

Guan, J. J. and Noronha, C. (2013). "Corporate social responsibility reporting research in the Chinese academia: A critical review," *Social Responsibility Journal*, Vol. 9, No. 1, pp33–55.

Hailey, V. H. and Balogun, J. (2002). "Devising context sensitive approaches to change: The example of Glaxo Wellcome," *Long Range Planning*, Vol. 35, No. 1, pp153–178.

Hannan, M. T. and Freeman, J. (1984). "Structural inertia and organizational change," *American Sociological Review*, Vol. 49, No. 2, pp149–164.

Hedberg, C.-J. and von Malmborg, F. (2003). "The global reporting initiative and corporate sustainability reporting in Swedish companies," *Corporate Social-Responsibility and Environmental Management*, Vol. 10, No. 3, pp153–164.

Hespenheide, E., Pavlovsky, K. and McElroy, M. (2010). "Accounting for sustainability performance," *Financial Executive*, Vol. 26, No. 2, pp52–58.

Holton, I., Glass, J. and Price, A. D. F. (2010). "Managing for sustainability: Findings from four company case studies in the UK precast concrete industry," *Journal of Cleaner Production*, Vol. 18, No. 2, pp152–160.

Hopwood, A. G., Unerman, J. and Fries, J. (eds) (2010). *Accounting for Sustainability*. Earthscan, London.

Hussey, D. M., Kirsop, P. L. and Meissen, R. E. (2001). "Global reporting initiative guidelines: An evaluation of sustainable development metrics for industry," *Environmental Quality Management*, Vol. 11, No. 1, pp1–20.

ISO (International Organization for Standardization) (2008). *ISO International Standards: Practical Tools for Addressing Climate Change*, www.iso.org/iso/climatechange_2008.pdf (accessed February 15, 2015).

Ivan, O. R. (2009). "Sustainability in accounting-basis: A conceptual framework," *Annales Universitatis Apulensis Series Oeconomica*, Vol. 11, No. 1, pp106–116.

Iyer, V. and Lulseged, A. (2013). "Does family status impact US firms' sustainability reporting?," *Sustainability Accounting, Management and Policy Journal*, Vol. 4, No. 2, pp163–189.

Jalaludin, D., Sulaiman, M. and Ahmad, N. N. N. (2011). "Understanding environmental management accounting (EMA) adoption: A new institutional sociology perspective," *Social Responsibility Journal*, Vol. 7, No. 4, pp540–557.

Jamali, D. (2005). "Changing management paradigms: Implications for educational institutions," *The Journal of Management Development*, Vol. 24, No. 2, pp104–115.

Jones III, A. and Jonas, G. A. (2011). "Corporate social responsibility reporting: The growing need for input from the accounting profession," *The CPA Journal*, Vol. 81, No. 2, pp65–71.

Joseph, G. (2012). "Ambiguous but tethered: An accounting basis for sustainability reporting," *Critical Perspectives on Accounting*, Vol. 23, No. 2, pp93–106.

Joshi, S. and Krishnan, R. (2010). "Sustainability accounting systems with management decision focus," *Cost Management*, Vol. 24, No. 6, pp20–30.

Kabanoff, B. (1991). "Equity, equality, power, and conflict," *Academy of Management Review*, Vol. 16, No. 2, pp416–441.

Kaeokla, P. and Jaikengkit, A. (2013). "Exploring the corporate social responsibility reporting: A case study in Thai listed companies," *African Journal of Business Management*, Vol. 7, No. 28, pp2794–2800.

Kauffmann, C. and Less, C. T. (2010). *Transition to a Low-Carbon Economy: Public Goals and Corporate Practices*, OECD, www.oecd.org/corporate/mne/45513642.pdf (accessed January/February 2015).

Kober, R., Ng, J. and Paul, B. J. (2007). "The interrelationships between management control mechanisms and strategy," *Management Accounting Research*, Vol. 18, No. 4, pp425–452.

Kolk, A., Levy, D. and Pinkse, J. (2008). "Corporate response to an emerging climate regime: The institutionalization and commensuration of carbon disclosure," *European Accounting Review*, Vol. 17, No. 4, pp719–745.

Kotonen, U. (2009). "Formal corporate social responsibility reporting in Finnish listed companies," *Journal of Applied Accounting Research*, Vol. 10, No. 3, pp176–207.

Lant, T. K. and Mezias, S. J. (1992). "An organizational learning model of convergence and reorientation," *Organizational Science*, Vol. 31, No. 1, pp47–71.

Larsen, S. V., Kornov, L. and Drissoll, P. (2013). "Avoiding climate change uncertainties in strategic environmental assessment," *Environmental Impact Assessment*, Vol. 43, November, pp144–180.

Lawrenson, D. M. (1992). "Britain's railways: The predominance of engineering over accountancy during the inter-war period," *Critical Perspectives on Accounting*, Vol. 3, No. 1, pp45–60.

Lee, B. and Humphrey, C. (2006). "More than a numbers game: Qualitative research in accounting," *Management Decision*, Vol. 44, No. 2, pp180–197.

Lee, J. and Pati, N. (2012). "New insights on the operational links between corporate sustainability and firm performance in service industries," *International Journal of Business Insights & Transformation*, Vol. 4, No. 3, pp80–93.

Lopez, M. V., Garcia, A. and Rodriguez, L. (2007). "Sustainable development and corporate performance: A study based on the Dow Jones Sustainability Index," *Journal of Business Ethics*, Vol. 75, No. 3, pp285–300.

Lusher, A. L. (2012). "What is the accounting profession's role in accountability of economic, social, and environmental issues?," *International Journal of Business and Social Science*, Vol. 3, No. 15, pp14–19.

Mark, N. (1998). "Beyond individual differences: Social differentiation from first principles," *American Sociological Review*, Vol. 63, No. 3, pp309–330.

Mezias, S. J. and Glynn, M. A. (1993). "The three faces of corporate renewal: Institution, revolution, and evolution," *Strategic Management Journal*, Vol. 14, No. 2, pp77–101.

Misiewicz, K. M. (2007). "The normative impact of CPA firms, professional organization and state boards on accounting ethics education," *Journal of Business Ethics*, Vol. 70, No. 1, pp15–21.

Mitchell, M., Curtis, A. and Davidson, P. (2012). "Can triple bottom line reporting become a cycle for 'double loop' learning and radical change?," *Accounting, Auditing & Accountability Journal*, Vol. 25, No. 6, pp1048–1068.

Morgan, G. (1986). *Images of Organization*. Sage Publications. Beverly Hills, CA.

Morgan Stanley (2014). *Morgan Stanley Installs Bloom Energy Fuel Cells at Purchase, NY Facility*, www.morganstanley.com/about-us-articles/d339e54b-370a-4834-a5cf-bfa6a80411db.html (accessed February 10, 2015).

Morgan Stanley (2015a). *Investing in Global Sustainability Themes – Executive Summary*, www.morganstanley.com/sustainableinvesting/pdf/Thematics_Aug14_Summary.pdf (accessed February 10, 2015).

Morgan Stanley (2015b). *Carbon Capture and Storage: A Realistic Solution? – Executive Summary*, www.morganstanley.com/sustainableinvesting/pdf/Carbon_Capture_Storage_Exec_Summary.pdf (accessed February 10, 2015).

Morhardt, J. E. (2010). "Corporate social responsibility and sustainability reporting on the internet," *Business Strategy and the Environment*, Vol. 19, No. 7, pp436–452.

Noronha, C., Tou, S., Cynthia, M. I. and Guan, J. J. (2012). "Corporate social responsibility reporting in China: An overview and comparison with major trends," *Corporate Social Responsibility and Environmental Management*, Vol. 20, No. 1, pp29–42.

O'Dwyer, B., Owen, D. and Unerman, J. (2011). "Seeking legitimacy for new assurance forms: The case of assurance on sustainability reporting," *Accounting, Organizations and Society*, Vol. 36, No. 1, pp31–52.

OECD (Organisation for Economic Co-operation and Development) (2010). OECD Publications on sustainable development. OECD Publications Service, Paris, www.oecd.org/home/0,2987,en_2649_201185_1_1_1_1_1,00.html (accessed January/February, 2015).

Ozsomer, A., Calantone, R. J. and Benedetto, A. D. (1997). "What makes forms more innovative? A look at organizational and environmental factors," *Journal of Business and Industrial Marketing*, Vol. 12, No. 6, pp400–416.

Parker, L. D. (2005). "Social and environmental accountability research: A view from the commentary box," *Accounting, Auditing & Accountability Journal*, Vol. 18, No. 6, pp842–860.

Perrow, C. (1986). *Complex Organizations*, 3rd edition. Random House, New York.

Pew Center (2011). *Pew Center on Climate Change Greenhouse Gas Reporting and Registries*, Pew Center on Climate Change, Arlington, VA, Mimeo, February 10.

Pfeffer, J. (1985). "Organizational demography: Implications for management," *California Management Review*, Vol. 28, Fall, pp67–81.

PricewaterhouseCoopers (2009–2015). *Global Sustainability and Climate Change*, www.pwc.com/gx/en/sustainability/services/monitoring-and-reporting.jhtml (accessed February 3, 2015).

PricewaterhouseCoopers (2010a). *A Framework for Greenhouse Reporting*, PricewaterhouseCoopers, New York, Mimeo, September 20.

PricewaterhouseCoopers (2010b). *Carbon Reporting*, www.pwc.co.uk/assets/pdf/carbon-reporting-may-09.pdf (accessed February 3, 2015).

Reverte, C. (2012). "The impact of better corporate social responsibility disclosure on the cost of equity capital," *Corporate Social Responsibility and Environmental Management*, Vol. 19, No. 5, pp253–272.

Ribeiro, J. A. and Scapens, R. W. (2006). "Institutional theories in management accounting change: Contributions, issues and paths for development," *Qualitative Research in Accounting and Management*, Vol. 3, No. 2, pp94–111.

Saravanamuthu, K. (2004). "What is measured counts: Harmonized corporate reporting and sustainable economic development," *Critical Perspectives on Accounting*, Vol. 15, No. 3, pp295–302.

SASB (Sustainability Accounting Standards Board) (2015). *Accounting for a Sustainable Future*, www.sasb.org (accessed January/February 2015).

Schaltegger, S. and Csutora, M. (2012). "Carbon accounting for sustainability and management: Status quo and challenges," *Journal of Cleaner Production*, 36, November, pp1–16.

Schulz, M. (1998). "Limits to bureaucratic growth: The density dependence of organizational rule births," *Administrative Science Quarterly*, Vol. 43, No. 4, pp845–876.

SEC (U.S. Securities and Exchange Commission) (2010). *SEC Issues Interpretive Guidance on Disclosure Related to Business or Legal Developments Regarding Climate Change*, U.S. Securities and Exchange Commission, Washington, DC, Press Release, January 27.

Sharma, S. and Henriques, I. (2005). "Stakeholder influences on sustainability practices in the Canadian forest products industry," *Strategic Management Journal*, Vol. 26, No. 2, pp159–180.

Siew, R. Y. I., Balatbat, M. C. A. and Carmichael, D. G. (2013). "The relationship between sustainability practices and financial performance of construction companies," *Smart and Sustainable Built Environment*, Vol. 2, No. 1, pp6–27.

Sisaye, S. (2011). "Ecological systems approaches to sustainability and organizational development: Emerging trends in environmental and social accounting reporting systems," *The Leadership & Organization Development Journal*, Vol. 32, No. 4, pp379–396.

Sisaye, S. and Birnberg, J. G. (2010a). "Organizational development and transformational learning approaches in process innovations: A review of the implications to the management accounting literature," *Review of Accounting and Finance*, Vol. 9, No. 4, pp337–362.

Sisaye, S. and Birnberg, J. G. (2010b). "Extent and scope dimensions of diffusion and adoption of process innovations in management accounting systems," *International Journal of Accounting and Information Management*, Vol. 18, No. 2, pp118–139.

Sisaye, S. and Birnberg, J. G. (2012). *An Organizational Learning Approach to Process Innovations: The Extent and Scope Dimensions of Adoption and Diffusion in Management Accounting Systems*, Studies in Managerial and Financial Accounting Series, Vol. 24, Emerald Publications, U.K.

Sisaye, S. and Birnberg, J. G. (2014). "Sociological approaches of organizational learning: Applications to process innovations of management accounting systems," *Advances in Management Accounting*, Vol. 23, pp1–43.

Sobhani, F. A., Amran, A. and Zainuddin, Y. (2012). "Sustainability disclosure in annual reports and websites: A study of the banking industry in Bangladesh," *Journal of Cleaner Productions*, Vol. 23, No. 1, pp75–85.

Teece, D. J. (1996). "Firm organization, industrial structure, and technological innovation," *Journal of Economic Behavior and Organization*, Vol. 31, No. 2, pp193–224.

Treffers, D. J., Faaj, A. P. C., Spakman, J. and Seebregts, A. (2005). "Exploring the possibilities for setting up sustainable energy systems for the long term: Two visions for the Dutch energy system in 2050," *Energy Policy*, Vol. 33, No. 13, pp1723–1743.

Turcsanyi, J. and Sisaye, S. (2013). "Corporate social responsibility and its link to financial performance: Application to Johnson & Johnson, a pharmaceutical company," *World Journal of Science, Technology, and Sustainable Development*, Vol. 10, No. 1, pp4–18.

Ussahawanitchakit, P. (2011). "Accounting sustainability, business ethics and corporate image: Evidence from listed firms in Thailand," *Journal of International Business and Economics*, Vol. 11, No. 4, pp1–10.

Vogel, D. (1987). "The new political science of corporate power," *The Public Interest*, Vol. 20, Spring, pp63–79.

Walker, B., Holling, C. S., Carpenter, S. R. and Kinzig, A. (2004). "Resilience, adaptability and transformability in social-ecological systems," *Ecology and Society*, Vol. 9, No. 2, 5, www.ecologyandsociety.org/vol9/iss2/art5 (accessed January/February 2015).

WBCSD (World Business Council for Sustainable Development) (2000). *Corporate Social Responsibility: Making Good Business Sense*. WBCSD, Geneva.

WCED (World Commission on Environment and Development) (1987). *Our Common Future*, The Brundtland Report. World Commission on Environment and Development (WCED) and Oxford University Press, New York.

Whitmeyer, J. M. (1994). "Why actor models are integral to structural analysis," *Sociological Theory*, Vol. 12, No. 2, pp153–165.

World Bank (International Bank for Reconstruction and Development) (2011). "Black carbon and climate change: Considerations for international development agencies," Prepared by Michael Levitsky, https://openknowledge.worldbank.org/bitstream/handle/10986/18317/673220NWP0EDP000Box367866B00PUBLIC0.pdf?sequence=1 (accessed February 13, 2015).

World Bank (2014). "Climate change and global warming: The role of the international community," Background Paper for WDR 2014 on Managing Risk for Development, prepared by Koko Warner, https://openknowledge.worldbank.org/bitstream/handle/10986/16366/WDR14_bp_Climate_Change_and_Global_Warming_Warner.pdf?sequence=1 (accessed February 13, 2015).

WRI (World Resources Institute) (2014). *Mitigation Goals Standard: An Accounting and Reporting Standard for National and Subnational Greenhouse Gas Reduction Goals*, www.ghgprotocol.org/files/ghgp/Mitigation%20Goals%20Standard%20-%20Executive%20Summary.pdf (accessed February 13, 2015).

WRI and WBCSD (World Resource Institute and World Business Council for Sustainable Development) (2004). *A Corporate Accounting and Reporting Standard*, revised edition, http://pdf.wri.org/ghg_protocol_2004.pdf (accessed February 13, 2015).

7 Contributions of the ecological approach to the integration of sustainability in accounting education and practice

The ecological approach views the integration of sustainability within the accounting curriculum as following the evolutionary process of organizational development. This approach suggests that organization systems undergo an evolutionary process of change and development. In organizational ecology and ecological anthropology, evolutionary changes are studied within the broader context of the environment – community, nation, ecosystem and organizational systems.

Accordingly, sustainability is an ecological resources management subject that can be best addressed from the perspective of organizational sociology and ecological anthropology. Sociology and anthropology have been concerned with the subject of sustainability and have developed ecological theories and methods that can be extended to examine the integration of sustainability into the accounting and reporting curriculum.

The Brundtland Report (WCED, 1987) embraced sustainability to address economic development issues related to natural resources management, agricultural production, food supply, environmental protection and global climatic changes and to address ecological changes related to drought, floods and other natural disasters. The social science disciplines, particularly anthropology, sociology and economics, have been concerned with sustainability. Sub-fields in ecology and evolution have developed to facilitate the study of sustainable development.

Accordingly, sustainability education has not only been covered in the social sciences, but also in the environmental, biological and agricultural disciplines. However, in accounting, sustainability education is non-existent, or if it exists, the topics covered are limited to focusing on both the internal and external dimensions of triple bottom line (TBL) reporting and disclosures to stakeholders and managers. Khan (2011) reviewed the sustainability course offerings in accounting in Canada, the United States and the United Kingdom from what was posted on the internet and found out that sustainability coverage is limited. Standalone courses are not commonly offered in accounting programs and most of the courses are elective.

This likely is the case because the subject of sustainability accounting and reporting is an emerging/current phenomenon. Sociological and anthropological approaches are used in this book because the subject of sustainability, conservation and ecological resource management are well established and well researched in these disciplines. Sustainability accounting research, education and practice have benefited from the work being done in these disciplines. Sociological and anthropological approaches have influenced accounting ethics education (Sisaye, 2011). Recently, the integration of sustainability into the accounting curriculum (Sisaye, 2012, 2013) has affected professional accounting education practices.

An overview of sustainability education in the accounting program: integration versus standalone courses

In business administration and accounting, sustainability has received a great deal of attention in the form of research and pedagogical publications. To meet the growing demands of interested organizations, professional accounting associations and practice and not-for-profit organizations (NFPs), most business schools and accounting programs have developed two types of courses – standalone or integrative – to incorporate sustainability into the curriculum (Vann and White, 2004). These approaches have helped them to realign their curriculum to increase coverage of sustainability topics by revising current course offerings at both the undergraduate and graduate levels.

However, the theory and methods in accounting education required for designing and delivering a standalone course in sustainability accounting are not yet entirely developed. For example, Hopwood (2009) suggested that an accounting theory with accompanying measurement techniques for sustainability has not yet been developed. It is, at present, only in its preliminary stage, as the subject of sustainability has focused exclusively on public interest and the corporate governance issues of business. Accordingly, sustainability has been viewed as a subject of corporate social responsibility that is consonant with accounting and business ethics.

Parker (2005) argued that social and environmental accounting falls under the general framework of stakeholder theory. Corporations provide social and environmental disclosures voluntarily in response to the interests/demands of stockholders. The stakeholder theory views profitability goals as requiring a tradeoff between social–environmental and economic objectives (Parker, 2005: 845–846), thereby expanding the scope of the groups to which the corporations perceive an obligation. This approach is nested in legitimacy theory as part of a corporation's role in educating the public about those environmental issues that affect society.

The legitimacy theory is focused on ensuring that the social, political and economic interests of corporations are in balance. Financial accountability then becomes a legitimate duty that requires corporations to provide reports of their business actions so that they can be made accountable and held responsible for utilization of the corporations' *financial* assets. Accordingly, moral and ethical dimensions are incorporated in order to justify financial accountability and legitimacy for the preservation and conservation of *environmental* resources. Companies can selectively prepare reports about their impact upon social and environmental programs such as pollution control and resource and environmental conservation in order to achieve broader market penetration which can sustain their products and services (Lorenz and Lutzkendorf, 2008). In that sense, there is awareness on the part of management that the theory and development of sustainability should be integrated within accounting education.

Ecologically, sustainability education can be best addressed through systemic/holistic integration into the accounting and business curriculum rather than in standalone courses. However, the process of sustainability integration is currently at the earliest stage of the ecological evolutionary process of educational development. Accordingly, the integration of sustainability into the accounting curriculum is likely to be subject to evolutionary changes in natural and resources management, the environment and competitive forces, as well as other external factors that shape the ecological processes of organizational change and development and accounting education.

From the standpoint of accounting education, the integration of sustainability into all facets of the accounting curriculum (i.e., financial, managerial and auditing courses) is argued to be an appropriate and viable format that would enable students to have the overall picture of the subject matter and its implications for organizational resource allocation decisions. The application of both sociological and anthropological approaches in accounting ethics education (Sisaye, 2011) suggests that the preferred approach to teach sustainability calls for the integration of sustainability into accounting education and professional practices (Sisaye, 2012, 2013).

The integration of sustainability within accounting education

Emerging trends

Sustainability has emerged as an important subject area of research and teaching in the business education curriculum. In accounting, there is a growing interest in sustainability. Recently, books and articles have appeared which discuss sustainability accounting and reporting (e.g., Aras and Crowther, 2008; Bowden et al., 2010; Epstein, 2008, 2010; Gray, 2006; Hopwood and Unerman, 2010; Hopwood et al., 2010; Unerman et al., 2007). A number of schools have developed standalone courses in sustainability accounting (Nicholas, 2010; Parisi, 2010; Senge, 2010; UNISA, 2010), while others have integrated sustainability into existing courses in accounting ethics or corporate social responsibility (see Becker Professional Education, 2010; University of South Florida, 2010; Wolcott, 2010).

Rationales

The argument in favor of integration of sustainability within the accounting curriculum in financial, managerial and auditing courses is that it is assumed that it has the potential to enable students to understand the overall picture of the business enterprise and implications in organizational resource allocation decisions. Recent developments in business and governmental policies towards environmental issues and sustainability have increased the need for a holistic view of business that calls for the integration of sustainability into accounting education – that is, into the curriculum rather than developing standalone courses. These concerns go beyond the public and/or stakeholder approach of business ethics, addressing the ecological, sociological and anthropological dimensions of business performance in societies and communities.

Gray (2013) applied the interpretive-critical framework and noted the difficulty of teaching sustainability in accounting conceptually and practically because the literature in finance and accounting is theoretically in conflict with sustainability. This criticism alludes to the current limitations in developing a single report that integrates financial, environmental and social data/measures. Nevertheless, there is a substantial literature in both sociology and anthropology that can be applied to frame the development of sustainability education in accounting. Both sociological and anthropological approaches have the potential to study the relationship between ecology, sustainability reporting and accounting education, which advances the integration of sustainability into accounting education and professional practices.

Integration requires linking accounting to the social and ecological resource contexts where sustainability evolved. In accounting, there is a movement towards the integration of topics that cover social, environmental and resource issues (Khan, 2011). Kolodinsky et al. (2010) reviewed four ethical attitudes – idealism, relativism, spirituality and materialistic behavior – to determine the extent to which they have influenced ethical education and students, attitudes towards corporate social responsibility (CSR). They associated ethical idealism as having positive influence on students' CSR attitudes because idealism promoted moral behavior that protects society and environment. On the other hand, relativism as a principle is when one rejects universalistic principles and tends to apply ethics in contextual situations (consequences) that raise moral dilemmas of ethical behavior, where the focus is on the most satisfying outcome from a given situation. This behavior does not, in general, support CSR activities. The third principle, spirituality, where there is a belief in a purpose or a divine power, may shape ethical behavior because of the interconnectedness of the individual with a higher spiritual order. This may positively influence subjects' attitudes towards CSR. The fourth attitude, materialistic behavior, may shape attitudes towards extrinsic values that do not support CSR or responsiveness to social and environmental issues. They concluded that, of these four principles, only idealism influenced CSR attitudes for those students who exhibited a high ethics of caring behavior (Kolodinsky et al., 2010: 170–172). They advocated the teaching of ethics to foster CSR among students.

The teaching of ethics in accounting is commonly associated with upper-level accounting courses, most notably in auditing courses. Fisher et al.'s (2007) study reveals an increasing trend towards ethics integration into accounting course offerings, which they attributed as one of the main underlying causes for a decline in standalone accounting ethics courses.

In reviewing sustainability education in the Western developed nations of the United Kingdom, the United States, Canada and Australia, Tehmina (2013) suggested that sustainability courses are commonly offered in natural and environmental sciences, engineering, social sciences, physical and biological sciences, and management. There are not that many standalone sustainability accounting courses. In the few that are offered, sustainability is covered at a limited scale as it relates to external reporting. The implication from this study is that accounting can benefit from work in the social, environmental, biological and physical science disciplines by following their approaches of integrating sustainability into the accounting curriculum. It can adapt sustainability content coverages in the allied disciplines of business, economics and management, advising on how best to integrate sustainability throughout the accounting courses at both graduate and undergraduate levels.

Business school and accounting administrators and accrediting agencies call for the integration of the social science disciplinary approaches of sustainability and ethics in business and accounting education

Sustainability has been a subject of interest in sociology and anthropology for many years because it addresses ecological resources, organizational development, community welfare, economic growth and national geographical boundaries. Accordingly, the integration of sustainability into the accounting curriculum has been influenced by evolutionary changes in natural and resources management, the environment and competitive forces, as well as other external factors that have shaped accounting education; the most notable is ethics, which preceded sustainability education and practice. Within the ecological approach, there is the presupposition that organizational systems undergo an evolutionary process of change and development. Accordingly, organizational sociology and ecological anthropology provide the evolutionary context for the integration of sustainability into financial and managerial accounting and auditing courses. The importance of multidisciplinary approaches, particularly in the social sciences, has long been recognized by business school and accounting administrators, the accounting professional community, and business school and accounting program accrediting institutions.

The movement towards integration has been spearheaded by the Association to Advance Collegiate Schools of Business (AACSB International), the organization responsible for accrediting business school and accounting programs. AACSB is in favor of integrating topics related to corporate governance, ethics and social responsibility within the business curriculum (Sisaye, 2011). Following the AACSB International guidelines, business school deans and accounting program administrators have advocated the implementation of integration as the best approach to any overhaul of the business curriculum. They have called for the integration of sustainability, ethics and social responsibility into functional business courses, including accounting, to provide students with an overall picture of the economy, polity and society that affect business organizations' resource allocation decisions and competitive behavior. Resource constraints, staffing shortages and limited availability of faculty expertise in the relevant subject areas, coupled with changes in the business environment, have supported integration as the best approach for incorporating current topics such as ethics and sustainability into the business and accounting curriculum.

In a *Wall Street Journal* (July 7, 2011) interview, Dean R. Glenn Hubbard of Columbia University Business School pointed out that the recent problems of the financial crisis could be attributed to "a failure by leaders to successfully see the big picture, focusing instead on their area of expertise." Accordingly, students and corporate leaders are not able to make the connections required to understand the issues. He suggested instead an emphasis in business courses on providing students with "a broader education in order to thwart an economic meltdown." He indicated that Columbia University Business School has emphasized the importance of integration by "deliberately weaving topics such as decision making and ethics into classes across all disciplines" (pB6). Dean Hubbard noted that students will not pay attention to issues of ethics and social responsibility unless these topics are integrated within existing finance and accounting courses. There is a tendency to marginalize standalone ethics.

Hopwood (2009), who chaired the Prince of Wales Accounting for Sustainability Forum, endorsed an integrated holistic approach for sustainability reporting, one that relates environmental and sustainability information to account for their consequences and their presentation in a "connected reporting framework" to report "the economic costs and benefits of environmental considerations" and to make sustainability a "more mainstream part of business," thus making the management of environmental issues "an increasing material factor in many sectors of the economy in the years to come" (p141; see also Hopwood and Unerman, 2010; Hopwood et al., 2010). Hopwood (2009) placed a sustainability agenda in an organizational life cycle (OLC) that has the potential to change corporate actions and policies to develop the "connected reporting system" (p141). Hopwood's suggestion underscores the importance of integration of sustainability into all aspects of corporate economic, social and environmental performances.

Following the recommendations of AACSB International, Dean Hubbard (2011) and Hopwood (2009), there has been an increasing trend towards the integration of the social and behavioral approaches of sustainability into business and accounting courses. These recent developments in sustainability management and reporting have been influenced largely by the ecological conceptual framework derived from sociology and anthropology. Given the co-evolution history of sustainability, ecological approaches suggest that external environmental conditions have shaped the integration of sustainability materials within the accounting curriculum. It is within the ecological context of external environmental factors that the integration of sustainability into accounting education is discussed.

Effects of external environmental factors on accounting ethics education: the background to sustainability education

The accounting and auditing education environment has significantly changed since the mid-1980s. The stock market crash, dissolution of savings and loans institutions, increases in business bankruptcies and liability suits against public accounting firms have all affected accounting and auditing education. The financial scandals at Enron, Arthur Andersen and WorldCom during the 2000s significantly increased governmental and public inquiries into whether or not accountants and auditors participate in covering up these scandals.

Gaa and Thorne (2004) attributed these financial crises to "the dominance of individual choice and behavior in ethics research" (p2). They attributed the lack of accountants' efforts to examine their decisions as being related to questions of character and value, as well as their effect on institutional well-being and economic impacts upon the welfare of their employees, investors and the local communities in which they operated. For example, Arthur Andersen's failure to audit the financial performance of Enron properly has been attributed to neglect of professional character and moral value/responsibilities that have been associated with the independence of the accounting profession.

The provision of tax and consulting services by accounting firms

Wyatt (2004) detailed the development of consulting services at Arthur Andersen from the 1960s to the early 2000s. He noted that, in the 1960s, "accounting firms 'provided clients with services' for improving their internal controls, their efficiency of operations, and even their business strategies" (p47). These services purported to improve auditing services provided by "audit personnel and were not the result of separate service engagements undertaken by non-auditing trained personnel" (Wyatt, 2004: 47). However, over time, during the 1980s and 1990s, these services evolved into consulting services, with the hiring of non-accounting graduates, particularly those with information system backgrounds, to integrate accounting and computer system services. This resulted in a disproportionate increase in consulting managers, who advanced in the hierarchy to become partners involved in policy decisions and in the strategic decisions of accounting firm policies (see also Zeff, 2003).

The mix of consulting and auditing business in accounting firms brought the potential for creating a conflict of interests between consulting and accounting personnel in the performance of auditing functions. Wyatt (2004) indicated that when the growth in consulting at Arthur Andersen and other certified public accountant (CPA) firms outpaced that of auditing and tax services, accounting firms hired more managers and personnel from outside who became partners. These managers did not have the background or the experience to "appreciate the importance of professionalism and ethical behavior in the practice of accounting" (p48). These conflicting services between auditing and consulting shaped the internal culture of independence of auditors in their opinions of clients' financial statements to the extent of accepting statements that "accelerate revenue recognition and to delay expense recognition," although these exceptions were not within the actual provisions or existing accounting standards (p50). He noted that the increased infusion of consulting personnel modified auditor–client relationships in such a way that auditors focused on keeping their clients rather than on losing them by applying strict accounting standards. They were also reluctant to question clients' financial statements (Zeff, 2003: 271).

Zeff (2003) suggested that auditing firms pursued their unrestrained commercial interests at the expense of "conservatism," "adherence to basic accounting principles," and "independence" (pp267–268). He named Arthur Andersen as the leading accounting firm in the consulting business generating the highest consulting fees in the 1990s, which averaged to over 40 percent of total gross revenue at that time. By 2000, that figure reached over 50 percent. The auditing firms became "full service business advisory firms," and non-CPAs were well represented in the top management of these firms (Zeff, 2003: 269–270; see also Wyatt, 2004: 46–52). These consulting services became profitable businesses. The issue was not only "auditors' lack of independence from their clients" (Zeff, 2003: 280), but also some of them were lobbying the Financial Accounting Standards Board (FASB) "on special technical issues" on behalf of their clients' interests (Wyatt, 2004: 52). Both Wyatt (2004) and Zeff (2003) questioned whether these conflicting behaviors eroded auditors' professional autonomy and independent judgment that the public was accustomed to and expected from accounting firms.

For example, because of the growing and profitable auditing and consulting services that it enjoyed with Enron, Arthur Andersen was reluctant to cooperate with governmental investigators in providing documents and testimonies against Enron, which eventually resulted in the collapse of both Enron and Arthur Andersen (Communale et al., 2006). In sum, these scandals and the collapse of Arthur Andersen, which reduced the number of big auditing firms from five to four, and of Enron, had significant economic impacts upon their employees, investors and the communities in which they operated.

The call for the integration of ethics and sustainability into accounting education

The outcomes of these financial scandals generated increased interest in accounting ethics instruction in higher education. It should be noted that ethics is a sustainability issue that is incorporated into CSR. It became apparent to accounting educators that ethics education should be incorporated into the curriculum for training students as well as accounting and auditing professionals in order to make them aware of the moral and social issues arising in an organization's decision-making processes (Waddock, 2005). Accordingly, ethics and social responsibility are now incorporated into the auditing curriculum. More recently, sustainability management courses expanded their ethics coverage to include environmental and ecological issues along with the economic indicators of performance as part of the overall business strategic planning processes.

The underlying rationale in formal accounting ethics education in the classroom is "based on the premise that moral development can be enhanced through the educational process" (Huss and Patterson, 1993: 235). Ethics increases the moral depth, cognitive development and analytical and ethical reasoning of students (Ponemon and Glazer, 1990). It allows higher-order thinking, objective reasoning and questioning of ethical issues and dilemmas (Shenkir, 1990). In general, ethics research in this area has focused on the ethical decision-making process of auditors as well as on the outcome of these decisions (Gaa and Thorne, 2004). Formal education thus provides the framework for addressing the questions of moral obligations and societal responsibilities. However, accounting and auditing policies affect public policy decisions with broader financial, economic and societal implications. Thus, accounting choices are contingent upon environmental and ecological factors which involve moral choices affecting organizations and society.

In accounting ethics education, there is currently an emphasis on the sustainability of ecological and natural resources management. This is prompted by the realization that future prospects for growth and survival of all levels of species are linked to current ecological and sustainability efforts to maintain reasonable living standards by protecting the environment. These issues are rich and complex, but they also have a long-term impact upon society and the world community at large (Parker, 2005: 856–857). Ecological issues call for collaborative research with other disciplines in order to make them relevant in addressing broader social and environmental issues pertinent to sustainability accounting and reporting (Adams and Larrinaga-González, 2007). The culmination of ecological and environmental issues in sustainability accounting and their subsequent impact on local, regional, national and global/international communities have broadened the scope of ethics research beyond corporate normative practices. Ecological and environmental accounting has broadened the functional focus of accounting ethics education beyond auditors' professional codes of conduct and corporate governance to incorporate ecological and environmental issues into ethics education.

Ecological and environmental approaches to accounting ethics education: implications for sustainability educational theory and practice

Many universities have incorporated sustainability as mechanisms for promoting changes in programs through the coordination of resources, environmental management, sustainable resources management, energy usage and garbage and recycling programs. They are leading in sustainability efforts to transform their administrative structures and academic programs (Ferrer-Balas et al., 2008). Ryu and Brody (2006) reported that university graduate programs and education in sustainable development have positively affected the sustainability and ethical behavior of students in ecological and land preservation, waste management and mode of transportation. They have augmented courses on ethics in accounting and auditing. They have altered student and consumer behaviors with regard to consumption of goods and services to favor companies with environmental management programs. These programs have improved universities' environmental and natural resources management performances consistent with business and community interests. Sustainability practices are used to support water management and energy and solid waste reduction, as well as the management of facilities and hazardous materials (Walton and Gales, 2005).

Ecological (land) ethics' linkage to sustainability

Ecological ethics has broader implications for environmental and resources management. Environmental ethics, as a subset of ecological ethics, focuses on human relationships with nature and the utilization and conservation of natural resources (Rozzi, 1999: 118). Sustainable management, the use of natural resources and maintaining the viability of the Earth's ecosystems are goals that are incorporated within the products and services of organizations for market planning and growth (Lorenz and Lutzkendorf, 2008). Accordingly, sustainable development can be referred as a subset of ecological ethics.

Anderson-Wilk (2008) related sustainability efforts in environmental conservation to land ethics. Land stewardship has emerged as an ecological conscience for environmental conservation, land management, the sustainability of ecosystems for future use of production, and resources to preserve land health and protect biodiversity. Sustainable health education has been implemented by many universities to integrate sustainability concerns across the curriculum, particularly in public health, to educate students about a wide range of ecological issues addressing environmental preservation and maintaining the well-being of human populations (Bajracharya, 2009). The integration of sustainability in health education has broadened the scope of health management to encompass environmental and ecological resources for the sustenance of health and wellness in communities with local, national and international boundaries. The ecological community has thus formed the core of land health ethics, focusing on biological systems as part of the environmental community (Curry, 2007). When land ethics is collectively viewed with regard to humans and other animals that live on land, the ecological interdependence of the entire community is recognized. Ethics education in financial and managerial accounting and auditing can emulate the manner in which the concept of land and environmental ethics has been incorporated into health education.

Ecological ethics thus goes beyond the spatial and temporal extension of environmental ethics to the human community. Thiele (1999) viewed interdependence as both genetic and cultural, whereas ecological ethics and morality "require viewing others along with the self as integrated parts of the larger whole. Ethics is largely about the obligations we have to sustain the community that sustain us" (p30). The moral obligation of ethics is rooted in religious and humanitarian issues where the common good (general welfare) of public life (goods) becomes intrinsically valuable for individual actions and relationships to fulfill community and society well-being (Cowdin, 2008).

Environmental ethics, costs and transactions

Evanoff (2005) outlined three objectives for environmental ethics that are pertinent to accounting ethics and sustainability education. The first issue is related to the transactional approach that focuses on the maximization of resource use to meet humans' material needs. The second aspect deals with maintaining ecological autonomy for society and nature whereby individual and societal interests are balanced. The third aspect focuses on promoting ecological sustainability and integrity whereby humans are viewed as a subset of natural and ecological systems. Evanoff redefined environmental sustainability as being based on a "transactional paradigm [that] would encourage human flourishing, social equality, and environmental integrity" (p111). These environmental objectives are inherent in accounting and auditing ethics education that is embedded in sustainability reporting.

The transaction cost approach assumes that human and societal decisions have economic consequences that affect sustainability business; and these transactions transcend economic and ecological objectives. Moreover, there are moral and ethical dimensions that are rooted in institutional arrangements which impact upon ecological transaction management (Beckman and Pies, 2008). Transaction analysis assumes tradeoffs will be made between economic profitability goals and ecologically formulated accounting principles. Accordingly, accounting and auditing ethics education should be restructured to include both normative – profitability and corporate governance – as well as moral dimensions of institutional legitimacy and accountability. Sustainability thus broadens accounting ethics education to include auditor professional codes of conduct as well as environmental, social and economic accounting reporting issues presented in TBL reports. Accounting ethics is now broadly embedded in ecological, environmental and philosophical ethics, where compliance reports of sustainable business environmental and natural resources management have become part of accounting reporting systems.

The background for sustainability in the accounting curriculum

The TBL reporting of environmental, social and economic objectives reflects business sustainable development strategies that are integrated within business organizations' core businesses. Transparency, accountability and sustainability have become indicators of both ethical and economic performances. Accordingly, corporations have expressed interest in the impact that sustainability has upon the well-being of communities where they conduct business.

Sustainability has now become the emerging business discipline that has incorporated environmental and ecological ethics into accounting and auditing education. The sustainability framework relates ecological and economic assumptions in corporate practices and behaviors to develop critical and reflective thinking by applying new and different perspectives from the social and environmental sciences (Onwue and Borsar, 2007; Stubbs and Cocklin, 2008). Accounting and auditing ethics education focusing on sustainability initiatives and reporting would now become part of the business ethics curriculum.

Corporate boards are realizing that sustainable development is an essential part of corporate ethical governance. Accordingly, the number of companies publishing sustainability reports – or those that focus on corporate economic, environmental and social responsibility (TBL reports) – continues to grow. These reports highlight policies and programs that companies have targeted using economic, environmental and social objectives. Sustainability accounting education has been largely limited to the TBL approaches of economic, social and environmental reporting.

Examples of sustainability education in the developed and emerging economies

In emerging economies, the transition from agrarian to industrialized and market economies has brought natural and environmental disasters. There has been concern over environmental degradation such as floods, drought and climatic changes. These countries do not have conservation policies to manage renewable and non-renewable resources. Commercialization of land and water to support industrialization policies has displaced many of the local indigenous populations.

There is the realization that sustainability education is the key for political, social and economic development in developing countries (Koehn and Obamba, 2014). For these countries, sustainable development addresses broader ecological, biological, health, agricultural and conservation and natural resources management (Koehn, 2014). In this context, natural resources management has embedded ecological ethics and land health. This has broader implications for sustainability education because ecology encompasses questions relating to the transactional use of the environment, land and natural resources, as well as the need for conservation and sustainability policies to sustain the well-being of present and future generations. There has been partnership and collaboration between the developing and developed countries to broaden the scope of sustainability education in curriculum development, research and outreach in order to promote change and development (Koehn and Uitto, 2014). While there has been substantial progress in the social and biological sciences, the pace of progress for sustainability education in the business and accounting disciplines has been limited. Nevertheless, ethical issues in accounting have recently been incorporated within ecological and environmental management, sustainability reporting and the ethical use of natural resources. However, the integration of ecological and environmental issues into sustainability accounting education is limited and varies, depending upon the economic development of the country: emerging or developed.

Two examples of emerging economies that have incorporated sustainability within accounting education are Malaysia and South Korea. In Malaysia, according to Zulkifli (2011), the focus has centered on the importance of social and environmental accounting (SEA) to teach students sustainability, environmental management and ethical issues. Malaysia is an example of an emerging economy that has several environmental problems resulting from the unplanned and illegal logging of forests, the pollution of rivers, the unintended exploitation of the natural habitats of fisheries, erosion and industrial waste, which has affected the quality of water and air and in general the well-being and standard of living of the local population in the community. These increasing social and environmental problems underscore the importance of SEA education in the accounting and business curriculum (Zulkifli, 2011: 77–82). While there has been an increase in SEA literature, accounting education in Malaysia has not been on a par with other business disciplines. Nevertheless, there is awareness among accounting educators in Malaysia of the importance of SEA education both to teach "social and environmental responsibility" to students and overcome the shortage of qualified accounting professionals at the workplace who are committed to ethics (p82). In this regard, SEA education has increased students' awareness of the social, ethical as well as financial/economic consequences of accounting decisions in Malaysian communities and society.

Zulkifli (2011) suggests that the drawback of the integration of sustainability education into the accounting curriculum can be related to the current state of accounting education in Malaysia, which has focused on technical skills in accounting, with less emphasis on integrating social, religious and cultural values pertinent to the Malaysian culture. The Zulkifli study points out that, if a convergence between sustainability and religion exists, religious studies in Malaysia can be extended to link ethics and sustainability to develop the moral behavior of accounting students (pp64, 82–83).

Tsuji and Tsuji (2011) compared the attitudes of Japanese, Chinese and South Korean students towards financial and CSR reporting. They found that cultural differences accounted for the results of CSR and sustainability information among these three groups of Asian students. They suggested that Korean students showed high awareness of and interest in CSR and sustainability/social information when compared to Chinese and Japanese students. They attributed these differences to the prevalence of Christian education and universities in Korea. This finding corroborates Zulkifli's (2011) study, which noted that religious studies (Muslim doctrines) can help to develop the moral behavior of students in Malaysia. This is comparable to the influence of the teaching of Catholic religious morals to South Korean students, who have demonstrated positive attitude towards CSR and sustainability. This suggests that religious studies have the potential to contribute to the advancement of sustainability accounting education through religion's emphasis on moral behavior and concern for others.

In contrast, in developed economies, sustainability education is broader and covers a wide range of environmental, social and ecological issues compared to those covered in developing economies. For example, Esmond-Kiger (2004) reported the use of articles and press reports of corporate actions and behaviors in developed economies to enhance student ethical awareness and social responsibility. These reports covered a wide range of corporate activities on social and environmental issues. The study highlighted the post-Enron period in which ethical awareness about the broader environmental issues facing societies and communities at large was raised with students. The Sarbanes-Oxley Act of 2002 formalized these concerns and broadened the scope of accounting reports to include sustainability programs. These concerns have been integrated by many organizations within their strategic planning processes.

Therefore, it can be argued that there are ethical obligations for both corporations and society at large to use natural resources responsibly with a focus on sustainability for future generations (Curry, 2007; Rozzi, 1999). It is, therefore, appropriate in accounting contexts to support ecological concerns that can develop individual convocation and responsibility to sustain ecological ethics for the preservation of the health of the land. In this context, land includes soil, water, plants, animals and other living organisms. The land ethics approach has an accounting ethics component that advocates land-use practices that are environmentally beneficial and restore ecological health to sustain community welfare (Anderson-Wilk, 2008: 142–144; Palmer, 2007).

Accordingly, social and environmental reporting has encompassed business sustainability programs. To this effect, Thiele (1999) elaborated upon the evolving relationships among ecology, environmental ethics and sustainability (see also Cowdin, 2008). She formulated that "ecology pertains to the study of relations of interdependence within biological communities. Ecology is inherently related to sustainability. The two concerns stand together" (Thiele, 1999: 29).

The basis of ethical principles in the ecology of sustainability education

In general, ecosystems are made up of interdependent co-existing environmental and social systems that have enduring and sustaining relationships. Ecology and natural resources management have sustainable relationships that are "amenable to ethical formulation. Ethics might be defined as a system of mores that arises out of and sustains certain relations of social interdependence" (Thiele, 1999: 29). These ethical considerations provide the foundation to sustain and conserve resources for future generations.

Sustainable development thus depends upon the moral dimensions of institutional legitimacy and structural arrangements. Sustainability concerns have advanced ecological and ethical issues covered in higher education (Ferrer-Balas et al., 2008; Ryu and Brody, 2006). Sustainability management is embedded in the Darwinian theory of natural selection as well as in individual actions and economic choices that make ethical education and training necessary (Leiserowitz and Fernandez, 2007).

Thus, accounting ethics education has become a component of sustainability management training that is shaped by ecological and environmental concerns. When ecological ethics focuses on sustaining the interdependence of social and biological relationships, accounting ethics education can be broadened to include issues related to human morality and individual responsibility. Accordingly, sustainability education is inherently an ethical issue that is embedded in conservation decisions and the development of ecological and natural resources to balance the economic, social and environmental objectives of organizations, communities and societies.

Sustainability accounting and reporting: evolving topics that call for integration

Sustainable development has been embedded in the ecology of natural and environmental resources management. Hopwood (2009) suggested that sustainability implies long-term interests where accountants develop "calculative devices" for investment, production and the preservation of natural and ecological resources (p433). He edited a collection of papers in sustainability accounting and reporting for a special issue of *Accounting, Organizations and Society* (AOS) (2009; see also Hopwood and Unerman, 2010). The 2009 AOS special issue has seven papers that address "the creation of a market in carbon emissions and the roles that accounting and calculative mechanisms can and cannot play in the environmental area" (Hopwood, 2009: 438). Some of the papers published in the collection employ critical perspectives to question "the role and functioning of accounting in the environmental and sustainability spheres" (p439). While Hopwood's contributions to behavioral accounting theory and research have been very substantial (see Chapman, 2010), it is in the 2009 issue of AOS where he noted the need for more research and education in sustainability accounting and reporting areas (Hopwood, 2009).

Following Hopwood's (2009) recommendations, the ecological framework has been extended to approach the integration of sustainability into accounting education (Sisaye, 2013). There are at least three subject areas where the sustainability concepts can be incorporated: financial accounting, auditing and managerial accounting.

Financial accounting: external reporting guidelines

This section covers the integration of sustainability within financial accounting course materials. It describes several external financial reporting guidelines that have recently emerged in order to incorporate sustainability into corporations' annual reports. These guidelines describe external reporting regulations that can be incorporated into a financial accounting course.

Some of these external reporting guidelines are outlined in the Global Reporting Initiative (GRI), the Dow Jones Sustainability Index (DJSI) and the Morgan Stanley Capital International Index (MSCI). They specifically address sustainability indicators to assess the performance of social and environmental programs. They are described in detail in Chapter 5 of this book. These guidelines have been favorably received by the Financial Accounting Standards Board (FASB) to develop Generally Accepted Accounting Principles (GAAP) to supplement the Sarbanes-Oxley Act of 2002 in order to provide a general framework and approaches for reporting on sustainability.

The GRI, DJSI and GAAP reporting guidelines raise a number of questions related to the integration of sustainability within the accounting curriculum. The first important question in the preparation of reports is the type of information contained in these reports. In sustainability, the question of corporate governance and accountability is crucial. As discussed earlier, accounting reports on sustainability have to address the economic, environmental and social performance of corporations. However, at present, environmental and social reports are voluntary; they are not required to be included with data on economic/financial performance in the organization's annual reports.

The accounting profession has stressed the importance of accountability and the verifiability of environmental and social information in annual reports. The AICPA and the big four accounting firms – for example, Ernst & Young (2010) – provide guidelines for the preparation of sustainability reporting. They have suggested that the auditing of information can be either voluntary or required, depending on the organization, and whether or not the disclosed information is of value to management, employees and shareholders. In general, Ernst & Young's (2010) *Sustainability Reporting* and KPMG's (2010) sustainability reporting focuses on the type of sustainability information (data) to be included in these reports. While it is important to note that the discussion has focused on the reporting format, the question of how to report and what data to use for the assessment and measurement of sustainability compliance have not yet been addressed. The big four accounting firms have focused on external reporting guidelines and possibly verification of information by CPAs. These are timely performance issues that need to be integrated and addressed in financial and managerial accounting and auditing courses.

Auditing and attestation: sustainability reporting issues in accounting education and practice

The role of auditors in the sustainability reporting system has become important (see AICPA, 2010). In the auditing curriculum, some of the relevant issues that call for integration are related to the role of auditors in sustainability reporting. These are outlined as follows: assistance in the design/implementation of a sustainability management system; facilitation with creating sustainability awareness or training employees; performance of limited-scope audits requested by top management; conducting supply chain audits; organizing compliance audits; advice regarding the appointment of outside assessors; coordination of audit activities by external assessors; pension reviews and retirement funding (investments); as well as pension liability disclosures.

Accordingly, the AICPA (2010) has issued broad guidelines in its *Auditing Firms and Sustainability Reporting Guidelines: The Trend Towards Comparability of Reports*. Some of the guidelines covered include good governance and sustainability fundamentals for improved business performance. They focus on integrating social and environmental performance with financial reporting rather than issuing separate reports; and advocate integration of oversight to review these reports (not necessarily mandatory) and the provision of assurance of integrated reports (external opinion validation). These are pertinent sustainability issues that require integration in the accounting curriculum to provide students with a holistic picture of organizational performance as well as of the economy and society.

Sustainability in the management accounting curriculum

The most important implications for the management accounting curriculum can be derived from the Sarbanes-Oxley (SOX) Act of 2002, which recognized the criticality of sustainability issues for management accounting decisions. Accordingly, sustainability is becoming part of an organization's strategic planning process – for example, in the balanced score card (BSC) framework for managing product and manufacturing cost analysis, new product development and organizational transaction cost management, as well as personnel training and development. Along with economic performance, environmental and sustainability dimensions can be integrated into the BSC framework as important determining factors in organizational resource allocation decisions.

Moreover, internal sustainability reporting provides information to management that can be used in managing the operational activities of the organization (see Accounting for Sustainability Group, 2006; Herzog, 2010; Isenmann et al., 2007; KPMG, 2008; Wallace, 2000). This information can be valuable for generating profitability, sustainability and continued productivity and performance of the organization (Bowden et al., 2010; Esty and Winston, 2006; Gray, 2006; H.M. Treasury, 2005; Savitz with Weber, 2006; Wiedmann and Lenzen, 2006; WRI and WBCSD, 2009). Accordingly, sustainability reporting prepared for internal use by management may include (among others): sustainability costs and benefits for decision-making; treatment of sustainability as a capital rather than as a revenue expenditure; when and how to treat sustainability as a cost (deferral) long-term asset rather than as an expense to be reported in the income statement of the current reporting period; identifying and separating the various costs associated with organizational life cycle (OLC) costs (i.e., product life-cycle cost assessment); approaching sustainability in terms of a transaction cost approach within a resource-based view of the firm; the application of activity-based costing (ABC) to develop sustainability cost drivers; and the use of sustainability in capital budgeting decisions.

Within the context of sustainability, ABC can be used as a cost control program to manage both costs and organizational change processes. New measurement and reporting techniques in management accounting are essential in sustainability management for changing the basis for cost allocation within a unit or division. Changes in accounting sustainability reports can be targeted to provide timely information ("score card") that enables managers to achieve desired profitability and income objectives that are consistent with sustainability goals/constraints.

These changes in reporting systems will require cooperation and teamwork among managers, corporate board members and employees for successful implementation. Similarly, in the BSC framework, some of the topics that can be expanded within the context of sustainability accounting include process improvements, market focus, organizational growth and development, and cost performance measures, as well as increasing the role and involvement of management/cost accountants in sustainable development (planning and control decisions). In other words, sustainability integration in managerial accounting, particularly ABC and BSC, involves planning, budgeting, internal control and reporting systems that shape managerial communication and decision-making processes.

Summary and conclusion

This book has discussed the extent to which the ecology of sustainability, particularly organizational ecology, has shaped environmental factors, industrial organizational structures, technological developments, government regulatory agencies and ecological resource endowment differences. In contrast, ecological anthropology has addressed how cultural and social forces have shaped sustainable development. The co-evolution of organizational ecological (sociological) and ecological anthropological views of sustainable development has related the overall resource-based approach framework for the integration of sustainability within the accounting curriculum. TBL reporting may indicate that a business organization has shown an appreciation or a commitment to conserve ecological and natural resources, and to support the environmental management objectives of sustainability. Accordingly, social and environmental data in sustainability reporting comprise interdependent and co-existing ecological natural resources and geographical systems that have enduring sustainable relationships. Ecology and natural resources management have sustainable relationships that govern individual, group and community behaviors, values, cultures and mores to conserve the current use of resources to sustain future generations.

Ecology has promoted sustainability topics in higher education. Sustainability management is thus embedded in the Darwinian theory of natural selection, individual actions and economic choices that make accounting education and training functional for the maintenance and stability of social systems. Accordingly, sustainability integration in accounting education has become a byproduct of organizational ecology, environmental resources management and ecological anthropology. Both the ecological anthropology and organizational ecology (sociology) aspects of sustainability are embedded in the conceptual framework of conservation and the development of ecological and natural resources to balance the economic, social and environmental ecological objectives of organizations, communities and societies. The integration of sustainability into accounting education and the role that the accounting practice profession has played in promoting sustainability reporting reflect the importance of environmental and ecological issues for the sustenance and long-term management of the natural resources of nations. Sustainability has both economic and financial objectives to advance business organizations' economic profitability simultaneously with social and environmental goals to promote the well-being of individuals, communities and societies at large.

Financial reporting guidelines in the GRI, DJSI and GAAP reports, auditing standards as required by the Financial Accounting Standards Board (FASB) and Public Company Accounting Oversight Board (PCAOB), and internal reporting (managerial accounting) use for strategic planning and control purposes raise a number of questions regarding the integration of sustainability into the accounting curriculum. The preparation of integrated reports is dependent upon the type, amount and depth of information disclosure contained in these reports. With respect to sustainability, the question of corporate governance and accountability is significant. It is imperative that accounting reports on sustainability address the economic, environmental and social performance of corporations. However, the inclusion of environmental and social reports with economic/financial performance at present is not mandatory but voluntary, and this dilutes the importance of sustainability data and information disclosure in these reports. It is hoped that when the FASB adopts the International Financial Reporting Standards (IFRS), sustainability reporting could become mandatory and, with uniform reporting requirements as outlined in the GAAP, will allow for verification and comparability of the reports among corporations within the same industry.

References

Accounting for Sustainability Group (2006). *Accounting for Sustainability: Introduction and Executive Summary*, Report from the Accounting for Sustainability Group convened by HRH, The Prince of Wales, December 5, 2006, mimeo.

Adams, C. A. and Larrinaga-González, C. (2007). "Engaging with organizations in pursuit of improved sustainability accounting and performance," *Accounting, Auditing & Accountability Journal*, Vol. 20, No. 3, pp333–355.

AICPA (American Institute of Certified Public Accountants) (2010). "Good governance and sustainability: Fundamental for improved business reporting," *Accountants Today*, July.

Anderson-Wilk, M. (2008). "Science and stewardship in a monolithic conservation movement: Facilitating positive change," *Journal of Soil and Water Conservation*, Vol. 63, No. 5, pp142–146.

Aras, G. and Crowther, D. (2008). "Developing sustainable reporting standards," *Journal of Applied Accounting Research*, Vol. 9, No. 1, pp4–16.

Bajracharya, S. M. (2009). "Emphasizing sustainable health and wellness in a health education curriculum," *American Journal of Health Education*, Vol. 40, No. 1, pp56–64.

Becker Professional Education (2010). *The Future of Corporate Sustainability Reporting*, CPE for CPAs, www.becker.com (accessed January/February 2015).

Beckman, M. and Pies, I. (2008). "Sustainability by corporate citizenship: The moral dimensions of sustainability," *The Journal of Corporate Citizenship*, Vol. 31, Autumn, pp45–57.

Bowden, A. R., Lane, M. R. and Martin, J. H. (2010). *Triple Bottom Line Risk Management: Enhancing Profit, Environmental Performance, and Community Benefit*. John Wiley, New York.

Chapman, C. (2010). "In memoriam, Anthony G. Hopwood, 1944–2010," *Accounting, Organizations and Society*, Vol. 35, No. 4, pp496–497.

Communale, C. L., Sexton, T. R. and Gara, S. C. (2006). "Professional ethical crises: A case study of accounting majors," *Managerial Auditing Journal*, Vol. 21, No. 6, pp636–656.

Cowdin, D. (2008). "Environmental ethics," *Theological Studies*, Vol. 69, No. 1, pp164–184.

Curry, P. (2007). *Ecological Ethics: An Introduction*. Polity Press, Malden, MA.

Epstein, M. J. (2008). *Making Sustainability Work: Best Practices in Managing and Measuring Corporate Social, Environmental and Economic Impacts*. Greenleaf Publishing and Berrett-Koehler Publishers, San Francisco, CA.

Epstein, M. J. (2010). "The challenge of simultaneously improving social and financial performance: New research results," in M. J. Epstein, J.-F. Manzoni and A. Davila (eds) *Performance Measurement and Management Control: Innovative Concepts and Practices*. Emerald, UK, pp3–18.

Ernst & Young (2010). *Sustainability Reporting: Seven Questions CEOs and Boards Should Ask about Triple Bottom Line Reporting*, www.ey.com/GL/en/SearchResults?query=sustainability+reporting&search_options=country_name (accessed January/February 2015).

Esmond-Kiger, C. (2004). "Making ethics a pervasive component of accounting education," *Management Accounting Quarterly*, Vol. 5, No. 4, pp42–52.

Esty, D. C. and Winston, A. S. (2006). *Green to Gold*. Yale University Press, New Haven, CT.

Evanoff, R. (2005). "Reconciling self, society, and nature in environmental ethics," *Capitalism, Nature and Society*, Vol. 16, No. 3, pp107–114.

Ferrer-Balas, D., Adachi, J., Banas, S., Davidson, C.I., Hoshikoshi, A., Mishra, A., Motodo, Y., Onga, M. and Ostwald, M. (2008). "An international comparative analysis of sustainability transformation across seven universities," *International Journal of Sustainability in Higher Education*, Vol. 9, No. 3, pp295–316.

Fisher, D. G., Swanson, D. L. and Schmidt, J. J. (2007). "Accounting education lags CPE ethics requirements: Implications for the profession and a call to action," *Accounting Education*, Vol. 16, No. 4, pp345–363.

Gaa, J. C. and Thorne, L. (2004). "An introduction to the special issue on professionalism and ethics in accounting education," *Issues in Accounting Education*, Vol. 19, No. 1, pp1–6.

Gray, R. (2006). "Social, environmental and sustainability reporting and organizational value creation? Whose value? Whose creation?," *Accounting, Auditing & Accountability Journal*, Vol. 19, No. 6, pp793–819.

Gray, R. (2013). "Sustainability + accounting education: The elephant in the classroom," *Accounting Education: An International Journal*, Vol. 22, No. 4, pp308–332.

Herzog, C. (2010). "Internet-supported sustainability reporting: Empirical findings from the German DAX 30," Centre for Sustainability Management, Leuphana University of Luneburg, Germany.

H.M. Treasury (2005). *Financial Reporting Advisory Board Paper: Sustainability Reporting*, U.K. FRAB (74) 03, June 24.

Hopwood, A. G. (2009). "Accounting and the environment," *Accounting, Organizations and Society*, Vol. 34, Nos. 3–4, pp433–439.

Hopwood, A. G. and Unerman, J. (2010). "Call for papers for a special issue on: The roles of accounting in advancing sustainability," *Accounting, Organizations and Society*, Vol. 35, No. 3, p11.

Hopwood, A. G., Unerman, J. and Fries, J. (eds) (2010). *Accounting for Sustainability*. Earthscan, London.

Hubbard, R. G. (2011). "Business education: Columbia's Business School dean on disclosure, leading, ethics," *Wall Street Journal*, July 7, pB6, reported by Melissa Korn.

Huss, H. F. and Patterson, D. M. (1993). "Ethics in accounting: Values education without indoctrination," *Journal of Business Ethics*, Vol. 12, No. 3, pp235–243.

Isenmann, R., Bey, C. and Welter, M. (2007). "Online reporting for sustainability issues," *Business Strategy and the Environment*, Vol. 16, No. 3, pp487–501.

Khan, T. (2011). "Sustainability accounting education: Scale, scope and a global need," *Journal of Modern Accounting and Auditing*, Vol. 7, No. 4, pp323–328.

Koehn, P. H. (2014). "Developments in transnational research linkages: Evidence from U.S. higher-education activity," *New Approaches in Educational Research*, Vol. 2, No. 2, pp52–58.

Koehn, P. H. and Obamba, M. O. (2014). *The Transnationally Partnered University: Insights from Research and Sustainable Development Collaborations in Africa*. Palgrave Macmillan, London.

Koehn, P. H. and Uitto, J. I. (2014). "Evaluating sustainability education: Lessons from international development experience," *Higher Education*, Vol. 67, No. 5, pp621–635.

Kolodinsky, R. W., Madden, T. M., Zisk, D. S. and Henkel, E. T. (2010). "Attitudes about corporate social responsibility: Business student predictors," *Journal of Business Ethics*, Vol. 91, No. 2, pp167–181.

KPMG (2010). "Reporting: Sustainability briefing paper," in partnership with *Accountability Journal*.

Leiserowitz, A. A. and Fernandez, L. O. (2007). "Toward a new consciousness: Values to sustain human and natural communities," Yale School of Forestry and Environmental Studies Conference Report, Aspen, CO, October 11–14, mimeo.

Lorenz, D. and Lutzkendorf, T. (2008). "Sustainability in property valuation: Theory and practice," *Journal of Property Investment & Finance*, Vol. 26, No. 6, pp482–521.

Nicholas, W. (2010). *ACCT 70161: Sustainability – Accounting and Reporting*, University of Notre Dame Business School, http://business.nd.edu/MSA/Academics/Elective_Courses (accessed January/February 2015).

Onwue, I. and Borsar, B. (2007). "The sustainability asymptogram: A new philosophical framework for policy outreach and education in sustainability," *International Journal of Sustainability in Higher Education*, Vol. 8, No. 1, pp44–52.

Palmer, C. (2007). "The future of graduate education in environmental philosophy/ethics," *Ethics and the Environment*, Vol. 12, No. 2, pp136–139.

Parisi, C. (2010). *HAHU1F – Principles of Sustainable Accounting and Finance*, University of Siena, Copenhagen Business School, www.cbs.dk/en/research/departments-and-centres/department-of-operations-management/staff/cpom#teaching (accessed January/February 2015).

Parker, L. D. (2005). "Social and environmental accountability research: A view from the commentary box," *Accounting, Auditing & Accountability Journal*, Vol. 18, No. 6, pp842–860.

Ponemon, L. A. and Glazer, A. (1990). "Accounting education and ethical development: The influence of liberal learning on students and alumni accounting practice," *Issues in Accounting Education*, Vol. 5, No. 2, pp195–208.

Rozzi, R. (1999). "The reciprocal links between evolutionary-ecological sciences and environment," *Bioscience*, Vol. 49, No. 11, pp911–921.

Ryu, H.-C. and Brody, S. D. (2006). "Examining the impacts of a graduate course on sustainable development using ecological footprint analysis," *International Journal of Sustainability in Higher Education*, Vol. 7, No. 2, pp158–175.

Savitz, W. with Weber, K. (2006). *The Triple Bottom Line*. Jossey-Bass, San Francisco, CA.

Senge, S. (2010). *ACCT 484-Environmental Accounting/Sustainability Reporting*, http://cbe.wwu.edu/acct/documents/accounting%20major.pdf (accessed January/February 2015).

Shenkir, W. G. (1990). "A perspective from education: Business ethics," *Management Accounting*, Vol. 71, No. 12, pp30–33.

Sisaye, S. (2011). "The functional-institutional and consequential-conflictual sociological approaches to accounting ethics education: Integration from sustainability and ecological resources management literature," *Managerial Auditing Journal*, Vol. 26, No. 3, pp263–294.

Sisaye, S. (2012). "An ecological approach for the integration of sustainability into the accounting education and professional practice," *Advances in Management Accounting*, Vol. 20, pp47–73.

Sisaye, S. (2013). "The development of sustainable practices in complex organizations: Implications and potentials for integration into the accounting curriculum," *World Journal of Entrepreneurship, Management and Sustainable Development*, Vol. 9, No. 4, pp223–245.

Stubbs, W. and Cocklin, C. (2008). "Teaching sustainability to students: Shifting mindsets," *International Journal of Sustainability in Higher Education*, Vol. 9, No. 3, pp206–221.

Tehmina, K. (2013). "Sustainability accounting courses, Talloires, declaration and academic research," *International Journal of Sustainability in Higher Education*, Vol. 14, No. 1, pp42–55.

Thiele, L. P. (1999). "Evolutionary narratives and ecological ethics," *Political Theory*, Vol. 27, No. 1, pp6–38.

Tsuji, M. and Tsuji, Y. (2011). "A comparative analysis of students' attitudes towards financial and corporate social reporting among Japan, China and South Korea," *Academy of Accounting & Financial Studies Journal*, Vol. 15, No. 2, pp73–94.

Unerman, J., Bebbington, J. and O'Dwyer, B. (2007). *Sustainability Accounting and Accountability*. Routledge, London.

UNISA (University of South Australia) (2010). *ACCT 3010: Sustainability Accounting and Reporting*, http://programs.unisa.edu.au/public/pcms/course.aspx?pageid=105462&y=2015 (accessed January/February 2015).

University of South Florida (2010). *MBA Program in Corporate Social Responsibility*, www.usfsp.edu/ktcob/academics-admissions/mba/mba-electives (accessed January/February 2015).

Vann, J. W. and White, G. B. (2004). "Sustainability reporting in the accounting curriculum," *Journal of Business & Economics Research*, Vol. 2, No. 12, pp17–30.

Waddock, S. (2005). "Hollow men and women at the helm ... Hollow accounting ethics?," *Issues in Accounting Education*, Vol. 20, No. 2, pp145–150.

Wallace, P. (2000). "Assurance on sustainability reporting: An auditor's view," *Auditing: A Journal of Practice and Theory*, Vol. 19, Supplement, pp53–65.

Walton, S. V. and Gales, C. E. (2005). "Some considerations for applying business sustainability practices to campus environmental challenges," *International Journal of Sustainability in Higher Education*, Vol. 6, No. 2, pp147–160.

WCED (World Commission on Environment and Development) (1987). *Our Common Future*, The Brundtland Report. World Commission on Environment and Development (WCED) and Oxford University Press, New York.

Wiedmann, T. and Lenzen, M. (2006). "Triple-bottom-line accounting of social, economic and environment indicators: A new life-cycle software tool for UK businesses," Third Annual International Sustainable Development Conference, Sustainability – Creating the Culture, Perth, Scotland, November 15–16.

Wolcott, S. (2010). "Sustainability accounting: What it is and how to teach it," American Accounting Association, CPE Workshop No. 40, San Francisco, CA.

WRI and WBCSD (World Resource Institute and World Business Council for Sustainable Development) (2009). "Product life cycle accounting and reporting standard," Review draft for stakeholder advisory group: The Greenhouse Gas Protocol Initiative, Geneva, November.

Wyatt, A. R. (2004). "Accounting professionalism: They just don't get it!," *Accounting Horizons*, Vol. 18, No. 1, pp45–53.

Zeff, S. A. (2003). "How the U.S. accounting profession got where it is today: Part II," *Accounting Horizons*, Vol. 17, No. 4, pp267–286.

Zulkifli, N. (2011). "Social and environmental accounting education and sustainability: Educators' perspective," *Journal of Social Sciences*, Vol. 7, No. 1, pp76–89.

Index